THE FRENCH
AT TABLE

The
FRENCH
at
TABLE

*Why the French know how to eat better
than any people on earth and how they have
gone about it, from the Gauls to Paul Bocuse*

Rudolph Chelminski

WILLIAM MORROW AND COMPANY, INC.

NEW YORK

Library of Congress Cataloging in Publication Data

Chelminski, Rudolph
    The French at table.

    1. Gastronomy—History.   2. Food supply—France—History.   3. Dinners and dining—France—History.
4. Cookery, French—History.   I. Title.
TX637.C44   1985   641'.01'30944   85-10469
ISBN 0-688-04459-X

Printed in the United States of America

First Edition

1 2 3 4 5 6 7 8 9 10

BOOK DESIGN BY ANN GOLD

The French word *sage* as an adjective means judicious or correct, and as a noun means a man or woman of wisdom. It is derived from the Latin *sapere*, to taste, have good taste, have sense. This book is dedicated to a few wise men and women whom I am lucky enough to count among my friends and acquaintances:

Fernande Allard,
Jean Banchet,
François Benoist,
René Besson,
Adrienne Biasin,
Georges Blanc,
Christian Bourillot,
Madame Cartet,
Madame Castaing,
Alain Chapel,
Robert Chavroche,
Bernadette Chestier,
Maurice Coscuella,
André Daguin,
Georgette Descat,
Jean Didier,
Georges Duboeuf,
Jean Ducloux,
Pierre Gaertner,
Jeanne & Jean Gouttebaron,
Marie-Claude Gracia,
Michel Guérard,
Paul & Jean-Pierre Haeberlin,
Hubert,
Pierre Jammet,
André Jeunet,
Philippe Lacharmoise,

Patrick Lannes,
Jean-Paul Lacombe,
Gilbert Laurent,
Gilbert Le Coze,
Gaston Lenôtre,
Daniel Léron,
Bernard Loiseau,
Jacques Manière,
Christiane Massia,
Marc Meneau,
Dominique Nahmias,
Gérard Nandron,
Albert Négron,
Louis Outhier,
Jacques Pebeyre,
Claude Peyrot,
Georges Pleynet,
Jacques Pic,
Madame Point,
Rénee Richard,
Lulu Rousseau,
Alain Senderens,
Alain Souffront,
Émile Tingaud,
Michel Trama,
Pierre Troisgros,
Shizuo Tsuji,
Roger Vergé,
Claude Verger

and, rather more than the others,

Paul Bocuse

With thanks and admiration

CONTENTS

THE FRENCH
AT TABLE

I.
DAMMIT, THE STORES ARE ALWAYS CLOSED HERE AT LUNCHTIME...

Midnight mass. The massive, gray-stone and red-tile church of Ville-Saint-Jacques, some fifty-five miles southeast of Paris, near the confluence of the Seine, the Loing and the Yonne, approximately on the border between the ancient Ile-de-France *pays* of the Brie and the Gatinais, was packed to the last pew, as it is once a year, and once a year only. Along the length of the sixteenth-century nave, built on much earlier Romanesque vestiges, as are so many of the churches of the area, and then spilling over into the aisles on either side, the peasants and bourgeoisie of the Seine-et-Marne *département* joined the weekend residents and odd transients in celebration of the eternal Christian mystery of the Virgin Birth, doing their duty by society and The Church while fetching their annual harvest of points with their Savior. To the left was the inevitable crèche, to the right the choir and in the center was Père Gelineau in his white linen robe, as gaunt and handsome and joyful as he always is when he celebrates masses, even the lesser ones, when the congregation numbers five or six instead of several hundred. The singers had reached approximately the middle of *Adeste Fideles* when the church's side door clattered open and a delinquent member of the choir hustled in, late but purposeful, and took his place among the singers, picking up the hymn on the fly and braying it out in a luxuriously resonant baritone half a note off key.

He smelled of food.

There must have been booze on his breath, too, as one could reasonably expect at midnight masses anywhere in the world—analysis surely would have identified it as champagne at this moment of the year—but what overwhelmingly dominated was the richly complex signature of the *réveillon*, the late holy day dinner which, quite clearly, he had been personally cooking for himself, his family and his guests, to be ritually devoured within minutes of leaving the church after mass and returning home. Only a person who had spent loving hours hovering over a serious stove in pursuit of a serious feast could have developed such an intense personal bouquet as now permeated his entire presence. The man was wearing his menu. There was the salty, vivacious ozone of flat Brittany oysters, shucked by the dozens; the unctuous continuo of foie gras, in a single, suave bass note; the powerful benthic aroma of lobster—or was it the cousin beast called *langoustine*, which, for want of a better English word we must call prawns?; and, over all, the principal melody line, familiar even to a visiting American, of *dinde farcie aux marrons*, the chestnut-stuffed turkey, which the French have now adopted as standard Christmas fare in place of the traditional—and usually much better—slow-cooked *daube de boeuf, boudin noir*, sauerkrauts, cabbage soups, stewed hare or simple roast chickens that used to grace holiday tables in the various provinces of this most gastronomically varied of countries.

Who was he? God knows. With his stately tummy, his hastily-donned black suit and prosperous countenance, as round and red as a *ballon* of Beaujolais, he could have been a butcher or a stockbroker or the owner of one of the beautiful sandstone farmhouses, the color of burnt cream, which lie among the easily sloping hills and valleys around Ville-Saint-Jacques, where properties are separated by ancestral boundary lines snaking along pathways and lanes and around the impenetrably dense copses that country people maintain for the express purpose of providing (temporary) sanctuary for game birds, rabbits and other comestibles, by the patchwork patterns of fields of wheat, corn and sugar beet that make this region one of France's most important breadbaskets and, just as much, by the time-honored custom of mistrusting your neighbor. But one thing about him was certain: he was typically, quintessentially French in his single-minded pursuit of eating copiously and well.

Contrary to what they might have you believe, the French did not invent eating. Nor are they the only people who like to eat, and not even the only ones who do it well. But history and accident and geography here have magically conspired over the centuries with climate and a natural Gallic penchant for revelry—the counterbalance to the more gloomy Cartesian endowments of analysis and perpetual complaining which also mark this civilization—to create a situation that remains unique even today, in spite of the fact that enormous armies of born-again *bons vivants* in every corner of the western world are doing their damndest to get into the act. The table in France is so much more than a simple place of nourishment that it must be regarded as a specific national phenomenon and point of cultural identification, like the struggle for personal success in America, the tradition of music in Italy or that of authority in Russia. True, things have been changing over the past few decades: the business-oriented structures of the Common Market, the American example of speed and efficiency in all things, the changing role of women in society, all of these have done their part to erode the traditions of small-town provincialism that are the true roots of the French gastronomic scene. True, the French don't wear *bérets basques* anymore, they rarely have Ronald Coleman mustaches on their lips these days, and precious few of them tool around on bicycles with *baguettes* under their arms, but the ageless atavisms die hard, and they are crouching there under the surface in spite of the insistent encroachments of the twentieth century. Scratch that surface, and out they leap, as healthy and debonair as ever. If, perforce, most peoples on our battered old planet eat to live, it is a relief of the last-ditch kind to consider how great are the numbers of French men and women who still live to eat. After all, what else is important in life? There is the family, of course, and maybe a little sexual hanky-panky, and possibly even an interest in work or politics or theater or sports, but more constant than any of these, less subject to the ravages of time, tedium or treachery, is the pleasure of eating and drinking. The French have made their choice, and it leans weightily in the direction of the knife and the fork.

What do the French talk about at table? They talk about food: other meals they have enjoyed previously and ones that they plan to attack very soon, all the while commenting on the merits of the one they are consuming at that minute. Meals past, present and future constitute the staple of social intercourse, without which hosts and guests would be reduced to the terror of conversational black holes, to be filled in panic with secondary subjects: films they have recently seen, television, vacation plans and denunciations of politicians with whom they do not agree, which means virtually all of them. Nowhere else in the world is so much thought, time and effort devoted to the arts of the table as in France, and nowhere else are these most ephemeral of arts—creation made for the very purpose of being instantly destroyed—honored with such persistent excellence. It was a Frenchman, Brillat-Savarin, who first postulated that you are what you eat, and then refined his gourmet's passion into a single lapidary phrase: "Animals feed; the savage nourishes himself; only the man of spirit knows how to eat."

Brillat-Savarin's contemporary, Marie Antoine Carême (1784–1833), "king of cooks and cook of kings," probably the most important member of the profession ever to grasp a pot handle, had a taste for pastry, complex sauces and unashamed hyperbole. He was not afraid to proclaim that "gastronomy marches serenely at the head of civilization," any more than he was to reshuffle the cards of the humanities with a marvelously presumptuous bit of didacticism: "The fine arts are in the number of five, painting, sculpture, poetry, music and architecture, the principle branch of which is pastry-making." An utterly humorless individual, but an untiring worker and codifier whose grand-style cooking matched the bombast of his pronouncements, Carême may be viewed with indulgent smiles today, but he believed every word he said and wrote. It was all so obvious. How could anyone doubt what he had spent so much time learning to understand?

"When cooking no longer exists in the world," he wrote in a fit of premonitory melancholy, "there will be no more letters, no more higher intelligence, no more meaningful relationships, no more social unity."

The odd thing is, most of the French would agree with him today, such is the importance of the table for social unity here. Certainly our off-key baritone with the Beaujolais face would agree, struggling as he was to ensure that Carême's vision of apocalypse never came to pass. And as I looked around the church that December night a couple of years ago, I could see plenty of others who were in league with him—not the least of whom was Père Gélineau himself.

"I used to be in the vineyards and in the wine cellar all the time when I was a boy," he had been saying a few days before that. "When you're the son of a *vigneron, caves* and wine sheds and pressing rooms are your playgrounds. It was as natural for me to play around the barrels as it was for a boy in Brittany to be around boats. I'll never forget the dim light of our *caveau* in Champ-sur-Layon, or the wonderful, sour smell of the earth floor there, where generations of Gélineaus had been spitting wine before I had been born, tasting it with customers or just seeing how the new vintage was coming along. And even today I can remember the taste of our 1927 *vin moelleux.* I could recognize it right now, among all the others, if we could arrange a hypothetical wine-tasting where all our vintages had survived the passage of time. It is astonishing how strong the impressions of taste are, especially the ones made on the young. Proust said it all with his *madeleine. Eh bien,* my *madeleine* was the 1927 Coteaux du Layon."

Little Joseph Gélineau, aged nine or so, didn't do much spitting on that hot summer afternoon when he methodically carried out his first *dégustation* and acquired his first oenological point of reference, one that would remain with him the rest of his life. After that, consciously or not, he would always be comparing those few chords of taste and bouquet to all the other wines that followed, developing the sensory memory that is the basic education on which any wine professional makes his livelihood. Alas, his promising career as a bacchic connoisseur was nipped in the bud when he received the call and became a priest, devoting himself to higher studies and pleasures reputed to be better.

Moving from barrel to barrel (they didn't use concrete or stainless-steel vats in those days), Joseph had gone down the entire line of the different years his father had in storage, dipping a straw down through the successive bungholes and cautiously sipping a taste from each one—a rite he had so often watched his father perform with his *pipette*, a long glass sampling tube in the form of an enormous eyedropper, and then with his *tâte-vin*, the shallow, dimpled cup, resembling a silver ashtray, which *vignerons* always keep around their *caves* for tastings with clients. The wines of the Anjou district south of the Loire, below the many-turreted fortress town of Angers, are like Vermont Yankees; honest but sharp, flinty and rather distant in character, making no particular effort to charm anyone they meet. As the Gélineau boy tasted, he may have been disappointed with the *blanc de blancs* and the *rosé*—why would adults like that?—but with the sweet, white, fat, fruity Coteaux du Layon he began to understand a little bit of the joys that big people took in wine. For his part, he took a second sip, because 1927 was an exceptional year.

"Eating and drinking are at the heart of social and religious structuration," the grown man had been saying, sounding more like the Jesuit he was than the gourmet he could have been. "Levi-Strauss says that the first two links of a culture are the rites of matrimony and cuisine. My father explained it more simply: '*Ça fait l'homme,*' he used to say. All the symbolic structure of a society follows its cuisine. You can understand why the pages of the Bible are filled with references to eating and drinking: they are the deepest roots of humankind.

"Specific dishes for certain days of the year and for holidays—

holy days—go deeper into the human experience than many realize. In the area of the Midi around Marseille, the *fête du chandeleur* (Candlemas, February 2) is the only day of the year when the churches are full all evening long. Everyone goes to church, and everyone eats a cake in the form of a little boat, a *barquette*, which the pasty shops make only at that time of year. What is it, this *barquette?* People in the Midi believe that it refers back to the three Marys and Martha, who were supposed to have been abondoned at sea in a little boat and who miraculously landed on the beach west of Marseille now called Les Saintes-Maries-de-la-Mer. But this is merely a Christianization of a much older pagan fecundity rite. In reality, the *barquette* represents the vulva, the symbol of female fertility.

"There have always been symbolic foods like this throughout the centuries, and if you dig a little bit you can peel the centuries away, deeper and deeper. I read somewhere that in the Vietnamese language, one third of the words have their roots in the words for 'eat' and 'rice.' In the same way, there are hundreds of proverbs about the word 'bread' around the Mediterranean. In the Provençale language there are eighteen different words for bread, depending on how it is cooked. We have only one word for 'snow,' but the Eskimos have fifteen."

Right there in the little town of Ville-Saint-Jacques, population 393, it was tradition that brought the parishioners out for midnight mass—they do the same for marriages and funerals, steadfastly avoiding the church the rest of the year—but tradition and true devotion would send them stampeding out afterward, into the black and humid December night, for the feast of *réveillon.* Matters of the stomach tend to hold traditions in place. The medieval city fathers of Ville-Saint-Jacques placed their village under the protection of Saint James when they gave their settlement a name, but as secularism gradually tempered religious fervor over the centuries the pilgrims who arrived there from Paris, Provins or Fontainebleau were a good deal more interested in buying wheels of the cheese bearing the town's name than they were in kneeling on the hard wooden *prie-Dieux* inside the church. And today, gourmandise oblige, this otherwise undistinguished town offers apprentice gourmets and food snobs a first-rate bit of esculent trivia: it is the home of the lost Brie.

Along with Camembert and Roquefort, the cheese of Brie is certainly one of the most universally known in the western world, even to the point of the nuance to be drawn between the wide, pizza-shaped Brie from Meaux and the smaller, thicker Brie from Melun. Many even know that the tall and fat Coulommiers, smooth as velvet, is also a Brie, and perhaps a handful of connoisseurs (more likely from Osaka or San Francisco than from Paris) are aware of the Bries from Montereau and Nangis. But how many know that until the fifties another Brie, the sixth, the lost tribe, as it were, was made on the farms around Ville-Saint-Jacques? If you take a stroll from the Place de l'Eglise and drop in at Chez Lucienne, the combination grocery store and bar facing out onto the Route de Nemours, Lucienne herself, a wispy old dear with thick glasses and a floral dress who looks like a Beatrix Potter creation, will tell you that she regrets that the cheese exists no more. It was smaller than the Meaux, she says, and also dryer, about the size of a dinner plate. They just stopped making it, maybe because not so many people keep cows anymore. But, she adds, you can drop in at the farm of André Haye, on the other side of town, and buy all the goat cheese you like, fresh or seasoned. *Plus ça change*, then, *et plus c'est la même chose:* the cheese of the cow is gone, but the goat has taken its place. Tradition continues.

Like the *barquette* fecundity symbol, the bonds between the French and the ever-so-distant past, when they were savages who had the good luck to have been born in one of the world's most fertile and varied areas (and one of the most beautiful, too, but that's another matter), are not always easily recognizable, but they are obvious just the same. What else beside primal instinct can be the force that drives sophisticated city people every autumn to invade forests and parks and return to the prehistoric rites of picking and gathering, until every last chestnut has been harvested and every last *cèpe* plucked from the dank soil? In the first few days when winter grudgingly lets go for springtime you will see them walking slowly, eyes glued to the ground, plastic bags in one hand and a fork or trowel in the other, sharing space with local peasants on the grassy embankments of superhighways, on the lookout for the first, fresh, bright-green shoots of the dandelions known here as *pissenlits*, or piss-a-beds, which, when married to thick, scalding-hot chunks of salt pork, make one of the finest salads imaginable. As springtime sets in for good they desert the malls of the *autoroutes* and plunge deeply into the forests again, where the *bolets, chanterelles, mousserons* and other coveted early mushrooms are hiding in the shade of the trees. As they tramp along, they can smell—yes, they can actually smell, just as Père Gélineau could still taste his father's 1927—the indescribably wonderful odor of these tender fungi softly cooking in butter, perhaps with a small note of chopped garlic and several generous pinches of parsley. If they are particularly lucky they will come upon a patch of morels, the prize of the prized, and they will exult as they mark down the location, because morels, like salmon, always return to their birthplace, having cleverly left colonizing spores in the humus below.

When the earth tilts frankly toward summer and the sun makes life impossible for any sensible mushroom, out come the snails—the famous *escargots* that foreign kids inevitably order the first time they enter a French restaurant, as a kind of rite of manhood, undertaken in the same manner as running the bulls at Pamplona, with a thrilling mixture of exaltation and terror (snails, uck!)—and now the plastic bags slowly fill with the whorled-calcium mobile homes, about half the size of a golf ball, of the gastropod crowd known here as *petit gris*. (They are not gray at all, in fact, but light tan with black racing stripes, irrefutable proof that Mother Nature has a sense of humor.) In the full flowering of summer, frogs—that second great symbol of French nutritional fearlessness—are pretty much spared these days because there aren't many of them left, the critters they eat having been ravaged by chemical insecticides, but the cockles, mussels, sea snails, limpets, sea urchins, crabs and any other beasts even vaguely edible, alive alive oh, then bear the brunt of the Atilla hordes of vacationers roaming Europe's beaches from Knokke-le-Zoutte to Cadiz for something to put into their mouths.

It is Père Gélineau's *barquette* all over again: as soon as they take off their clothes and step into their vacation loincloths, the millennia fall away and the French behave as their distant ancestors, foraging for nature's gifts. And nature is kind in every season: scarcely is the vacation season finished than it is time to hop into the car and go out after the berries which have been considerate enough to ripen during one's absence at the seaside. After which the chestnuts are ready, and the wheel has come full circle.

"Dammit, the stores are always closed here at lunchtime," a visiting American friend complained to me the other day. "It's just not convenient for shopping."

He hadn't learned yet. My unacclimated friend was being perfectly silly. Of course the French stores are closed at lunchtime. The French are at table, they take lunch seriously around here and their approach to it is fundamental: they eat it, fancy that, either at home on a properly set table or in a proper restaurant. What my friend also hadn't noticed is that French *commerçants* make up for this concession to sanity by opening earlier and closing later than any American, Canadian, English, German or Scandinavian merchant would ever think of doing. Moreover, if Sunday is the proverbial day of rest just about anywhere else in the western world—try to buy anything more than a newspaper on a Sunday in London or Stockholm—in France it is the best day of the entire week for doing your marketing, because all the food stores are open and offering their best and freshest supplies. Why? Because of *le déjeuner de dimanche*, the provincial Sunday lunch, copious enough to stupefy a wild boar and only slightly less important than the Christmas and New Year's *réveillons*. When something as serious as that is on the line, you will not settle for day-old lettuce, tomatoes, lamb chops or tripe, not if you are a French cook, and certainly not if you are the one who will eat what he or she puts together from the ingredients in the market.

When I am in America, Sunday morning is predicated on *The New York Times*. Giving it merely a cursory reading with a few tentative forays into the crossword puzzle pretty much takes care of the time that remains after sleeping late. It is only after this that thoughts turn toward lunch, or the particularly important ball game that happens to be on the tube. In France, there are no Sunday papers, none that merit attention at any rate, and even if there were no one would take the time to read them. More important things are in play, like finding the perfect cabbage to go with the partridge.

Watch the French picnicking. When the weather is fair, they're all doing it, all the ones who aren't crowding into the roadside restaurants, leaving the roads miraculously empty from noon to two o'clock. None of this crude Anglo-Saxon blanket-on-the-ground business for them. When the French picnic, they first pull a card table from the trunk of their car, then the folding chairs, then the tablecloth, napkins, cutlery and glasses, and only then the food itself. It is in proper pomp, then, that they consume their pâté, cold chicken, salad, cheese and wine, enjoying the spectacle of the passing traffic.

If, on occasion, the French are caught by surprise and organize a picnic impromptu—hardly their style, but it can happen—they are usually able to make up for the faulty seating arrangement by improvising menus properly vast and varied. Such is the lesson to be learned from Henry Hope's *"Déjeuner sur l'herbe."* Henry is an old friend, a gent and a scholar, a retired college professor and a connoisseur of everything that is worthwhile in life, like painting and music and literature and boats and women, and not necessarily in that order. Henry also knows a thing or two about friendship and food and drink, having spent his young manhood in France doing research on these. It was during this period of cultural basic training, during the Depression, that he bumped into the ultimate picnic.

"I don't believe any of us thought of Manet's great painting," Henry wrote me, "but that's what it was, a picnic on the grass, although unlike the Manet party, the ladies, mother and daughter, were quite properly clothed. But it was no ordinary meal, such as one sees every day along the roadsides of France. It differed in the choice of food, of place and, if I do say so myself, the people."

Having suitably charmed a girl named Lulu at a ski lodge in Megève, Henry had the pleasure of meeting her mother when she dropped by in her auto, en route for Nice. What a coincidence, ad-libbed our boy, I was just about to leave for Nice myself, and quicker than you could say Jacques Robinson, Henry found himself invited to ride with the ladies on the trip south. Madame Rosenberg, Lulu's mother, was a former opera singer with the classical build of Wagnerian sopranos, and she filled the little car with airs from *Carmen, Rigoletto, La Traviata* and *La Bohème* as they drove downhill toward the Mediterranean.

"Whenever Lulu, the driver, sang," Henry's letter went on, "I could relax because she would moderate her breakneck speed, and since she was singing she couldn't shout obscene remarks at passing motorists. On our second day we were in Avignon. You could park in the center of town without difficulty then, and we stopped on a little street appropriately named Saint Agricole. It was lined with food shops; not only fruits and vegetables, but all kinds of delicacies were in the windows: chocolates, candied fruits, bottles of fine wine, various pâtés, tins of foie gras and caviar. Nearby were a *boulangerie*, a *pâtisserie*, a *fromagerie*, a *saucisserie*, and Madame Rosenberg was a discriminating shopper.

"Soon we were on the road again. The two ladies amused themselves, and me, imitating the local accent. We passed Aix, then Toulon (this was long before the *autoroute*), then on a narrow road Lulu drove into the hilly country back of Hyères, where she chose a perfect spot for a picnic. After climbing over a low stone wall, we were in a little olive grove. It sloped upward toward hills thick with cork oaks. Far below was the Mediterranean. To one side was a field of silver-leaved artichoke plants laid out in formal rows, very much in contrast to the gnarled olive trees standing together like a group of bent old men. Beneath their branches the ladies spread a blanket and Madame Rosenberg began to lay out the goodies and a bottle—or was it two?—of *rosé* of Tavel. I can't remember all the delicacies, but there was Parma ham, *saucisson d'Arles, pâté de campagne*, goat cheese, long sticks of bread, still warm, a sort of Bavarian cream that Madame Rosenberg seasoned with vanilla sugar, fruits, and little cakes and tarts. Every few minutes, between mouthfuls, one or the other of the ladies would break into song, and sometimes they sang together, in duet.

" 'Come, Henry,' said Lulu, 'sing us something American.'

"The only songs I could think of were 'Down by the Old Mill Stream' and 'Sweet Adeline', but I was not about to make a fool myself. So I squirmed out of it by offering to join Lulu in singing *Buvons du vin*, which she couldn't resist. Presently the picnic came to an end and we were on our way to Nice. Lulu, contrary to my fears, drove with moderation, perhaps lulled by the drink.

"I had a very special feeling of elation. Not that this was a gourmet picnic, which it was. Not that the company and the music was pleasurable, even rare, which they were. And it was not only for the place itself, the olive grove, the hills, the distant sea. It was the perfect moment that gave me a sense of suspension in time which comes to you occasionally in your existence."

Ah, Henry. He put his finger on it, as he always does. This fleeting feeling of communication and compatibility, this euphoric sense of being in touch, however tangentially and however briefly, with the perfectability of humankind, of having snatched a moment of transcendence and grace from a function that is entirely animal, this is the secret they are always chasing, the riddle that lies behind the French passion for the table—as it does, come to think of it, for sex, although that particular riddle is rather more complicated. (When they're put together, the permutations for euphoria are absolutely dizzying, which explains why restaurants have always been, and remain, prime venues for seduction.) I'm not sure that cooking can be ranked along with the Fine Arts, and even less so that eating can, but I do know that the French at table, more than any other people, reflect something higher than the usual blood and mire of the human condition, something that is a lot more than mere gluttony, nourishment or even epicureanism.

It is, as Henry said, a kind of suspension. Not always, to be sure, but when it is there, it can produce much the same effect as one of the greater arts, like painting or music. "A poem was never worth a dinner," wrote Joseph Berchoux, a French poet and gourmet who lived between 1765 and 1839. That's nonsense, of course—or is it? With a little effort we could find plenty of pompous nineteenth-century Alexandrines or windy imitations of Wordsworth that I would hesitate to match against a *pâté chaud* by

Claude Peyrot or a *gâteau de foies blonds* by Alain Chapel. Let's say a bad poem was never worth a dinner. Berchoux, either lucid or modest, was no doubt thinking of his own production.

If the perfect suspension and elation are not always on call, their shadows are there often enough to transform time. I cannot count the hundreds of solitary and otherwise depressing evenings filled and warmed by a good restaurant or bistrot in a strange city, after another hard day's reportorial labor on the road. A hospitable *salle*, a knowledgeable waiter, a menu with some interesting specialties and a mock-grumpy *patronne* to explain them for you: this and the presence of like-minded members of the human herd can go a long way toward reconciling a person to his mortal condition. This complicity between diners has probably existed since the cavemen stopped fighting over bones and sat down together, but it is in restaurants in France that it has developed to its highest degree. Henry Hope saw it years ago, when he began frequenting these harbors of peace and learning what they were all about.

"At first my observations were concentrated on the food, usually with admiration. As I became more familiar with the traditional dishes and the usual fare in the modest places which were what I could afford, I began to broaden my food research by observing the people who ate it. Thus it was that I discovered a kind of silent language that flashes back and forth among diners. An attractive lady enters the restaurant. You admire her, then you look at the next table to see if they noticed her, and perhaps the man will raise his eyebrow slightly to say 'Yes, I noticed her, too.' Or I might eavesdrop on an animated discussion about what the party opposite me will decide to order. Not only was French cooking so different from what I had been accustomed to at home, but so were French diners: their conversation, their manners, their vivacity, their discrimination."

A generation or so after Henry, I finally had the chance to see what he was talking about, when I came to France for a year of studies. My experience wasn't as picturesque as his, because it happened in Paris—you have to leave the capital to find out what this land is really about—and because it happened in the much more modern times of the early sixties, and the shadow of the American model was already creeping up on the country, bringing with it shopping centers, motels, superhighways, business schools, real estate promoters and other such horrors. Still, Paris was not lacking in charm, and old Lutetia had done what she could to resist the wreckers and craven profiteers who were tryng to turn her into Fort Worth. The cops still wore capes in those days, and when they walked against the wind they resembled magnified swallows about to take off. The streets were filled with the low rumble of the now-defunct Renault busses, the great old green beauties with the squared-off radiator snout, the open-air balcony in the back (the greatest fun was to sprint after a departing bus and leap gracefully up onto the balcony through the gap in the railing, as an understanding passenger lifted the protective chain away from its anchor point to allow you through) and with the *contrôleur* who signalled stops and starts to the driver by grabbing a wooden handle hanging from a chain at the rear and whanging it down to ring an anemic bell up front: one whang for go, two whangs for stop. The Métro didn't run on rubber tires yet, and the clattery old wooden cars made an amazing racket, even in first class. But the very idea of having a first and a second class in a subway was so preposterous and so wonderful that I occasionally allowed myself the luxury of riding with the swells (padded seats—wow!).

Most of our meals were in the cheap (one-franc, at that time) student restaurants. They were correct, but boring: the usual self-service trays, steam tables, cheese in aluminum foil and yogurt in waxed cardboard containers. The real pleasure came on the days when I and a few friends decided to cast economy to the winds and treat ourselves to a "real" restaurant or an urban picnic in one of the rooms of our student hotel a hundred yards from the Luxembourg Gardens.

The "real" restaurants that gained the honor of frequentation by high rollers like us must have been among the cheapest commercial establishments in Paris—we rarely spent more than ten francs apiece—but for us it was the big time, being young American hicks for whom the mere appellation "French restaurant" had always meant the most expensive joint in town, with supercilious waiters, too many forks and baffling dishes named *chausson belle Aurore*, *veau Orloff*, *pommes duchesse* and the like. About the only element of this secret code that we thought we had mastered in America was "à la mode." Great was our surprise, therefore, when in Paris we discovered that *boeuf à la mode* most definitely did not mean steak with a scoop of vanilla ice cream on top, but rather one of the great classics of home-style cooking: a piece of pot roast marinated in red wine, larded and cooked (for hours and hours) with carrots and onions.

Even our cheap restaurants, though, were wonderlands for the neophyte gastronomes that we were then, with their astonishingly long menus—only one per table, mind you, because these people, too, were economy-minded—written by hand or typed and mimeographed on equipment so venerable that most of the menu was blurred and half-incomprehensible. Never mind: you could always count on finding the traditional dishes which, though they may appear banal to habitués of three-star restaurants, were for us, the zero-star crowd, nothing short of revelations: *boeuf bourguignon*, *daube*, *blanquette de veau*, *coq au vin*, *fricassée de volaille*, *gigot d'agneau*, *cassoulet*. . . . Each new dish was more desirable than the last, and we quickly fell into the honorable habit of sharing and tasting—gimme some of those *champignons à la grecque*, and I'll let you have a taste of *terrine*—and mopping up juice, sauce or *vinaigrette* that remained with pieces of bread from the basket which the waiters always kept filled for us. Here, too, my mentor Henry must have the last word, because in the French provinces they always surpass Paris, even when it comes to matters of *étiquette* like this. He and a friend named Mario were the witnesses to the scene.

"We were in a little *pension* in the Haute Savoie," he recalled, "when a couple of locals came in. They looked like hunters: caps, bright-colored flannel shirts, boots. One was a husky peasant, the other short and squat. He might have been the village postman. After our first curious glances we paid no further attention until, some time later, a delicious smell wafted across the room. The two hunters were being served what looked like *civet de lièvre*, brought in by the *patron*. Obviously he had done the cooking himself. It would make the story better if I could say that the men had just shot the hare and brought it into the café to be cooked, but that couldn't be true. For one thing, we saw no hare, nor rabbit nor any other game when they came in. More important, that dish needs a couple of hours to prepare—even a couple of days if it were marinated. But all supposition aside, the rich, spicy aroma caused us to sneak glances across the room. One didn't want to stare rudely, but we managed to watch the two men finish very large servings. (*La nouvelle cuisine* was unheard of in those days.) As we expected, each man wiped up the sauce with chunks of bread—a fitting conclusion to a knuckle-deep sauce like that. But then came the *coup de grace:* together they produced hunting knives, cleaned the gravy from under their fingernails, spread it on bread and ate it.

" 'That's really gourmet eating,' said I.

" 'You mean gourmand,' said Mario, the purist."

In Paris, our choice of restaurants was dictated in large part by a golden rule that still holds good today: stay away from places with real tablecloths. Everywhere in France, it seems, restaurants can be divided into two categories, according to how the table is covered. If it is paper, it is bound to be reasonable; if it is linen, it is almost surely expensive, at least by student standards. The paper squares of our bistrots, about a yard by a yard, not only protected the tables, but were disposable and hence free to be used by the client as he wished: for doodling, for adding up the bill, for writing down the Great Thoughts that came with the third or fourth glass of wine, or for composing a letter home whining artistically for more money. Paper tablecloths are one of mankind's more useful inventions.

Halfway between the restaurants and the student canteens in price were the urban picnics, often organized on Sunday mornings, when there were no classes, which meant we had plenty of time to do a proper job on our marketing. The pleasures of marketing in Paris—or in Lyon or Strasbourg or Nîmes or Gap or Clermont-Ferrand or just about any place you can imagine in this unbelievably rich country—are all the greater for having been raised, as I was, in the area of the supermarket and the shopping mall. Since our area of town was in the vicinity of the Sorbonne, we used to frequent the open-air markets on rue de Buci, near Saint-Germain-des-Prés, and rue Mouffetard, running downhill from the tiny, circular Place Contrescarpe, and occasionally the covered Marché Saint-Germain, around the corner from the enormous stone battleship known as the Church of Saint-Sulpice. There were dozens of other ones just as good in different quarters of the city, but these were the ones we knew best.

My friend and mentor in those early days of gastronomic apprenticeship was Chuck Krance, a renegade heller who missed his life's calling when a promising career as a leather-jacketed, motorcycling proto-rocker was terminated by his unfortunate discovery of Beckett, Proust and Céline. He is now paying for the error of his ways by laboring as a professor of French literature at the University of Chicago, where he directs the renowned Centre Universitaire d'Engrais Hippique (C.U.E.H.), an international organization devoted to clarity of scholarly expression. In his student days, though, Chuck was an admirably expert marketer, foraging through the nutritional paradises of Buci, St. Germain or La Mouffe with an unfailing eye for freshness and a ferret's nose for a bargain. Since our cooking facilities were limited to the weak hot plates that some of the boarders sneaked into their rooms—Madame, who ran the place, didn't approve of them at all, and she was right, because the current greedily sucked up by the orange-glowing electric coils inevitably meant blown fuses and shouts of outrage up and down four floors of the hotel—the picnics were usually room-temperature affairs made up of fresh fruits and vegetables and a selection of the wonderful precooked dishes available at the *charcuteries.*

In my book, that is to say right here, where I'm in control of things, the *charcuteries* rank along with the wheel, gunpowder and Catherine Deneuve as fundamental contributions to civilization. Literally, the word refers back to cookers of meat—in medieval French, *chaircuitier*—but in modern terms it has come to mean a very special kind of artisanal food shop halfway between a butcher, where everything is raw, and the grocery store or supermarket, where everything is cooked, canned, conserved and industrially embalmed in one way or another. The *charcutiers* are more cooks than grocers, and what they sell is meant to be taken out and eaten at home or in the office. All of them offer the usual selection of cooked and smoked hams, of course, and sausages and cold cuts and pickles and even some canned and dried goods, but the heart of the *charcuterie* is in the dishes which the *patron* has cooked up fresh for the day: the whole chickens roasting on the *tournebroche* out on the sidewalk; the vats of the peculiarly bland French version of sauerkraut; the pork and veal roasts, and the *rosbif* French style, so rare that the middle is hardly cooked at all. Around these staples, artfully arranged in the front window and then behind display counters inside, are several cornucopias of salads, cold omelets, smoked salmon, scallops on the half shell with *béchamel* sauce, decorated with little crescents of *pâte feuilletée:* these and a score of other delicacies, all of them sultry and seductive and ready to go home with the first customer who addresses them a kind word and a small banknote. A *charcutier*'s front window display is enough to make grown men weep with pleasure and anticipation. I always carry a handkerchief myself, just in case.

Many eyes more distinguished than mine, and many noses more noble, had been afflicted with similar symptoms in centuries past. If Paris had always offered her exceptional siting to foreign visitors, and her churches, cathedrals, *hôtels particuliers* and eminent centers of learning, at around the period of mid-Renaissance she added the magic ingredient that has stuck with her ever since, as much a part of her image as the Seine, the two islands in mid-stream and the twin heights of Montmartre and Belleville: food.

"What did foreign visitors speak about when they returned home?" rhetorically wondered French historian Pierre Labracherie. "Notre-Dame and her lofty towers? The city's twenty-four churches? The Cours de la Reine? The galleries of the Louvre? Not at all! What they raved about as the marvels of the great city were her *tavernes* and *rôtisseries*, the new sauces, the ragouts unknown elsewhere."

This kind of reflection has always been a double-edged sword for the French. Naturally, they are proud—often to the point of unbearable snobbery and ignorance of what goes on beyond their frontiers—of their traditions of *haute cuisine*, but at the same time they detest being placed inside a ghetto of good living when it is a question of their image abroad. Their national vanity tends to become hypersensitive on the subject. Watch what happens when a well-meaning foreigner continues just a little bit too long with his paens of praise for a culinary creation and the people responsible for it. Ever so gradually, his French interlocutor's face will change from delight to pleasure to manifestations of impatience and finally forthright irritation, until he makes the declaration that every visitor who has stayed for more than a couple of months knows by heart: "We don't just make food and perfume and fashion, you know. We have heavy industry, too, and the Concorde and the TGV."

The TGV, the Train à Grande Vitesse, the 150-m.p.h. bullet train which now connects many major French cities, is, indeed, a nice technical achievement, as is Concorde and probably any number of abstruse industrial products like high-pressure valves and extruded cast-iron cylinder linings, but there is nothing in any of these that is truly unique: military planes have done what Concorde does for decades, the Japanese made fast trains long ago, and everyone makes abstruse industrial products. Worse, Americans make perfume and fashion, and so do the Japanese and Italians and Germans and British and even the Russians, Lord help us. But like it or not, there is one thing that is absolutely unique about the French: nobody handles food the way they do. And that, *chers amis*, is what brought the silken handkerchief to the august nose of Jerome Lippomano four centuries before mine. As ambassador to Paris from Venice, he knew the city well, and took pleasure in writing home about what he discovered there in 1577.

"Paris has in abundance everything that could be desired," he observed. "Merchandise flows in from every country. Provisions are brought in by the Seine, from Picardy, from Auvergne, from Burgundy, from Champagne and from Normandy. Thus, although the population is innumerable, nothing is ever lacking. Everything seems to fall from the sky."

I couldn't have put it better myself, four centuries later, as I went shopping for my urban picnics. If the denominations of the various food trades have changed since the Renaissance, the wonderment that Lippomano expressed at the food scene in Paris was just the same as mine when I first discovered the *charcuterie.*

"For nothing else do the French as readily spend money," Lippomano went on, "as for eating and making what they call good fare. This is why the butchers, the meat-sellers, the roasters, the street peddlers the pastry-makers and the owners of taverns and cabarets are there in such quantity that it is a real confusion. No street, however small it might be, does not have its share. Would you like to buy animals at the market, or just meat? You can do so all over town, and at any hour. Would you like your provisions all ready to go, cooked or raw? The *rôtissiers* and *pâtissiers,* in less than an hour, will arrange dinner for you, or a supper for ten, for twenty, for one hundred persons.

"Pork is the customary food of the poor, but only of those who are truly poor. Every worker, every merchant, however wretched he may be, intends to have mutton, venison or partridge on meat days, just like the rich; on lean days [he has] salmon, codfish, salted herring from the Netherlands in great abundance. The stores of Paris are overflowing with them."

Our student expeditions into the *charcuteries* inevitably began with one kind or another of France's limitless varieties of pâtés, terrines or *rillettes,* and it didn't take us long to distinguish between the different kinds of liver employed in that most ubiquitous of confections, *pâté de foie.* Foie gras, the entire liver, cooked and potted, of force-fed ducks or geese, was a noble delicacy so far beyond our budgets that we didn't even give it a thought, but the generic term *pâté de foie* exhibited such a striking range of prices that it was obvious to us, even in our puerile ignorance of *res gastronomica,* that this reflected some drastic differences of composition. The smooth and rather cloying *mousse au foie,* attactive in appearance and terrific in price, which we snapped up in the early days and slathered over bread like peanut butter, was most likely composed, I now reckon, of pig liver and anything else that was left over or unused for some other, more avowable purpose (I will spare you the hideous details). Pâtés can be a marvel for using up odds and ends, and as long as it's got liver in it, you can call it *pâté au foie,* in the same manner as the classical French joke about the recipe for *pâté aux grives*, or thrush pâté: one horse, one thrush, one horse, one thrush. . . .

At the same time as we became more discerning in our choice of livers, the simple meagerness of our budgets forced us into a wisdom about fruits and vegetables that any good professional respects by instinct: stick with the seasons. Why buy a tomato from a Dutch hothouse in March—the appearance is beautiful, but the inside is mush—when it will cost you three or four times as much as if you waited for summer, when tomatoes will taste like real tomatoes? Apples can be stored the year round without too much problem, and bananas can ripen in the boats from Africa, but buying strawberries or peaches out of season was an idiocy that we were happy to leave to the bankers, stockbrokers and hairdressers who lived in the sixteenth arrondissement and shopped at Fauchon or Hédiard, the deluxe and ridiculously expensive food emporiums on the Place de la Madeleine.

In our student hotel, as in most of the poorer quarters of the city, the outside of the windowsill was the fridge, and the ledge where it extended inside served as the buffet where our picnics would be laid out. Mary Ann, Chuck Krancé's gorgeous blond wife, did what she could to bring some order to the proceedings, but the room was so small and so strewn with books and papers that we usually ate standing up, moving in on the victuals in turn, helping ourselves from the little cardboard containers of *salade niçoise, rillettes du Mans, galantine de canard* or whatever else was on the day's menu, spraying the floor with thick, golden crumbs from the *baguette* as we broke it up into large, crackly pieces (poor Mary Ann), alternately swigging from a bottle of *gros rouge*. God, it was good!

Being blond and American and presenting to the world the external architecture not unlike that of, say, Betty Grable, Mary Ann naturally had to undergo the persistent raillery of the vendors in the open-air markets. These market food-hawkers are a very special race, both the men and the women: hangovers from the Middle Ages who mix commerce, theater and social commentary in an ongoing chatter that is designed as much to amuse and entertain as to sell. Like *chansonniers*, the best ones can draw crowds when they are performing well. For some curious reason which I have never been able to fathom, the stars of the trade, the ones most thoroughly infected with *joie de vivre* (and, I suspect, *joie de boire*) are invariably the vegetable and fish people. Butchers are vastly more reserved, as befits millionaires, as are the B.O.F. (*beurre-oeufs-fromage*) ladies, silently dignified in their white smocks, and the tripe dealers—the offal organ grinders, as they are known around my house—tend to lurk in the shadows at the back of their sinister shops, amid their treasured collections of ears and snouts and lungs and intestines and pancreases and other unmentionables which the French know how to make edible. When a vegetable man is in good form, his voice and imagination fueled by a few litres of antifreeze, the merits of his radishes, celeries or artichokes become positively epic, possessing every virtue known to humankind and instantly available at a miraculous price, which would be even lower if it were not for those criminals who run the government.

A good sport if there ever was one, Mary Ann accepted the vendors' ad libs concerning her own comely person as one of the trials to be endured in return for the pleasure of living like a pauper in the world's most beautiful city, but her French was never good enough to offer any rejoinders better than a gaze of superior disdain. It remained for my own wife, Brien, to avenge Mary Ann a few years later, when we were living in Paris ourselves, and she frequented the same market and came under the fire of the same heavy-handed mockery.

"Does this remind you of something?" asked the vegetable man in a loud stage voice, brandishing a long, slender, obscenely red eggplant and leering like a Gallic Groucho Marx, even more hyperbolic than the original.

"Yes," she shot back with a sweet smile. "Your nose."

But victories like this were rare. Usually the other side won, because they were quick-witted and were playing the game on home ground against opponents, in our case, who were in deep water over their heads, completely outclassed: innocents abroad. The Krances and I discovered to our discomfort that market people possess an undying love for practical jokes—it extends to the highest echelons of the French cooking establishment, as we shall be seeing a bit later—when we decided to try a plump and devilishly attractive cheese that we came across in a stall of the *marché* on rue de Buci. In fact I now realize that it was only a kind of gouda, and not particularly distinguished at that, but what made it irresistible to our untrained eyes was the bumpy black crust that surrounded it. It was composed, we guessed later, of dried grape pits.

"Make sure you eat it with the crust," the cheese man solemnly enjoined us and, naturally, we did just as he said, back in the hotel room with his blackened gouda serving as the climax of our Sunday lunch. Crunch, crunch, crunch went our teeth as we tried to follow the *fromager*'s injunction, but the cheese formed an obstinate, waxen ball in our mouths, and its armor of crackly pits that felt like pebbles, made swallowing painful and got stuck between our teeth.

"Um, I fink we've been had, Chaz," I managed to articulate through the spinous mass clogging my palate.

"Yup," he agreed. "better ftick wiv Camembert fum now on."

Never mind. Misadventures like that only served to sharpen our sense of joining a kind of cabal by learning about eating. An occasional, minor humiliation was like a friendly form of hazing, an initiation rite, the dues to be paid for getting into the club. If that was the price to pay for Paris and French food, well, it was a bargain. Berkeley and Chicago and Cambridge may possess more profoundly innovative seats of learning, and in hundreds of other university towns around the world the student activities are surely planned more rationally, but that doesn't make any difference: the foreign students who roam the Latin Quarter from the Luxembourg to the Seine, from Saint-Germain-des-Pres to the twisting, medieval pathway-streets by the Église Saint-Séverin know that they are privileged just for being in Paris and bathing in its atmosphere. It was about one of these ancient streets near the Place Saint-Michel, rue de la Huchette, that Rabelais made a famous profession of faith:

I would concede all the rest of Paris for this blessed street which emcompasses more marvelous things than the Temple of Solomon. There is, in this little corner of the earth, more philosophy and wisdom than in the Sorbonne and in the University, for it is there that the art of eating is taught.

The nice thing about history and Rabelais is that not only is the rue de la Huchette still there, but it also continues to be one of the city's great centers for the arts of the belly, and most especially for the student crowd, because the restaurants there are frank, simple, unsophisticated and polyglot. The cuisine in that area isn't very traditionally French nowadays, but it certainly is colorful. In the rabbit warren of streets down by the river across from Notre-Dame and the Sainte-Chapelle, a nonstop theater of edacity plays to a milling throng of young *flâneurs*, standing room only, who slalom with delectation between fire-eaters, panhandlers, resuscitated Christs, real and imagined intellectuals, cops, and other kids of every imaginable national origin and physical appearance. Food is everywhere, fairly leaping out at you from the artfully arranged storefronts of dozens upon dozens of restaurants, assailing you with an irresistible bouquet of odors that mingle and clash in the middle of streets hardly wider than the average suburban driveway. No cars are allowed on Huchette anymore, and if it weren't for the electricity and the twentieth-century clothing, it would be easy to imagine yourself writing as Lippomano all over again:

> Would you like to buy some *souvlaki* dripping juice on its spit, or would you prefer a whole roast lamb? Would it please you to try a polychrome shishkebab, or do you like Chinese food better, or perhaps Italian? You can have them at any hour on any one of the streets. Would you like to have your sausage or your egg roll there, or take it away? The restaurants are only too happy to oblige you.

The purveyors of food who have flooded into the Huchette area may be more Greek or Italian or Chinese or Vietnamese or Arab than French today, but the mere fact of setting up their shops in this most eating-oriented of countries has transmuted them into something other than what they would have been back home. By serving the French, by becoming a part of the enterprise of feeding this giant, voracious but still discriminating maw, they have become accomplices of Rabelais and Henry Hope and the unknown parishoner in Ville-Saint-Jacques who smelled of food instead of aftershave. Willy-nilly, they have become a little bit French themselves: they are in on the joke.

The joke is on Eternity, of course, a momentary thumbing of the nose at the Big Brother, whoever he may be, who has stuck us down on this mortal treadmill and is waiting for us at the other end. On the lesser plane, it is also a Bronx cheer and a *bras d'honneur* in the direction of the speakers of gloom, the yogurt and carrot juice fanatics—*ptoouie!*—the aerobics bores, temperance lecturers and all the other humorless Stakhanovites who would impose a totalitarian efficiency upon our sovereign persons for our own good. As Lenin said to the kulaks, this hurts me more than it does you. A likely damn story.

Let the joggers jog and sweat and be miserable and suffer jock itch, if that pleases them. As long as they keep their dark secrets to themselves and refrain from bothering me, I will leave them alone in turn. Me, I cast my lot with the Henry Hopes of the world, and with the guy in Chez Jacques.

The guy in Chez Jacques would have been just another forgotten stranger if it were not for the fact that he was eating osso buco and he was alone. For that, he stuck in my memory forever as another symbol for the French at table. Chez Jacques is an unprepossessing little bistrot with good food, on a side street near the Faubourg Saint-Antoine furniture-making district, behind the Bastille. Osso buco happened to be on the menu that day—an Italian dish, in fact, but Jacques could have served the same thing and called it *jarret de veau braisé au vin blanc*—and the man at the table opposite us was having a solitary lunch. No. Correct that. He wasn't having a lunch: he was existing it.

He must have been about fifty. By his correct but simple dress—gray jacket, blue tie—and slightly world-weary manner, I took him to be a moderately successful dealer in varnish, hardware or other furniture accessories. His face was round and reposed, and he had a large brush mustache. I noticed him when he began communing with his osso buco, respectfully lifting the fat pieces of bone from his plate, carrying them to his mouth with his hands and delicately divesting them of their cargo of meat with his teeth. It was so good that his eyelids drooped as he ate, savoring every privileged second of contact between the tender veal, his teeth, his tongue and his palate. With his round face, mustache and half-closed eyes, he might have been purring, for he looked exactly like a great, big happy cat. I would not have been surprised if he had ended his meal by licking his paws. He was great. Today still I salute you, guy in Chez Jacques. If there were more people like you around, there would be more good cooks in the world, and the franchised hamburger joints would all go broke, and a signal service would have been done to mankind. *Bon appétit* to you, sir.

A couple of years after I quit the student scene I returned to work in France, and it was only then that I was able to make the discovery that too many foreigners miss by limiting their tourism to Paris: the real gastronomic truth of this country is out there in the heartland, in the provinces, where people are not so self-conscious about food and drink, neither trying to flash and dazzle with false *nouvelle cuisine* foolishness nor to re-create a fictitious rural authenticity, because they are already right in that, up to their ankles. It was in the provinces, not in Paris, that the contemporary school of French cooking developed between the two world wars, took root in the fifties and sixties and flowered in the seventies. Of the twenty or so cooks who are generally considered giants of the profession, no more than three (and maybe not even that many) exercise in Paris, while the rest are out there with the Bocuses, Troisgros, Blancs, Chapels, Guérards and company. It is also in the provinces that you can have the pleasure of meeting the real French, the friendly and funny and generous ones, who more than make up for the Parisians, who have been renowned as irascible, vain and arrogant since approximately the days of Vercingetorix, and each one of whom is sincerely convinced that his belly button is the center of the world.

The men and women who compose the industry of the stomach in France today, especially in the provinces, are an extraordinary bunch of people, as endearing as they are admirable. That I find them commendable far, very far, beyond the common range of mortals—how infinitely more estimable is a man with a reputation for a special touch with green beans than a senior vice president of Megalo Motors or Imperial Toilet Tissue (ITT)—is not just for their constantly bubbling inventiveness, which has carried French cuisine to an apogee of creation probably unmatched at any other time in history; not just for their instinctive intelligence, which, with the best of them, matches that of any company director, politician or scientist I have ever met; and not just for the astonishing professionalism that allows them to keep from sinking with enterprises that any business analyst would qualify as pure folly: labor intensive, unmechanized, inefficient, agonizingly subject to public whim, low in profit margin, generally mistrusted by the tax authorities and demanding working hours that are so absurd that any other trade would reject them out of hand. All that is there, but there is something more, too. What separates these people from almost everybody else is the conviction and passion and joy with which they run their establishments.

"You've got to have *le feu sacré* to succeed in this business," Alain Senderens told me years ago. His sacred fire glowed for years in a small, ultra-chic and ultra-inventive restaurant called l'Archestrate, on a side street next to the Invalides in Paris, until he took over the *monument historique* named Lucas-Carton (where he had worked as a *sous chef*), but the same flame crackles in Puymirol and Digoin and Rive-de-Gier and any one of a hundred other oddly named localities where some stubborn young person buys a long white apron and the goofy-looking bonnet called the *toque* and decides to strike out on his own, away from the crowd that prefers to stay by the edge of the shore, plashing in the lukewarm water. *Le feu sacré* is a phrase that recurs time and again when chefs try to articulate thoughts about their trade. There is a second recurring phrase, too, and it is just as significant: *se donner des coups de pied au cul*, which means to kick yourself in the ass. A psychiatrist might call it voluntarily-imposed motivation.

Certainly their places have to be classed as commerces, but a restaurant is not the same as a factory or a garage or a boutique. By their acts of receiving and feeding, cooks are charged with symbolism and move into the shadowy realms of the mystery of human existence. They are—or can be, on good days—part friend, part mother, part priest, and the plentitude they find in this odd profession is in large part explained by the pleasure of giving pleasure. There aren't many trades like that, and no one honors it with the devotion and intelligence that French professionals lavish on it. *Casser la croûte* (literally, breaking the crust) is the French everyday expression for having a meal, and the man who breaks bread for you partakes of the same symbolism of bodily and spiritual sustenance as Jesus with his disciples on the eve of His crucifixion. The symbolism precedes Jesus in time, of course. When He said an act of grace before feeding His disciples He was only doing what any Jew of His time did before eating: thanking the divinity for His nourishment. Go to the French countryside today (you can forget the Parisians, because they have lost the habit) and watch the Frenchman cutting his loaf of bread at the family table. He holds the big, round loaf against his stomach and cuts the opposite way an American would, toward him rather than away from him. But before cutting, he enacts a little gesture with his knife, so quick and so practiced that most visitors don't even notice it at all, zipping the knife up the long way and then at right angles the other way: the sign of the cross. He will never cut into a new loaf without this ancient, instinctive gesture.

If my best experiences with the French at table lean heavily to the provinces, my preferences among the provinces are even more heavily weighted in favor of Lyon, France's second city and the world's greatest center of good eating and drinking. Stick a pin in the center of Lyon on your Michelin map and draw a circle with a radius of fifty or so miles around it, and you have captured the biggest and best fish in your net. To be sure, there are plenty of others swimming outside, and that is what makes touring around France so enjoyable: wherever you are, it is hard to go wrong. I don't pretend to any comprehensive listing of the French restaurant food or drink scene here—I leave that to the guides, which are much better at it than I—and if I give any recipes they are purely incidental. Many of the people I write about on these pages are good friends with whom I have shared my adventures in the empire of eating, so of course I am prejudiced. Don't expect me to tell you that Paul Bocuse uses too much thyme in his *bouquets garnis,* that Georges Duboeuf vinifies too young or that Georges Blanc has a heavy hand with *filets de bar*. I have sold out: I am on the side of the home team.

The names I mention will change within a few years as the older ones shuffle off to the great cuisine in the sky (ambrosia soufflé! nectar cocktails!) and the kids move in to take their places, but the spirit that drives them will surely stay the same, even if most of humanity is nourishing itself on soybean pellets or petroleum-burgers by the year 2000. There are, after all, some things that simply cannot be allowed to change. As long as the industrialists and the developers and governmental geniuses leave a little bit of this fat, rich land's countryside out of their plans for a Radiant Future, as long as chickens run around farmhouses in Bresse and cows make *créme fraîche* in Normandy, there will be French cooks to make *poulet sauté à la créme* and western civilization will be saved.

You think I'm speaking figuratively, don't you, and probably with a pinch of irony, right? *Eh bien*, not at all. Who else is going to do it for us? Jerry Falwell? Jane Fonda? Ol' Blue Eyes? El Ron Hubbard? The vegetarian (*pouah!*) lobby? Not bloody likely. Utopians and intellectual activists have done more to mutilate, bend and staple humankind than any other single historical category, and if there is to be any bearable future on this planet, I would prefer it to be in the hands of artists and artisans who touch and feel life every day, who have not divorced themselves from common sense and reality, and who limit their assassinations to oysters, roosters, lobsters and snails. I see the fright mask of militancy everywhere around me, and I am scared. Why don't all these people go out and have lunch instead of running about brandishing their fists and their slogans?

Why can't everyone be more like Père Baroillet? I met Raymond Baroillet during a lunch with Pierre Troisgros in Roanne, the little city halfway between Vichy and Lyon which has strictly nothing to recommend it beyond Le Restaurant Troisgros opposite the railroad station. Because of the excellence of his cuisine and the warmth of his welcome (Gault and Millau once called his place The Greatest Restaurant In The World, a bit of hyperbole that is both forgivable and understandable), Pierre has a faithful clientèle of the international elite, who gladly detour into the middle of nowhere to taste his salmon scallops with sorrel sauce, his scrambled eggs with sea urchins, his *poulet au vinaigre* and other such trifles, but this day it was *table d'hôte*, at the round table inside his kitchen, where he and his staff and his friends take their nourishment before each *service*.

There was nothing special that day—cooks rarely eat *haute cuisine* in their own places—but Père Baroillet attacked the stewed veal and fresh egg noodles with the appreciative and discriminating attention that is the mark of the dedicated gourmet, and he expertly extracted every last atom of goodness from his wine by first vacuuming its complex aroma of vapors into his inquisitive nose, then obliging the liquid to travel the familiar, circuitous path from lips (slurp) to palate (clack) to the back of the tongue (chew chew chew), before it was permitted to continue downward. A final retro-olfaction, back up through the nether passage from the mouth to the nose, and the glass returned to the table. It was pure, practiced beauty, as pleasurable to watch as an olympic hurdler getting his steps right.

Father Baroillet had been *curé* of Meursault before the war, Pierre explained, and both his skill with wine and his physical appearance reflected the precious experience he had gained in the salons and wine cellars of that blessed corner of Burgundy. He was seventy-three when I met him, wearing the inevitable shiny gray suit of the impecunious country priest, with the little silver cross pinned to his lapel. He was a small man, slightly stooped, with an aureole of wispy hair, the odd dishwater color that happens when blonds turn white, ringing his head, the centerpiece of which was a marvelous, crimson, roadmap nose. His brilliant blue eyes belied his seven decades, and his perpetual good humor bespoke a person who had found peace with himself many, many years earlier.

Père Baroillet had been the Troisgros family priest almost ever since Pierre could remember. He had confessed them when they were kids, married both Pierre and his brother, Jean, buried first their father, Jean-Baptiste, and then, quite recently, unexpectedly, tragically, had done the same for Jean, who had been struck down out of the blue with a heart attack. He was a part of the family and had his napkin ring by the table in the kitchen. He had been around them for so many years and had been so imbued with the world of food and drink that he was virtually a professional himself. But the full extent of his dedication had come home to Pierre a few years earlier, when he and Jean were attending a private commemorative mass for their father. Père Baroillet followed the approved routine for the mass, as he had done hundreds of times before, for other departed souls, but at the moment of Consecration, as he tenderly cradled the chalice of wine in his hands, he turned to the brothers to ad lib a little piece of information which he was sure would interest them.

"*C'est un petit aligoté de chez Colin,*" he announced before tasting it and getting on with his work.

II.
BARBARIAN TO
GOURMET IN A FEW
EASY CENTURIES

In spite of my considerable erudition (that is to say, one
year of utter bafflement a hundred years ago, at age
fourteen, struggling with *De Bello Gallico*, followed by a pleasure
cruise a few months ago through a wonderful modern translation by
John Warrington), I have been unable to find any reference by
Julius Caesar to the eating habits of the proto-French, then known
as the Gauls and who were, as everyone knows, tripartite. He describes all manner of scheming and treachery—treachery for Caesar
meant anything this side of total, abject submission to Roman
rule—which he punished with the most appalling bloodbaths, spar-
ing neither women nor children nor cattle nor the villages in which
they had been living in relative peace until he came clanking along
with his legionnaires and his obdurate certainties. As for their native *spécialités de cuisine*, though, *nihil dicit*. He honors the Germans, the most terrifying of all the barbarians—they were
communists with no upbringing who wore bikinis the year round,
and if you have any bones to pick with my historical accuracy I in-

vite you to read paragraph II of Bell. Gall, IV; either that, or go to a beach in Bulgaria, where you will find the same thing—with a brief summary of the transrhenane diet: few cereals, chiefly milk and meat gleaned from stock-raising and perpetual hunting.

But for the Gauls, nothing at all: just plots and blood. The only hint comes backwards, by extrapolation from another reference to the Germans: "Imports of wine are absolutely forbidden on the grounds that it makes men soft and unequal to hard work." Well, who did import wine, then? Among others, the Gauls, that's who, because their love for this Roman specialty is well documented elsewhere. In the beginning, they traded for amphorae of the thick, syrupy stuff—you cut it with water, two to one or three to one—before they planted their own vines and developed their own industry. A good deal more sensible than the Germans, the Gauls had nothing against getting soft and unequal to hard work, and they worked hard at it.

Before they learned to make wine, their native drink was *cervoise*, a primitive beer, and their preferred dish was wild boar, roasted on a spit over an open fire, stuffed with garlic, then flanked with roast hare, chicken, geese, grouse or whatever edible creatures they happened to have on hand. That was good, healthy, honest fair, and I could go for some right now. It contrasted favorably, indeed, with the stupid excesses of the Romans back home, who lounged about and horizontally ingested the most absurd, rare and *recherché* dishes that orgy-fevered imagination could conceive: nightingales' tongues, field mice, ostrich brains, parrots' heads, camels' heels, elephant trunks and even, it is said, carp which had been tenderly fattened on a diet of slave meat. No wonder they had problems finding help.

Caesar's silence on Gallic food (he was a humorless old bastard and I am sure didn't approve of anything that looked like fun for others) was made up for by his successor in the emperor's executive suite, Septimus Severus, who reigned from 193 to 211 A.D. Septimus said it all with his famous observation that "eating heavily is gourmandise for the Greeks, but natural for the Gauls."

As the Gauls began the long march toward the civilization that eventually became France, developed towns which turned into cities, and restructured themselves into the medieval Christian society which, once more, was divided into three—the Church, the aristocratic soldiery and the peasantry—a new gastronomy evolved, and it was heavily influenced by the bad example of the Romans. In *châteaux* and palaces, where the folks could afford the luxury of actually thinking about the day's menu, eating with a gaggle of guests was like taking them to your garage to show off your 1959 Cadillac. It was all display and pomp, more carnival than dinner. It was food for social climbers and parvenus, out to impress, and at its extremes it was perfectly ludicrous: immense constructions of meat, fish and fowl, cheek by jowl in wiggly-jiggly, gelatin-bound cohabitation, toted in from the kitchens by strong-armed lackeys who paraded them up and down the long tables on stretcherlike palanquins before setting them down in front of the lord or guest of honor at the head of the table. The bigger the construction—the *pasté*, which later became known as the *pièce montée*—the better it was for the show. It was all the rage to stuff animals with animals, so an ox could enclose a deer over a sheep over a kid over a chicken, the whole massive mound of flesh roasted, dripping with fat and surrounded with sausages and ragouts and thick sauces, ready to be hacked apart and eaten by the fistful. Sometimes the constructions were so big that human actors—pipers piping—would be enclosed within an outer shell of pastry and burst forth like the high-kicking dancer inside mafia birthday cakes.

Four and twenty blackbirds baked in a pie, indeed. That was amateur stuff. The feudal French had a specialty that was half pyrotechnics and half nourishment: *paon cracheur de feu*, or fire-spitting peacock, created by sticking a piece of burning camphor inside the gilt beak of the roasted bird. Why a peacock? Because it looked so terrific with its feathers reconstituted around its skinny little carcass, just as a swan did with its graceful (roasted) neck in a fluffy, reupholstered white S-curve. The fact that both swans and peacocks make lousy eating didn't concern anyone: they made a gorgeous parade.

In the reign of Charlemagne (who loved the cheeses of Brie, by the way, and had a regular ration of them sent to his court in Aix-la-Chapelle), ladies were finally admitted to the seigneurial tables on the condition that their perfumes not be so strong as to bother the men in their eating. Neither plates nor spoons nor forks had yet made their appearances, and the he-men of the Middle Ages ate off flat pieces of unleavened bread called the *toastée* (they were distributed to the poor afterward), carrying the food to their mouths with their hands and their knives, with which they served themselves from communal pots placed at convenient intervals. With the copious ingestion of wine, the sport of serving oneself from the pot could be as risky as a duel, and trenchermen often wore gloves to protect their hands against impetuous stabbings from across the way.

Perhaps because of the sexual revolution by the presence of the ladies, etiquette became stricter, and it was no longer considered genteel to blow one's nose on the tablecloth or wipe one's hands on one's dog. The real dandies took to wiping their mouths with the back of their hands instead of the tablecloth, but this bit of effeminate affectation required many years to be accepted as part of courtly *savoir-vivre*. After all, there are limits. Erasmus, the scholar-monk, found the happy middle ground for table manners when he wrote a little precept that, everything considered, seemed reasonable to most gourmets:

> It is a mark of incivility, when your fingers are sullied and greasy, to carry them to your mouth and suck them, or to wipe them on your jacket. For this, it is better to use the tablecloth or your napkin.

Still, old habits die hard. As late as the mid-1600s, when the fork was beginning to come into common use, it was still ridiculed by the equivalent of the beer and pizza crowd, who used it exclusively to pick their teeth, and even Louis XIV, the bulimic Sun King, preferred to eat with his hands at Versailles, even though it is known that he possessed at least one fork. His chancellor, Pierre Séguier, one of the most important men of the realm, mixed all his food together into a single polychrome hash and rinsed his fingers in the bowls of sauces which were always nearby. Versailles may have been grand, but table manners and notions of personal *hygiène* weren't quite consonant with the glorious architecture of Jules Mansard, who seems to have entirely neglected the thought of toilets.

Back when Charlemagne died, the Holy Roman Empire and any nascent moves toward refinement in eating crumbled. In fact, eating itself became an uncertain proposition. It was a time of invasions, famines, plagues and misery, and French peasants were obliged to mix their poor, grainy flour with whatever might help them fill it out: beef blood, roots or even earth. For at least three centuries, historians tell us, the French turned to occasional cannibalism, gobbling each other up with the same delectation that Hottentots are said to have reserved for missionaries. As famine and the pest receded, though, they discovered that other beasts tasted better than the human one and, apart from an occasional eccentric, forswore anthropophagy for good around the twelfth century.

This does not mean, however, that they took to T-bone steaks and lamb chops. Being a serf or a peasant in Europe was never a sinecure and not particularly stomach-filling. French history primers teach that country folk fed on "grasses and roots" (although in medieval parlance this could refer to such things as carrots, cabbage and turnips), and it was not until our own twentieth century that they consumed meat regularly. As late as the nineteenth century, most peasants ate meat only once a week (Sunday lunch, of course), while bread and cheese—"the meat of the poor"—were the more usual daily fare. In the Middle Ages, the commonest country food was *fromentée*, a kind of boiled wheat mush or pudding that was very similar to the diet of the Roman lower classes, those underprivileged souls who never knew the taste of nightingale-tongue soufflé. In fact, this primitive nourishment, born in the dawn of time, survived right up to the last century in England if we are to believe Thomas Hardy. Let the wheat mush—fromenty, furmenty, furmety, or furmity, depending on who was saying it in which dialect—ferment a little bit, and you get the rustic beer that caused dire trouble for Henchard, the man who went on to become the mayor of Casterbridge. After tarrying too long at the counter of the furmity woman, the impetuous young bloke sold his wife off at auction, which seems like a rather strong reaction to a couple of drinks, but that's the English for you: just can't hold their Wheatena.

The French finally began putting some order into their gastronomy toward the end of the fourteenth century, when Guillaume Tirel rose through the ranks to become *premier queux,* or first cook, to King Charles V. Nicknamed Taillevant—the best restaurant in Paris today honors his memory by taking his name—Tirel is especially appreciated by historians because he sat down and wrote *Le Viandier* (The Victualer), the first French cookbook of all. Because of this epochal monograph, we have an idea of what passed for *haute cuisine* in France at about the period when Falstaff, over on the other side of the Channel, was cavorting with Prince Hal in Eastcheap, stuffing himself with capons and washing them down with tankards of sack. *Le Viandier* shows us that the French were on the road to a certain culinary sophistication compared to Shakespearean fare, but I'm not sure that I wouldn't prefer Falstaff's menu: Taillevent boiled meats before roasting them, thickened sauces with bread crumbs, audaciously mixed sweet and sour flavors—would you believe sugared fish?—and in general so chopped, mashed, disguised and spiced his dishes that they resembled Indian food more than what we know today as French. Naturally there were the "re-dressed" swans and peacocks, pigs and calves roasted whole, but hardly ever any vegetables. They were a carnivorous lot, the nobles of France, entirely dedicated to hunting when they weren't out bashing each other with broadsword and morgenstern, and they were happy to leave the "roots and grasses" to the peasants.

As with the growing of grapes and the making of wines, the French owe much to the Italians, that admirable people of precursors, in the field of culinary expertise. Although scholars do not entirely agree on the scope of Italian influence over the development of *la cuisine française,* it is certain that French noble houses as a general rule were still waddling about in their hodge-podges and gelatinous ragouts when the fourteen-year-old Florentine princess named Catherine de Medici crossed the Alps to marry the Dauphin Henri II. A thoroughgoing sensualist with an imperious appetite, she mistrusted the food up north (clearly uncivilized) and so brought her own Florentine cooks with her, along with her perfumers and other purveyors of daily necessities. She had an especial weakness for artichoke hearts, it is said, and cockscombs and kidneys, so much so that at one banquet she ate enormous quantities from which she almost suffocated. But that didn't hold her back. This is how Pierre de l'Estoile, a contemporary chronicler, described a little party she threw in the beautiful, river-straddling château of Chenonceaux in 1577, two years after her heroic indigestion:

> For this marvelous banquet, the most beautiful and honest ladies of the court, half-naked, their hair down on their shoulders, were employed to wait on table. This feast was held next to the entry giving onto the garden, where the main pathway starts, next to a fountain which sprang from a rock through a series of tubes. Everything was in good order.

I believe it. Catherine was clearly a girl who knew how to live, and I gladly accord her a place in my Hall of Esteem, right next to Henry Hope and the guy in Chez Jacques. Her appetites and the force of her character are legendary, and the importance which she attached to matters of the table profoundly impressed her contemporaries. By her own example, then, and by the presence of her personal Italian cooks, she was in an ideal position to become the grandmother of gastronomy in France. Historically, this was the period of the Renaissance, and as far as cooking was concerned, France was ready for a simple *naissance*.

Refinement in cooking doesn't necessarily mean refinement in eating, though. The *noblesse* who hired the cooks still had one foot in the Middle Ages, and it took them a long time to wrench it entirely free. Henri IV, the good king who brought prosperity to the land, a chicken into every pot and innumerable ladies to his couch, enjoyed gardening, cooking and shooting gamebirds with his royal harquebus, but when it came to curing himself of the grippe, he fell right back upon the medieval approach of a sink-or-swim shock treatment: against the earnest entreaties of his court physicians, he devoured double portions of sardines and oysters and washed them down with the spiced wine called hypocras. It worked fine.

If this was imprudent eating, it was nothing as compared to the titanic gluttony of Henri's grandson, Louis XIV. As the representative of God on the face of the earth (about the best credentials you could get in those days), Louis doubtless felt he owed it to the courtiers who had the honor of watching him eat to do justice to the table at Versailles, and the stories of his appetite were repeated over and over again. He employed more than fifty cooks and helpers in his palace, and they labored to produce an enormously varied and impressive display of dishes, all of which were then laid out at the royal board for everyone to admire. The magnificence of Louis' table soon became a subject of international wonderment, a reflection of the country and of the king himself. As such, it was an instrument of state. Louis initiated at Versailles what was to become an important and on-going tradition of French foreign policy: the diplomacy of gastronomy. Presented in the carefully arranged tableau of abundance known as the *service à la française*, Chinese banquet style, the repasts were exhibits as much as nourishment. For an idea of the kind of meals that Louis was accustomed to eating, we have the menu of a little something he trotted out at the Hôtel de Ville in Paris for a distinguished foreign visitor in January of 1687: it included 22 "large" and 64 "small" soups, 21 main entrées, 44 different kinds of roasts, 63 side dishes, 36 salads, and 12 sauces.

"I have seen the King eat, and this on many occasions," wrote his sister-in-law, the Duchess of Orléans, "four plates of different soups, an entire pheasant, a partridge, a large plateful of salad, a helping of mutton with garlic, two healthy slices of ham, a plateful of pastries followed by fruits and jellies."

Louis' bulimia may have been provoked, as some have theorized, by a tapeworm, but it was a habit that stayed with him throughout his long life. In 1708, when Bach and Handel were composing music to the glory of God in Germany and Cotton Mather was writing puritanical tracts (Essays to Do Good) in America, Louis was a tired old man obliged to watch his health, and who had cut his dinners down to virtually nothing: toast (*croûtes*), a bowl of pigeon soup and three roast chickens. By this time, on doctors' orders, he had sacrificed the still wines of Champagne which had been his preferred drink as a young man—champagne didn't become bubbly until the last twenty years of his reign—in favor of the more "tonic" Burgundies.

Whatever his own excesses at the table, it was during Louis XIV's reign that classical French cuisine, in its full, confident separation from any apery of the Italian style and from its own medieval past, took form. For the first time ever, France had a *"nouvelle cuisine."* There would be many, many more, over the years. This new style was a growing thing, of course, a process that developed over many years, but the signal that it had arrived for good came with the publication in 1651 of *Le Cuisinier François*, by François Pierre de la Varenne, a gentleman cook (*écuyer de cuisine*) of the Marquis d'Uxelles, a man whose name is remembered with suitable respect every time a professional cook chops mushrooms. La Varenne's work, which ran into fully thirty editions, was doubly important in that it was the first real cookbook to appear since Taillevent's almost three centuries earlier. Never again would there be such an interval between publications of this sort. From that time onward, French cookbooks have appeared regularly, being written in the geometric progression of numbers that has culminated in the overwhelming flood that we know today. There is a balance in life, though, and sometimes even justice: just as Taillevent, the best restaurant in Paris, honors the most important cook of the Middle Ages, so does La Varenne, the best cooking school in Paris, honor the first of the "modern" French cooks.

Cooking by now had become an art, and the seriousness with which the French approached it will forever be symbolized by François Vatel, *maître d-hôtel* of Louis II de Bourbon, Prince de Condé, who owned, among many other properties, the lovely island château at Chantilly, thirty miles north of Paris. Sleepless, nerve-wracked and exhausted from days spent in preparing to receive Louis XIV and his retinue—he needed twenty-five tables to seat them all—Vatel was crushed with humiliation when he discovered that the roasts were lacking for two tables at dinner. (It was hardly his fault that some noble hangers-on had crashed the party, but he didn't see it that way.) That evening, cloudy weather ruined the firewords display and Vatel wandered around the sleeping château all night, worrying about redeeming himself the next day with a meal that would be, well, fit for a king. *Horreur:* the next morning at 4 A.M. he saw only two carts of fresh fish arrive from the Atlantic seaports to which he had dispatched orders many days before, in anticipation of the royal Friday appetite.

"Is that all?" he asked, aghast. He had been expecting twelve carts.

"*Oui, Monsieur,*" answered the unwitting delivery man, and Vatel stumbled up to his room, jammed his sword against the door and hurled himself against it. The poor man was obliged to give it three tries, having missed his vital organs on the first two, but on the third one he got it right, and expired in a Wagnerian pool of gore. No sooner was he breathing his last earthly sighs than the rest of the fish arrived, according to plan.

In 1680, nine years after Vatel did himself in, a very signal event happened on a Paris street then called rue des Fosses Saint Germain, but now renamed rue de l'Ancienne Comédie: a Sicilian with the prettily euphonius name of Francisco Procopio opened a café, where he sold fruit syrups, tea, liqueurs, chocolates and the new-fangled invention called *glaces* (ices), the forerunner of today's ice creams and sherbets. And coffee, of course. This exotic brew, introduced into France by the Turkish ambassador to the court of Louis XIV, swept irresistibly over France, as it did England and the rest of Europe, first in the royal courts, then in noble residences and soon afterward into the streets themselves. Procopio's was not the first café—the word in French simply means coffee, of course—in Paris, but it was the first to offer a certain elegance allied to the gastronomic novelty of ice cream, which became as much of a rage for the ladies as coffee was for the men. This marked the beginning of an entirely new style of civilization. The cafés quickly became what they remain today: forums, places of gathering and discussion where strangers met who never would have met in other circumstances. Procopio's place has survived a good deal longer than most works of mice and men: it is still there at its original address on rue de l'Ancienne Comédie, halfway between Place de l'Odéon and the Carrefour de Buci, and it has been declared a *monument historique*. It is more restaurant than café now, and it might be just a leedle bit touristy, but that's all right. What is important is that history has not been forgotten.

Café society flourished in Paris. "Decent" ladies avoided the places when alone, but the males of the bourgeois species flocked in, to smoke and drink, do business and tell lies, plot revolutions and seductions. And to play chess. Probably no café anywhere, at any time, can rival the importance of the game of kings at the Café de la Régence in Paris, next to the Palais Royale. Chess carried the name of this male Mecca around the civilized world, and anyone with a brain in his head and a whiplash combination of bishop, knight and queen which he imagined to be new hurried to the Régence to watch the fabulous play of Philidor, Mayot or Légal—or even to challenge them. Who knows? With a little bit of luck and some good play, a patzer could immortalize his name as the man on the other end of the Legal Sacrifice (Hey, look, guys, I got his queen, I got his queen!) which is to chess approximately what the first slam dunk is to basketball.

Cooks followed cooks and kings followed kings as the French ate their way into the reputation that they are now stuck with. Everyone was cooking and everyone was inventing. If Louis XIV had amused His Majestic Person by brewing his own coffee, his great-grandson Louis XV was both a fine gourmet and a serious cook (chicken with basil was a specialty), and he surrounded himself with a like-minded court. Charles, prince of Soubise, was a wretched general who collected battlefield defeats but always found grace in his sovereign's eyes for his imaginative cooking, resulting in things like an omelet of pheasant and partridge eggs. Historians remember him today for his ingenuity in snatching defeat from the jaws of victory at Rossbach, but to cooks and epicures (and, presumably, to Louis XV) his name means only *purée Soubise*, an unctuous sauce of onions, butter and sometimes rice, to be served with roast meats.

When Louis XV died in 1774, the French Revolution had already begun, although no one had any way of knowing it at the time. School books traditionally linger over the date of 1789 (the storming of the Bastille, the founding of the National Assembly, the Declaration of the Rights of Man, and so on), but the times were changing long before that, and anyone who cared to tend an ear and listen attentively could clearly hear the distant thunder of the hoof-beats of history, bearing down directly upon the poor, hapless, fat but regal head of Louis XVI, the Bourbon for whom was coined the famous phrase: "They never forgot anything and never learned anything." After the Boston Tea Party a year earlier, the Americans were already in virtual insurrection against the British crown and Paul Revere's ride was only a year away. James Watt had patented his condenser, suddenly making steam power really feasible, while Hargreaves and Arkwright, with invention after invention, were wrenching the spinning industry from the cottage to the factory, as the network of industrial canals linking mines and production centers was growing apace all over England. If France was somewhat slower with these physical manifestations of change, she, too, would know them all quite soon. On the theoretical side of things, however, the French are never far behind anyone, and Mirabeau had already published his *Essays on Despotism*, of most premonitory ring. (Across the channel, in a nicely symbolic metaphor for what was looming for the *ancien régime*, Gibbon was scribbling monumentally away on his *Decline and Fall*, the first quarto of which was published two years later, as was Adam Smith's apologia of capitalism, *The Wealth of Nations*.) Mozart was still composing, but Beethoven had been born. The old road was rapidly aging.

And, in 1765, the first restaurant was opened.

It always comes as something of a surprise, this date, because the automatic assumption is that restaurants had been there, well, sort of forever. Not at all. In the old world of horseback transportation, post carriages, small family enterprises and cottage industry, travel was infinitely slower and more arduous, and western civilization's entire social structure tended to keep people close to home. Hence, they usually ate at home, either by cooking themselves or buying in the street from those *charcutiers, rôtissiers* and *traiteurs* who had so dazzled Lippomano, Rabelais and anyone else of any good sense at all. For those persons who were obliged to travel, there were the various *auberges* (inns) and post houses, located at strategic towns along the track of the main roadways, while in the large cities the cabarets were rustic bars first and foremost, "places of debauch," where wine was drawn from the barrel and beer served in pots. In the slightly more recommendable *tavernes*, customers could have wine by the bottle and, if they were in luck, perhaps find some chickens roasting on the spit. Apart from these, though, the choices for nourishment were limited in the extreme. Brillat-Savarin, the wonderful old judge from Belley (which isn't French for belly, but ought to be), summed up the dilemma in his *Physiologie du Goût*, when he listed the options available to visitors to the capital:

> They were forced to have recourse to the cuisine of the *aubergistes*, which was generally bad. There were a few hotels with a *table d'hôte*, which, with only a few exceptions, offered only the strict minimum, and at fixed hours.
>
> There was the recourse of the *traiteurs;* but they delivered only entire pieces, and anyone who wished to entertain a few friends was forced to order in advance, with the result that those who had not had the good fortune of being invited to some opulent house left the great city without knowing the resources and delicacies of Parisian cuisine.
>
> An order of things which went against the most basic daily interests could not last, and already a few thinkers were dreaming of improving matters.

The birth of the modern age of French gastronomy took place on the rue des Poulies in Paris, which now bears the name of rue du Louvre, when someone put out a few marble tables in a ground-floor room and began serving bouillons, chickens, various egg dishes—known as strength-giving restoratives in those days, much as chicken soup is known as Jewish penicilin in America today—to a clientèle of passing pedestrians. I say "someone" here because historians don't seem to know whether the man's name was Boulanger (Baker), or whether it was a baker of now-forgotten naming who cooked these dishes in his big oven and offered them for sale as a sideline to his regular business. Whatever the truth, his was an idea whose time had come, and he further embellished his niche in the history of the stomach by coining the phrase which led to the actual word "restaurant." He did so by hanging his profession of faith on a sign outside his establishment, phrased in outrageous kitchen Latin:

> *"Venite ad me omnes qui stomacho laboratis et ego restaurabo vos."* (Come to me, all of you whose stomaches are in distress, and I will restore you.)

Come they did, so much so that we now possess a quote from Diderot himself, writing in 1767 that "I went out to dine at the restaurateur's of the rue des Poulies; it is comfortable there, but rather expensive." It is nice to know that the first restaurant was also the first to have customers complaining about the bill. Come to think of it, this was not really the first restaurant, but the first *restaurat.* As with most neologisms, there were different versions of the word at the start—what do you call a place where you eat restoratives?—and it took a few years for the version with the "n" in it to become the accepted norm. It is still a gross error, however, both in France and America, to refer to the owner as anything but a *restaurateur,* without the "n."

With the double whammy of cafés and restaurants now at their disposal, the French bourgeoisie had a serious armlock on the Good Life, and they plunged into it with a gusto unmatched anywhere, many of them boozing and carousing like their ancestors the Gaulois around their wild boars, but just as many inventing, refining, analyzing and philosophizing as only this people knows how to do about what they put into their mouths. As the bourgeois booted the aristocracy out of power and poor old Louis XVI out of life itself—off with his head!—the nation was already on its way to becoming a gastrocracy, and its motto might just as well have been Liberté-Égalité-Gastronomie, because they have never been as keen on Fraternité over here as reputed.

Did you say *nouvelle cuisine*? The French have been saying it for centuries, and every time, like falling in love, they think it is the first time. In 1739, fifty years before the Bastille was taken, the preface to a new cookbook by one François Marin contained this self-satisfied assertion: "Modern cuisine, established on the foundations of the old one, with less pomp and impediment, although with just as much variety, is simpler and perhaps more complex."

By the time history had almost caught up with Louis XVI—1786—the Parisian playwright and critic Louis Sébastian Mercier was asking:

> Who can enumerate all the dishes of the nouvelle cuisine? It is an idiom that is absolutely new. I have tested some dishes cooked in such a manner and prepared with such art that I could not imagine what they could be.

I know how he felt. Kiwis, no doubt.

For you lovers of the absurd and the macabre, we have a few last gluttonous slings and arrows to throw in the direction of Louis XVI. They concern his marriage, his downfall and his demise. On his wedding day, when he was sweet sixteen, hungry but not horny, he ate himself "breathless," and when Louis XV, his grandfather, thinking solicitously of the bridal chamber into which he would be shooed a few hours later, warned him about charging his stomach too heavily, he gave an answer that is a classic of boobery: "Why not?" he burbled. "I sleep so much better that way."

Even better known is the story of his botched escape on June 21, 1791. Having safely slipped out of revolutionary Paris the night before, he was on his way to join loyalist forces at Metz. His carriage was racketing along at a fine clip, and it looked like he would make it to the happy ending, back in the arms of the friends and sycophants, for whom he was officially known as *le bien-aimé* (The Beloved, no less). But what had to happen happened: The Beloved got hungry. He had already devoured the provisions in his carriage by the time he got to Sainte-Ménéhould, where the local specialty was then, and remains today, pigs' trotters. The mere thought of this falsely humble delicacy, lengthily simmered in water or bouillon, then covered with bread crumbs and melted butter and baked in a slow oven until golden brown, fairly bursting with juicy essences, its delicate little bones so tender that they can be ground into delicious submission by the royal choppers, the meat surrounding them so fat and hammy and gelatinous that it makes the royal lips sticky—the mere thought, then, of all this goodness must have been far too much for Louis to bear, and so, groaning and squealing with the delicious pain of anticipation, joyously treasuring the hunger that he knew would soon be assuaged, he ordered a northward detour to the town of Varennes-en-Argonne, where his former first *valet de chambre*, Chamilly, was living in comfortable retirement.

When Monsieur Chamilly recovered his senses and finished bowing and scraping he whipped up a dinner that couldn't be beat, as refined as it was copious. *Hélas*, His Majesty had been recognized by a fink, name of Drouet, in Sainte-Ménéhould—his carriage and his beautiful horses were about as discreet as a shocking pink Rolls with Abarth pipes. With no telephone or telegraph in the kingdom, Louis had been able to keep ahead of trouble until then, but the three hours lost in comforting his hunger proved fatal. He was arrested and returned to Paris and never again got the chance to flee. A bit more than a year later, Louis ate a cold roast chicken under the eyes of the revolutionaries who had judged him, and when he returned to his cell after the death sentence was pronounced, he had supper: six cutlets, a big portion of chicken, eggs and three glasses of wine.

Marie-Antoinette, his wife, is said to have completely lost her appetite as she perceived the shadow of the guillotine approaching—obviously the Austrian royal family was not cut of the same cloth as the French. In contrast to her sorry fast, her executioners of the revolutionary tribunal, on October 27, 1793, offered themselves a celebration dinner in honor of their swift removal of her aristocratic head. They ate at the fashionable Restaurant Méot, and their menu included turkey wings stuffed with foie gras, roast chicken, quail, larks, champagne, but no cake. I'll bet they put it on the expense account.

III.
GROWING UP:
The Intemperate Nineteenth Century

After the Terror had run its bloody course to give way
to the Directoire and then the Napoleonic empire, history hiccuped when the Bourbons returned during the Restoration,
but the good old days for royalty in the grand style that accompanied them were finished, in eating as well as in politics. The Bourbons exited for good with the Second Republic, which Napoleon III
was happy to bury with his own imperial reign, but, like his uncle,
he made the mistake of arm-wrestling with the Prussians and came
off second best in 1870. The democratic régime that followed stayed
in place throughout the rest of the century and staggered on all the
way to 1940, when the Wehrmacht retired the Third Republic's
presidential jersey for good. The rich, turbulent, truculent nineteenth century had been a time of great events and considerable
growing pains for France, of colonization and imperialism and
much shoving of the national elbow against neighbors, of the renovation of Paris by the Baron Haussmann, the building of the Eiffel
tower, the apparently endless flowing of prose, poetry and even art

from Victor Hugo, the flowering of the music halls, Offenbach and zee French cancan, the glorious explosion of French painting in the persons of Delacroix, Renoir, Dégas, Monet and company, sculpture with the inimitable Rodin, and innumerable inventions and advances in the sciences.

Following it all, on a parallel line of succession, were the arts and sciences of the stomach. After the rue des Poulies set the example, restaurants sprang up throughout Paris (and the larger provincial cities, too) like mushrooms after a spring shower. Now that the *noblesse* no longer held the reins of power, the lackeys and artisans who had been in their employ were out on the street without work. For those of the cooking trade, what could be more natural than to open a restaurant? They did, with the verve of pioneers, and some of them went on to build fortunes that could compare favorably with those of their former masters. Of the great names of nineteenth-century Parisian restauration we still have the Grand Véfour and the Tour d'Argent, but most of the other celebrated temples of gastronomy from that period are now things of the past: Riche, Hardy, Les Frères Provençaux, Véry, Marguery, La Maison Dorée and the aforementioned Méot leave us only memories of their incredibly lengthy menus, famous feasts and an overabundance of personnel that would be impossible today, when unions, the spoilsports, will no longer allow owners to exploit their workers 16, 18 or 20 hours a day. In the gilt dining rooms of the bourgeois *nouveaux riches*, plotting and trickery of all manner were hatched to persuade great cooks away from other households with an energy and devotion scarcely ever expended for the seduction of another man's mistress or wife. The best of the cooks were sitting as pretty as tight-end free agents who can run the 40 in 4 seconds flat.

The numbers of gourmets and refined drinkers were surely great in this roaring, self-confident century, but what most strikingly remain with us today are the tales of alimentary excess, the enthusiastic, even fanatical, overeating by which segments of the bourgeoisie distinguished themselves. Having grasped the power and amassed their fortunes and fearing naught for their waistlines—a courtly, portly silhouette was a sign of importance, authority and success—they plunged into gluttony with fearsome energy and dedication, eating in a manner that now seems scarcely credible. And yet it is true; the accounts repeat themselves over and over again. Every factory owner, it seems, every real estate profiteer, railroad tycoon and financier wished for nothing more than to imitate the Sun King at his most egregiously horrible.

If Victor Hugo set the example by devouring nourishment the way he devoured life—he is said to have had the teeth and appetite of an ogre—the one who bore the flag of gluttony the highest and proudest was Honoré de Balzac, author of *La Comédie Humaine*. Balzac had a notorious insatiability for praise, women and food, and since the first two were never enough or never quite right, *naturellement*, he made up for their failings with the third. I am not certain how history will judge his literature a few centuries from now, but I do know that writers everywhere around the world ought to erect a monument to the man who really knew how to deal with their slave drivers. "Care for a bite, Honoré, old boy?" his unsuspecting editor asked the star workhorse of his stable, and Balzac, who was in form that day, said, "Sure, why not?" They repaired to Chez Véry, near the Palais Royal, a fittingly posh and expensive beanery, and while the dyspeptic editor picked at a bowl of soup and a portion of cold chicken, Balzac gave him something to test his credit with: he devoured a hundred Ostende oysters, twelve cutlets, a duckling with turnips, a pair of roast partridges, a *sole normande*—the real *sole normande* as they used to make it, with oysters and mussels and shrimp and mushrooms and truffles and smelts and proper croûtons fried in good Normandy butter—a monstrous selection of cheese and desserts and untold bottles of wine.

How many bottles of wine? Maybe three, maybe four, maybe five. Who knows? What those people were capable of in those days before the invention of cholesterol or the *crise de foie* properly beggars believing. Napoleon, for example, had a general named Bisson, whom he referred to as "Gargantua," who used to consume eight bottles of wine every day for lunch. I looked this character up to find what distinguished military feats he had signed, but the only reference I could find to any battlefield triumphs concerned the time he challenged an English admiral to a duel at Boulogne-sur-Mer. The weapon he chose was food, of course, and the menu was a yard or so of blood sausage, *boudin noir*, followed by six chickens and six legs of lamb. When the Englishman gave up, Bisson placidly ordered his cheeses and desserts. Eventually, many meals later, he died of apoplexy.

Apoplexy was something of a chic affliction in the nineteenth century, like *anorexia nervosa* for Scarsdale schoolgirls today or the cocaine twitch for their daddies and mums. Probably the most famous of its carriers in the select circle of full-time gluttons was a certain Monsieur Gourier, otherwise known around expensive Paris restaurants as *l'assassin à la fourchette*, or the fork murderer. Gourier had enough money, time, appetite and obsessive determination to turn nourishment into a deadly duel, much like General Bisson, but on a permanent basis. He "invited" his opponents to eat for free, with the sole stipulation that they join him for every meal and keep up with him. Then he ate them to death. Two victims had already gone to their rewards when he encountered the sinister figure of a man named Ameline who, fittingly, was an undertaker by trade. Ameline matched Gourier plate for plate for three full years, until the murderer, hoist by his own petard, expired at lunch, over his fourteenth sirloin.

Compared to accomplishments such as this, Brillat-Savarin is positively virginal when he tells the tale of Prosper Sibuet, another general, who was a boyhood friend of his. As a young man of eighteen, in the full flower of youth, Prosper had just finished lunch at a good restaurant in Belley when, passing through the kitchen on his way out, he spied a magnificent cock turkey, roasted golden brown and sweating with fat. His jaws ached.

"I've just finished eating," he announced, "but I'll bet I can eat this whole turkey myself."

A prominent local farmer who was nearby took up the challenge, promising that he would pay if the presumptuous young pup finished the bird, but adding that Prosper would have to pick up the tab if he failed. Not only did Prosper do it, but he pushed the cruelty to the point of leaving not a scrap for the hungry farmer, causing him to cry out in distress: "Since I've got to pay, at least leave a little piece for me."

If Rabelais had already coined the word *gastrolâtre* to denote one who revered his stomach like a god, it remained for the jovial and genteel Brillat-Savarin to refer to himself as a *gastrophore*, or one whose body was invested with one principal duty: to carry his stomach. There were some pretty big-league stomach-carriers waddling around Paris in the age of Brillat-Savarin, and they weren't all necessarily French. The City of Lights was by then an imperative point of pilgrimage for famished tourists from every corner of the globe, and many of them comported themselves honorably, even by French standards. There was, for example, the anonymous and taciturn Englishman who became something of a minor celebrity around town by demonstrating his devotion to food and drink at La Maison Dorée, where he arrived every evening promptly at six o'clock. Silent as a mole, he ate twelve dishes until ten o'clock, continued to drink until midnight, gobbled a pickled herring and then went on drinking until five in the morning when, with no more word than to ask for the bill, strode out into the rosy-fingered dawn to repose himself until the next evening.

But when the situation is truly desperate and the national honor is at stake, the French can always be counted on to do better than Perfidious Albion. The Big Stomachs proved that beyond the shadow of cavil. Le Club des Grands Estomacs was a gastronomic society, if you can call it that, made up of wealthy Parisians who met every Saturday at 6 P.M. at a restaurant called Pascal and ate for eighteen hours straight, in 3 servings of 6 hours a piece. One of their menus has come down to us. Six P.M. to midnight: several glasses of bitter wine to whip their appetites into top form, followed by carrot soup, turbot with caper sauce, filet steak, leg of lamb, braised chicken, veal tongue, kirschwasser sherbet (to cool the laboring palate), roast chicken, creams, tarts and pastries, all of which was accompanied by six bottles of Burgundy per person. Midnight to 6 A.M.: several cups of tea, turtle soup, a chicken curry, salmon with spring onions, peppered venison cutlets, filets of sole with truffle sauce, peppered artichokes, rum sherbet, grouse *au whiskey*, rum pudding, spiced English puddings, with three Burgundies and three Bordeaux a piece. Six A.M. to noon: peppery onion soup with crackers and biscuits and then unsugared pastries in unlimited quantity, accompanied by four bottles of champagne apiece, coffee and an entire bottle of cognac per man. *Et vive la France!* Hell, that Englishman couldn't even have made the jayvees.

Eating and drinking societies are a peculiarly French invention. The spiritual father of the hundreds of such clubs that abound today was a deformed, eccentric and immensely wealthy tax-collector's son named Balthasar Grimod de la Reynière, who began life under the reign of Louis XV, studied law, surveyed the world and apparently came to some far-reaching philosophical conclusions, then passed unnoticed through the dangerous turmoil of the overthrow of the monarchy into the Revolution, the Napoleonic era, the Restoration, the Revolution of 1830 and finally the reign of Louis-Philippe, mentally shrugging his shoulders and thinking about the only thing that really mattered: his stomach. A practical joker with a penchant for black humor, but intelligent and sensitive as well, he was marked for life by the birth defect which left him with two weird, stumplike excrescences instead of hands, but with which he was remarkably skilled at wielding knife and fork. One of his favorite tricks, by which he paid back normal people for their good luck, was to place his gloved finger—a wooden one—on a red-hot stove, remarking that it didn't seem warm enough and innocently asking his guest to test it, too. Another time, Grimod sent announcements to his dining partners that he had died and convoked them to a mortuary service at his mansion, at the site of the present United States embassy. By seeing who showed up, he was able to judge who his real friends were, and he replaced the "service" with a massive meal.

With all his crankery, though, Grimod was an eminently talented gourmet, and both his *Almanach des Gourmands*, the ancestor of all present-day exercises of food criticism, and his Jury-Dégustateur, or tasting panel, an exclusive and radically limited group of Parisian *fines gueules* whose duty was to taste-test new products and new dishes once a month, were important innovations that marked the gastronomic landscape and continue to spawn untold imitations today still. Being one of Grimod's jurors was such a distinction and rare honor that even Talleyrand himself, the great Talleyrand, the archetypal statesman, "who betrayed every master but the cheeses of Brie," plotted and schemed to gain

membership. (He never made it.) In the years since, Grimod's original idea has burgeoned into innumerable academies, brotherhoods,
associations, clubs and orders, giving Frenchmen a virtually permanent justification for getting together to eat too much and drink too
much and be in good company while doing it. In France today there
is an Order of the Taste-Quiche, a Brotherhood of the Companions
of the Plate of Tripe, an Order of the Necklace of the Burgundy
Snail and the Golden Spurs, a Most Serene Order of the Ardèche
Chestnut, a Gastronomic Brotherhood of the Companions of the
Golden Trotter of Sainte-Ménéhould, a Worldwide Order of
Bearded Gastronomes, a Brotherhood of Jubilation, an Association
Amicale des Amateurs d'Andouillettes Authentiques (A.A.A.A.A.),
a grouping of connoisseurs of tripe sausage, with a total membership of five, an Académie des Abats, whose menus are made up exclusively of innards. You name it, they've got it. Less exclusive than
A.A.A.A.A. but nevertheless the most prestigious of them all are
the Club des Cent, limited to one hundred members, whose canteen
for a weekly lunch is Maxim's in Paris, and the Académie des Gastronomes, whose members must demonstrate the same kind of
gourmet knowledgeability that Grimod demanded of his jury. The
infinitely more renowned Confrérie des Chevaliers du Tastevin de
Bourgogne in Clos de Vougeot has a membership made up almost
exclusively of German machine tool salesmen and American oph-
thalmologists but, even so, has one of the nicer historical touches
attached to its name: it was the same General Bisson, the Gargantua
of the eating duel at Boulogne, who instituted a custom still respected in the French armed forces today by having his regiment
present arms as they trooped past the grand old château (which itself was built by Cistercian monks, fellows who knew a thing or two
about architecture, agriculture and alcohol).

If Grimod de la Reynière elevated gastronomy to something of
a science, it remained for two extraordinary French statesmen of the
revolutionary and post-revolutionary period to refine its use as a political weapon, far beyond the mere pomp and panoply routine at
Versailles. Jean-Jacques Régis de Cambacérès and Charles-Maurice
de Talleyrand-Périgord were born one year apart (1753 and 1754,
respectively) and enjoyed careers that were in many ways parallel.

Both began by serving the monarchy, both turned their backs on it at the advent of the Revolution, became important figures of the new order, abandoned it for the Napoleonic empire and then once again threw in their lots with the house of Bourbon when it came charging back into power after Napoleon's defeat at Waterloo. Both men were ambitious and brilliant, not particularly burdened with moral scruples, and both were passionately devoted to the table.

"Receive in my place," Napoleon ordered Cambacérès, who had the title of *archichancellier*, and Talleyrand, *grand chambellan*. "Let your tables do honor to France."

The Emperor himself had a bad stomach, detested ostentation (said he did, anyway, before he crowned himself in Notre-Dame and started imitating Julius Caesar) and ate as he was reputed to make love—very, very quickly—and with no particular grace or decorum, often standing up when he was in a rush. Cooks tore their hair when working for Napoleon, because it was impossible to tell when he might wish to take time off from his work for a little food (he might order a meal at any time of night or day), with the result that dishes were regularly overcooked, burned to a frazzle or improvised at the drop of an imperial whim. Furthermore, he had no taste for refinement, and preferred rough soldierly victuals and soups so thick that his spoon would remain standing "at attention" when he plunged it in.

With Cambacérès and Talleyrand, though, formal dinners were things of high statesmanship, designed to create the aura of wealth and magnificence so dear to Louis XIV, but also an *ambiance* propitious for the kind of negotiation that can be carried out only in the presence of truffles, crayfish, turbot and other persuasive diplomatic credentials, as efficacious for the construction of treaties as they are for seduction. (Is there a difference?) All the great and powerful in Paris, French and foreign, flocked to the régime's two most coveted tables, and woe unto him who did not abide by the rules. Prince Wilhelm of Bavaria learned this cruel truth when his carriage was delayed by traffic (the French were terrible drivers even then) and he arrived at Cambacérès's *hôtel particulier* after six o'clock, the fateful and immutable hour when guests passed from the salon to the table. The dining room was locked up tight, and not even Wilhelm's august title and anguished *Gott-in-Himmels* could gain him access.

Cambacérès and Talleyrand resembled each other for their political importance, their taste for a glittering *mise en scène* at the table, their lofty opinions of themselves and their waspishly inventive tongues—and, for that matter, in their sexual non-conformity. The Arch-Chancellor was something of a gourmand in his bisexuality, while the Grand Chamberlain, though strikingly heterosexual, gave his libido freest expression when, as a young man, he was bishop of Autun. (Do women find red skirts on men erotic? I leave this important socio-historical question, a fitting subject for a doctoral thesis, for future scholars to debate.) Talleyrand, even when occupying the most important functions of the empire, spent an hour in his kitchen every morning, composing menus with his cook, the great Carême, and he watched over every detail of presentation when the dishes came to his table, carving the roasts himself and serving his privileged guests one by one. It was Talleyrand who coined the famous advice about the proper method of enjoying a fine Cognac, Armagnac or other prestigious liqueur:

> You take your glass in the palm of your hand, warm it, agitate it by giving it a circular movement, so that the alcohol can release its fragrance. Then you carry it to your nostrils and you smell it. And then you put your glass down and you talk about it.

The noses of gourmets at this rarified level of performance are developed like biceps at Muscle Beach, but the only outward sign of their terrifying skill is a discreet rubescence from the tracks where veins have worked overtime to carry blood to the finely-tuned sensory cells hiding within the nostrils. These are Formula-I schnozzles, and they poke, inquire and analyze with such efficiency that on occasion one has the impression that the mouth is almost superfluous to the act of appreciation. "Ah," I once heard Georges Duboeuf mutter with joy as he found a Beaujolais that at last was absolutely perfect. "This one's so good I'd almost drink it." How *raffiné* can you get?

I'll tell you how *raffiné* you can get. Cambacérès demanded that his guests make themselves as presentable as the dishes he was offering them and did not hesitate to reproach the most noble ladies if he found their dresses and jewelry below the standards of his table. He was also famous for becoming nervous and testy if the conversation around him grew too loud: "Speak more softly, I beg of you," he would say on those occasions. "I can't tell what I'm eating."

But the greatest tangible service rendered by gastronomy to statesmanship came at the Congress of Vienna in 1815 when France, defeated, prostrate and without friends after Napoleon's last fling at Waterloo, was delivered to the allies "to see with what sauce she would be eaten." As Talleyrand boarded the coach that would carry him to Vienna, his new master, Louis XVIII, anxiously inquired whether he could use any more ministers, position papers or advisors to accompany him on the fateful expedition.

"Sire," said Talleyrand, "I need casseroles more than any written instructions."

As much as the French adore *bons mots*, this was far from being a mere joke. Talleyrand did, in fact, bring his casseroles with him to Vienna, and the sumptuous dinners he offered there, combined with the fearful dissension he sowed in the ranks of the allies—divide and conquer—are seriously credited by apparently respectable historians as saving the day for France at the negotiations. His secret weapon was twice dangerous: his own devious mind coupled with the prodigious talents of his cook, Carême. Not until Peewee Reese and Jackie Robinson came along to offer pure, Mozartian beauty on the move from short to second to first did history give us such a double-play combination again.

Marie Antoine Carême is one of the few names that anyone with even a passing interest in food ought to know and salute with respect, because he is unquestionably a seminal figure in the history of French cooking. Indeed, Anne Willan, the many-talented food writer who divides her time between England, France and America, does not hesitate to describe him as "the greatest cook of all time."

He is an interesting case, Carême: pretentious, affected and self-important, he irritates by the vaingloriousness of his prose (like many amateurs, he took himself for a writer), but the several books he produced finally brought together, codified and cleaned up the disparate mass that French cooking had been when he encountered it, taking it out of the Middle Ages and into the modern world. Certainly his taste (and that of his masters) ran to the overelaborate, but this was a forgivable last echo of the circus at Versailles and the *service à la française*, when all the dishes were presented in great pomp on the table together, making a show of their massed beauty. Soon this old style would be supplanted by the *service à la russe*, in which the dishes were served more intelligently, one after the other, as they are today.

But Carême stayed faithful to the grand banquet manner all his life, and if his ostentation grates present-day sensibilities, we have to give him his grudging due: he earned it. In the last quarter of the eighteenth century, when he was born, there was scarce quarter or pity wasted on the poor, and he was, quite literally, pushed out into the street at age eleven to fend for himself. One of twenty-five children in the family of a day laborer, he was one mouth too many on the tightrope above starvation; everything he accomplished afterward, every mouthful of food, every bit of education, every *louis d'or*, every higher post, every honor, he got on his own, and it wasn't easy.

"Go on, boy, and fare thee well," he wrote later, describing his forced exit from the bosom of his family as his father pushed him into the street. "There are good trades out in the world. Leave us to languish here. Misery is our lot, and we will die of it. There are fortunes to be made out there. You have to be bright to make one, but you are. Go on, boy, and maybe tonight or tomorrow some good house will open its door to you. Go now, with the gifts God gave you."

You can almost here the violins playing in the background, but the fact that Carême obviously brocaded around his papa's parting words doesn't alter the reality of an eleven-year-old in rags walking the streets and wondering where he would eat next. The lad eventually found work—unpaid, of course—with a *pâtissier* and began the long apprenticeship that would finally bring him to the top of his profession. Carême was a demon for work (it's a good idea to have that capacity in the trade even today) and when his long day as an apprentice was over he spent the few hours that remained before sleep overwhelmed him studying prints and engravings of architectural antiquities, so that he could copy them later in lard, spun sugar or chocolate. Those were the days of the *pièces montées*, the elaborate decorative constructions—Greek temples, Roman ruins, landscapes, imaginary cities—that served as eye-pleasing pedestals in, on and over which equally elaborate dishes for consumption would be presented. It was the painstaking craftsmanship and attention to detail which he lavished on these *pièces* that moved Carême to make his famous claim for *pâtisserie* as the noblest expression of architecture. The worst reminders we have today of the prodigious creations commonly assembled in Carême's time are the multi-tiered wedding cakes, over which plastic bride and groom reign in industrial bliss, and the occasional swan, carved from a block of ice, its back burdened with a selection of technicolor sherbets. Carême obviously had artistic talent as well as energy, and he brought the *pièce montée* to a peak outstripped only by later cooks who turned his kitsch into purest caricature.

Having learned everything there was to know about *pâtisserie*, he rapidly assimilated the knowledge of the greatest cooks under whom he worked, and soon surpassed them all. The first to be referred to as "king of cooks and cook of kings," he was also the last of the great masters of the trade to limit himself to private kitchens. After Carême, all the best cooks would be found in hotels and restaurants. But what a list of individuals he served: Talleyrand, the Tsar Alexander I, Lord Stewart, the English ambassador in Vienna, the English prince Regent, later King George IV and, at the end of his career, the house of Rothschild in Paris. Carême was a star of truly universal proportions, the Horowitz of the casserole, and in spite of his taste for the grandiose (labor wasn't expensive in those days), he was the one who made the framework on which modern French cooking was built. Perhaps even more important was the social phenomenon he represented: for the first time, with Carême, cooks began to be treated as *artistes* rather than dumb servants. The road to liberation was open.

One evening, the story goes, Gioacchino Rossini, having successfully polished off several Oldies but Goldies like *Othello* and *The Barber of Seville* and *William Tell,* was on the lookout for other fields to conquer and, while dining *chez les Rothschild* in Paris, spoke of the offer that he had received for a grand tour of the United States. Would Rossini board the boat and cross the Atlantic, or wouldn't he? Such was the question ardently debated at the Rothschilds' table that evening, and finally the maestro made his decision as he ingested the last morsel of *bombe glacée* prepared by The Greatest Chef in the World:

"I will go," he announced, "if Carême comes with me."

"Oh, master, you do me too much honor" (or something of the sort) protested Carême, who had been summoned from the kitchen for the proposition. But beneath his varlet's manner the king of cooks had the unbudging, steely determination of the eleven-year-old who had survived and prospered in an indifferent city. He had other projects. He had already done his traveling. Now, as he was drawing near the end of his life, he wanted to complete his writings. And so it came to pass that Carême refused, and Rossini cancelled his trip.

The gourmet composer was rewarded for his dedication by another cook, Georges Auguste Escoffier, whose creation of the much-praised and much-decried *tournedos Rossini* gives me the perfect historical peg for passing from the Bach to the Beethoven of cooking. Escoffier, a tiny little man in bowler hat, brush mustache and platform shoes, took the relay stick from Carême—he was born just fourteen years after Carême died—and carried it almost all the way to the Second World War, finally expiring, rich and famous and adulated, in 1935 after an active career spanning fully sixty-two years. Escoffier-style cooking is often dismissed as overwrought "palace food" these days, especially by practicians of the kiwi and raw-fish school, but what they forget is that this dedicated craftsman and fundamentally important author (*Guide Culinaire, Ma Cuisine*) took the needless ostentation out of Carême's teachings, and brought French cuisine from the baroque to the classical. His writings, especially the *Guide Culinaire*, constitute, today still, the grammar on which the trade is built. Every French cook of talent and conscientiousness begins with Escoffier, both with his basic preparations and his organization of kitchen personnel, before moving on to other things. You have to learn about subject-verb-object before you can write a sentence, and you have to know Escoffier's ordering of culinary technique to become a master cook.

In partnership with César Ritz, hotelier, promoter and PR man of uncommon genius, Escoffier reigned over the world of cooking as he moved from Nice to London to Paris, making the reputation of hotels like the Savoy and Carlton in London and the Ritz in Paris, where the *gratin* of international wealth flocked to taste the new creations, be seen and discreetly ogle the greatest stars of the age, who were on virtually permanent display there. There were the odd emperors and kings at Escoffier's table, of course, but times had changed since Carême, and now what counted the most was to cook for the likes of Sarah Bernhardt, Enrico Caruso and the Australian soprano Nelly Melba, the apple of the public's eye but the peach of Escoffier's heart, and whose *pêche Melba* lives on forever. There were hundreds of other creations, many of them less felicitous than this most-copied of desserts (fresh peaches, vanilla ice cream and raspberry purée), but all of them redounding to the benefit of the already unequalled reputation of *la cuisine française*. And if today it has become fashionable to sneer patronizingly at the famous *tournedos Rossini* because it seems too complicated, too rich and too pretentious, try it some day if you ever find the right cook with the right ingredients, and who knows what he is doing. He will start by frying up a large croûton in butter. On this base he will deposit a rare filet mignon just off the grill, on top of which he will gently place a scallop of fresh foie gras which he has rapidly sautéed in butter, adding three or four generously thick slices of truffle and lastly a light Madeira sauce. Don't try to make it at home (virtually impossible), but if you find the right restaurant and the right cook, if your appetite is good and you fear not for cholesterol, why, then the nineteenth century won't seem so bad. *Bien au contraire.*

IV.
THE HOLY TRINITY:
Point, Pic and Dumaine

The year 1933 was as rich in historical events as a *sauce espagnole* burbling on the back of a chef's coal-fed *piano* was in aromatic ingredients. Things weren't going too well in Austria, where parliamentary government was being suspended, or in Germany, either, whence the Allied troops of occupation had decamped just in time for the fall of the banks and the rise of the Nazis. These charmers had begun by winning the majority in the Reichstag and then, after a diseased music-hall Napoleon named Adolph Hitler had been named Chancellor, consolidated their power by the simple expedient of outlawing all other parties. German voters demonstrated their outrage at Hitler's heinous policies by voting for the Nazis with a 92 percent majority—read 'em and weep. In New York, both the Empire State Building and the George Washington Bridge were just completed, and in Washington, Congress had made Francis Scott Key's awful bit of jingoistic doggerel the National Anthem. Kate Smith was carrying musical culture toward new summits with "When the Moon Comes Over the Mountain," doing what she could to make up for the loss of Dame Nellie Melba, the toast (sorry for that) of three continents, the very one for whom Escoffier had created the Peach Melba, deceased two years earlier in Sidney. Calvin Coolidge, too, went to his reward in 1933, but the real talk of America then centered around two lumbering giants who had risen to sudden, surprising notoriety: Primo Carnera, the Italian heavyweight who knocked out Jack Sharkey, and King Kong, the ape with the jerky movements and a weakness for blondes.

In France, the year 1933 marked the beginning of a new epoch: La Pyramide in Vienne was awarded three stars in the *Guide Michelin*. One year later, the same distinction came to a restaurant called Pic, in the village of Le Pin, near Valence, and one year after that it happened to La Côte d'Or in Saulieu.

Something was afoot. Certainly there were other three-star eating places in France at the time—names like the Poste in Beaune and La Tour d'Argent and Lapérouse in Paris spring to mind—but these three establishments, located in secondary provincial burgs, were different and special, and it was no accident that they met with this rapid-fire consecration, one after the other, among the elite of restauration. It meant that Michelin had sensed something: a new style was hatching, a new school amaking. It was still far too early to perceive where it all was leading, but these first probings toward a new order can be recognized today as a turning point in French gastronomy. In a way, it could be said that these three restaurants were the first to bring French cuisine into the twentieth century, and for this they deserve very special mention. It is significant that the names of the establishments count far less here than the *patrons* who ran them: Fernand Point, André Pic and Alexandre Dumaine. They are the pioneers who showed the way for the chefs who have brought French gastonomy today to a point probably unequalled in history. Point, Pic and Dumaine had the good fortune to be located along the road south to the Côte d'Azur at a time when the wealthy French bourgeoisie was becoming accustomed to travel by car. But their contributions to the progress of the table transcend mere geographical accident. Proprietors of their own restaurants rather than employees like Carême and Escoffier, they set their own rules and developed their own new style. After their passage through history, the French table was never quite the same. Precursors and trailblazers, they are the Holy Trinity of the table.

For all his brush-clearing and simplification, Escoffier was a man of the nineteenth century, formed by the teachings of Carême and employed almost exclusively in the vast kitchens and manpower-heavy *brigades* of the luxury palaces of the capital cities, seaside resorts and watering spots where the rich came to dally. Because of the tremendous pedagogical influence of his writings and his extraordinary longevity, he pulled the nineteenth century right along with him into the twentieth, and there it remained until the Second World War. Like Marxist-Leninist philosophers, who conclude that they've got humanity all figured out and scientifically ordered in neatly predictable categories because the guy with the beard said so, chefs in the first half of this century tended to drug themselves with Escoffier and did their cooking by dogma: *sole Alice* was made one way and one way only, as was *veau Orloff, soufflé Rothschild, purée Crécy* or what have you. That was that, and please don't ask any questions. Escoffier had laid down ideal proportions for mandatory ingredients, and, with few exceptions, cooks dared not gainsay him. It was because of this timidity, born of the conviction that the rules of cuisine had now been graven in marble, that the high-level French cooking in the first half of this century reflected the atmosphere of the *palaces* in which Escoffier toiled: the complicated dishes with incomprehensible names; the sauces based on variations of sauces, themselves based on hours and hours of the painstaking alchemy of reduction to essences; the headwaiters, either cloyingly obsequious or overweening, depending on how they eyeballed you; wine stewards who seemed so snobby that it was a wonder they allowed clowns like you to have a drink; and a general attitude that suggested both mystery (the chefs were druids, wielding arcane formulas and "secret" recipes) and haughtiness, in the face of which the client was made to feel like a cloddish intruder.

Point, Pic and Dumaine were the exceptions, both in their

manner and in their cooking. To begin with, all three of them were blessed with genius, and their command of the trade could compare favorably with any of today's great chefs. Although they all sprang from Escoffier's teachings, each man in his own way began to take certain liberties with The Master, modifying here and there, further simplifying what he had already simplified, adopting regional tradition with their *haute cuisine* skills, reducing their *cartes* from the portfolio menus of the *palaces* to only a few daily specialties and placing emphasis on faultless preparation of the best produce rather than on superfluous complication of production and presentation. The three provincial geniuses knew each other well, and often telephoned back and forth to exchange professional gossip and tips about where to find the perfect asparagus, the sea bass with the brightest eyes, the mellowest of coffees and other such subjects of abiding concern.

In itself, this attitude of friendship and respect between *confrères* was something new for a trade traditionally riddled with parochialism and jealousy. The Holy Trinity showed the way here for the next generation, the one that is at the top now. An amazingly vast collection of contemporary stars among provincial France's senior *cuisiniers-patrons* was either taught by or influenced in one way or another by Point, Pic or Dumaine. Those who are practicing today have been given credit for building the modern style of restauration sometimes referred to as *nouvelle cuisine*, but the hinge on which the door between the centuries swung was mounted at Vienne, Valence and Saulieu.

"My father was an Escoffier man," explained Jacques Pic, André's son and now the man in charge *chez* Pic. "He had *Le Guide Culinaire* and *La Cuisine Moderne* on his bedside table, and I do, too. The best books on cooking are Escoffier's. But then each of us approached him differently, with our own style. That's how it was for Dumaine and Point and my father."

"What triggered everything," said Pierre Troisgros, a man who knows a thing or two about Escoffier himself, having learned his classics under the old school of *coups de pied au cul*, "was the realization that you could modify and personalize Escoffier and play with his rules a little bit. Before, that had always been considered *lèse-majesté*. In those days, if an apprentice had an idea and came up to the chef to ask him about it, the chef would give him a kick in the ass and tell him to get back to his *partie* and shut his mouth."

What Michelin was discovering as it began showering stars over Vienne, Valence and Saulieu was that provincial food could be as good as food in Paris. This was of fundamental importance on the French gastronomic scene. Along with a few rare pioneers like Curnonsky, "the prince of gastronomes," a journalist who devoted his life to promoting intelligence at the table, Michelin broke ranks with the Parisian gourmet establishment, which was busy (as Parisians usually are) with patting itself on the back and congratulating itself for being the biggest, brightest and best. In time, this important discovery was carried to its ultimate logic: that provincial cooking was, in fact, *better* than in Paris. And this is where we are today. The seed of the modern school of French cooking was planted in the provinces and there flourished. When it degrades into the grotesque caricature of *la nouvelle kiwisine française*, more often than not the crime is committed in Paris.

Food, Curnonsky postulated, should look like what it is and taste like what it is, neither disguised into ridiculous, humiliating shapes or camouflaged by excessive mixtures of seasonings or spices. How simple and obvious the idea seems—and yet how great was the difficulty for the French gourmet establishment to understand it, splashing around as it was in all those wonderful complications. It was within the capacities of very few Parisians, indeed, to understand the grandiose simplicity of the prewar menu of the Côte d'Or which I have before me at this instant. For the sum of 18 francs, the passing motorist would find himself offered: a variety of hors d'oeuvre; butter (listed that way on the menu, as a separate item); peasant omelet; little French peas; roast chicken; green salad; cheeses, desserts and fruits. If anted up 2 more francs, he could add a *feuilletée* of crayfish tails between the hors d'oeuvre and the roast chicken. And if he was dying of hunger and was filthy rich (30 francs—hang the expense!), he could enjoy a poached trout before the crayfish tails.

Ah, but what poached trout, and what roast chicken! The former were plucked from the River Cure, a chilly, undefiled affluent of the Yonne, and the latter had spent their abbreviated lives galloping hysterically around barnyards in the blessed Bresse district, building the world's most seductive fowl thighs to sexy perfection, pigging out on corn and discussing the ethical imperative of pecking orders before encountering the hatchet. The butter was cut from unctuous, light yellow, basketball-size *mottes* (mounds) fresh in from the Deux-Sèvres *département*, the eggs and lettuces were from local peasants, and the crayfish, like the snails and frogs served on other days, were privileged citizens of bog, swamp and fen who had never heard the word "hatchery." Flawless produce cooked exactly right, by professionals who have learned their grammar and only afterward add their intelligence and creativity: such is the sophisticated simplicity that marked the Holy Trinity of Point, Pic and Dumaine, and it is to their glory that they swung closed the door on the nineteenth century by imparting their vision to those who have now successfully imposed their teachings wherever French cooking is practiced seriously.

For the literate among gastronomes in France, the generation gap between the old and the new style of cooking will always be exemplified by a wonderful book which anyone who would understand this people and their devotion to good eating would do well to digest, preferably in French: *The Life and Passion of Dodin-Bouffant*. This minor masterpiece, by a gourmet writer named Marcel Rouff, one of Curnonsky's best friends and *compagnons de table*, was published in 1924, seven years before the *Guide Michelin* even began the practice of awarding stars, but everything about the novel shows that Rouff had already traveled enough around France to come to the conclusion which the red guide would reach a few years later. What little plot the novel contains is centered around the luxuriant sensuality of a retired provincial judge (clearly, Rouff had Brillat-Savarin in mind, and the book is set in the nineteenth century, in an unnamed provincial town that could well be Belley) whose life is devoted to eating with perception and elegance. So great is Dodin's gastronomic wisdom and so vast his erudition that he is renowned far and wide as the country's greatest gourmet, an eater of taste so sublime that he is referred to simply as *l'artiste*. So strict and so restrictive are his standards that he accepts as his table companions only two men, both of them local notables. None other is worthy of breaking bread with him until the town librarian, a man of sensitivity and scholarship, creates for Dodin a dish of lobster *bouchées* so extraordinary, so unexpected that he is accepted forthwith into the select circle, and weeps with pride and joy at the culmination of a life's ambition. The world's most exclusive eating club, then, has one president and three members. No one but a French writer could take such a situation and imbue it with so much grace and humor and, yes, love: love for the fat, rich, beautiful land, love for the endless flood of esculence which it so generously produces, love for the enlightened persons who commune intelligently with it. Rouff sings his love song as his hero is borne through the countryside in a carriage, accompanied by his faithful friend and fellow gourmet Rabaz:

> The voyage was an enchantment. The blue mountains appeared distant through the warm haze. The cows, already taking their ease in the cool fields, ruminated fragrant grasses. The thatched roofs of villages were awash with joyful light, and even the shadows cast by trees gleamed brightly. The route was abrim with happiness. Partridges shook fields of wheat in their mad dashes, like sudden bursts of wind, and Dodin, pointing to a hare that darted between the muddy legs of a cow that stood before the shaky old stone wall of a vineyard, cried out:
>
> "What an admirable country! Look at the synthesis, Rabaz, see how it all comes together: animal, cream and wine . . . just the ingredients for a civet!"

The true measure of Dodin's devotion to the arts and sciences of the stomach is demonstrated when he reaches the great crisis of his life—the threatened departure of his cook Adèle Pitou, the simple peasant *cordon bleu* whom he had painstakingly formed into a

Galatea of cuisine—and solves the cruel dilemma by taking her as his wife. But the book is not entirely frivolous, and Rouff brings it to a climax that is both an apologia and a *prise de position* about what cooking is and how it should be approached. It is not unlikely that this very chapter influenced Point, Pic and Dumaine to take the route they did and—who knows?—maybe even the mighty Michelin, that never admits to being influenced by anything. It is the famous *pot-au-feu* sequence, one of the finest examples of one-upmanship anywhere.

A fabulously wealthy "prince of Eurasia," an esthete and sensualist who prides himself on his refinement and profound knowledge of the finer things in life, sends a messenger to Dodin's provincial village, praying The Master to deign come and join him for the proverbial humble repast, in one of the residences that he maintains in France. Dodin accepts and, accompanied by his friend, makes the trip across the lush land to the mansion where the prince is eagerly waiting, self-confident and smug, to display the magnificence of his table. The three men are ushered into the dining room as if into a sanctuary, and the prince's *officier de bouche*, hand on his *épée*, announces the menu in a voice charged with the gravity of the occasion:

The soups will be:

One of bisque of pigeon,
One of quail, *coulis à la reine,*
One of crayfish,
And one of stuffed sole.

For the succeeding dishes, a young wild boar, preceded by a *pâté royal* and followed by a pheasant terrine with young truffles.

The hors d'oeuvre will be:

One of spit-roasted partridge in *fines herbes* with essence of ham,

A *poupetin* of turtle-doves,
Two sausages *à la dauphine,*
One of stuffed pike.

The main entrée will be:

Two stuffed chickens in cream,
Hare *à la Saingaraz,*
River birds with oysters.

And the wines of the first service will be: after the soups, dry sherry and, for the whites, Carbonnieux, Langon, Meursault and Pouilly; for the reds, Chainette, Thorins and Saint-Éstèphe.

And while the second service is being dressed, Cypriote malvoisie and madeira will be served.

The second service will be of two removes preceding the four large dishes of roasts:

One of Lake Geneva burbot *à la vestale* and the other of trout *à la Chartreuse.*

And the dishes of roasts will be:

Young turkeys *à la daube,*
Beef ribs *à la hollandaise,*
Breast of veal *au pontife,* accompanied by veal sweetbreads and dumplings,
And stuffed filets of leg of lamb.

There will be four sauces:

Sharp,
Pauvre homme,
Celestial blue,
And *à la nichon.*

And three salads:

Of herbs,
Of oranges,
And of olives.

And the warm side dishes of this service for the remove of the roasts and salads:

Stuffed *chanterelle* mushrooms,
Cocks' combs *en pagode, au champagne,*
Asparagus,
Carp roe *à la béchamel,*
And truffles *à la maréchale.*

The wines of this service will be, for the whites: Haut-Preignac, muscatel of Frontignan, Jurançon and Seyssel; for the reds, Côte Saint-Jacques, Cortaillod-en-Neûchatel, Richebourg and Romanée-Conti.

And while the third service is being dressed, there will be served:

Maraschino sherbets,
Wines of Tokay, grenache and lacryma-christi.

The third service will be, for the soups:

One *panade* of chicken breasts,
One bouillon of *metonnage,*
And one of *ouille.*

For the entrées:

Terrine of salmon,
Rabbits *Père Douillet,*
Goose *à la carmagnole,*
Alouettes *au gratin,*
Pheasant *en gondole,*
Terrine of woodcock.

For the hors d'oeuvre for the remove of the entrées:

Fish sausages,
Blanc manger fritters,
Foie gras *à la cendre.*

The desserts will be:

Four dishes of compotes, preserved fruits and marmalades:
Of quince compote in ruby jelly,
Of peach compote,
Of nut paste,
Of marmalade of violets.

There will be:

Sweet oranges and pears in *eau-de-vie*
Candied cinnamon and jonquil,
Waffles in Spanish wine,
Little pastries,
Marzipans,
Macaroons in syrup,
Ices of rose, barberry and pomegranate,
Almond paste sculptures,
Fresh cheeses,
And refreshing drinks of fennel, pistachio and orgeat.

The wines for this service will be, for the whites:

Yvorne, Rochecorbon, Puy Notre-Dame and Vouvray; for the reds: Chambertin, Mouton-Lafite, Hermitage and Lunel. After which will follow red champagne of Bouzy, Verzenay and Port.

Moka coffee. Ratafia liqueurs of Grenoble apricots, muscatel and anis."

It is fiction, of course, but this manner of banquet, presented in the *service à la française* as in Versailles, might well have happened in the excessive days of the Big Stomachs. It is Carême caricatured, a good thing carried far too far—and there were fiendish chefs in practice around the time that Escoffier was writing who were perpetrating precisely this kind of nonsense. They were convinced that it was wonderful, too. Their tables resembled those overcrowded late-Victorian parlors, so chockablock with bibelots, lace and statuary that it was almost impossible to navigate within them. First Escoffier, and then Point, Pic and Dumaine after him, skinned off the superfluous and stripped away the pretension, leaving the purest expression of true gastronomy. For Rouff, this meant Dodin-Bouffant's *pot-au-feu.*

Naturally, the prince's gastronomic Götterdämmerung inspires Dodin to pick up the gauntlet and offer his meal in exchange. And his stroke of genius is to return the favor not by another belly-burster, but rather by a lesson in simplicity and finesse. With suitable ceremony, then, Dodin invites the prince to his house on a warm summer afternoon. When they are comfortably installed in his dining room, he rises at the head of the table and reads the menu:

> "Delicacies before the soup,
> *Soupe* Adèle Pitou,
> *Fritures* Brillat-Savarin,
> *Pot-au-Feu* Dodin-Bouffant with its vegetables,
> Purée Soubise,
> Desserts,
> White wines of Dezaley and Château-Grillet,
> Red wines of Châteauneuf-du-Pape, Ségur and Chambolle."

Terror, disappointment and discomfort seize Dodin's regular eating partners, while the prideful prince inwardly debates whether he ought to flounce away home, but *l'artiste* knows what he is doing, and the meal which he has brought forth from Adèle (not yet his wife) is a wolf in sheep's clothing, an apotheosis of sophistication disguised as common fare. Dodin's triumph is total, and the prince accepts his punishment with grace: "Dodin, perfectly happy, held the hint of a smile on his lips. To the vanity of the prince's culinary sumptuosities he had replied with a meal that was simple, short and bourgeois, but one whose art was so profound that even he who had dispensed such ostentation understood his own indignity."

As the vanquished gourmand mounts into his carriage for the long journey homeward, Dodin offers him his definition of cuisine in an aphorism worthy of Brillat-Savarin: "A work of choice, demanding much love." How French. I know dozens of chefs, male and female, to whom this truth applies in the full depth of its exhausting reality today, exactly as it did for Pic and Dumaine a generation ago—and even more especially for Point. If the Holy Trinity is One and Equal in theology, it turns out that in gastronomy one of the component parts is more equal than the others: Fernand Point is by far the most important of the most important. He is God the Father.

The influence of Fernand Point today is immeasurable, as great as was the fabulous reputation of La Pyramide, the paradise he began creating in 1924 in Vienne, a city of small industry lying between granite cliffs and the river Rhône, twenty miles south of Lyon. A haven of calm, comfort and refinement which was arguably the greatest restaurant in the world during the postwar period (although such superlatives are as dangerous as judging Manet against Monet), La Pyramide's kitchen was graced with an astonishingly great number of internationally recognized names of French gastronomy today. They came to Point as *commis* or *apprentis*, *Wunderkinder* of the casserole, gifted children who were long on energy and short on experience, but hoping to learn a trade. Point took this juvenile material and turned them into masters. Paul Bocuse was Point's preferred pupil and surrogate son, and he was also the one who stayed the longest: six years. But so many other cardinals and archbishops of today's eating establishment passed under Point's benign pedagogy that it seems scarcely believable: Pierre Troisgros (his brother, Jean, too), Roanne; Louis Outhier, La Napoule; Alain Chapel, Mionnay; and Claude Peyrot, Paris. All of these, like Bocuse, run three-star establishments now. In the two-star category were François Bise, Talloires; Maurice Coscuella, Plaisance, and Pierre Gaertner, Ammerschwihr. Add to this illustrious list Jean

Banchet (Le Français in Chicago), Georges Pleynet, of the one-star Les Grillons in Champagne-au-Mont-d'Or, plus the occasional lesser celebrity whom I may have forgotten, and you have a bouquet such as no other single person had ever put together: The only student of Pic who has made an indelible mark is his own son, Jacques, and Dumaine seems to have left behind him no one of note but Jean Ducloux, owner of the admirable two-star Restaurant Greuze in Tournus.

If the main difference between Point and his eminent colleagues, then, was in pedagogy, he also was more radical in his departures from Escoffier doctrine, experimenting more daringly with The Master's precepts, not hesitating to adopt regional specialties and ancient *bonne femme* recipes into his *haute cuisine*. The same dishes, personalized according to each man's style, now appear on the tables of Bocuse, Troisgros and Chapel: *poulet en soupière, gratin dauphinois, gâteau de foies blonds de volaille* and all the rest of the marvelous panoply of domestic masterpieces which had developed over centuries in obscure kitchens of farm and village. But perhaps even more important than his creativity and professionalism was the intangible: Point's personality. A gentle tyrant, he was as generous and forgiving as he was intractable about the quality of every aspect of his house, and his young workers both loved him and respected him. With his vast knowledge and perfectionist's stubbornness, he could have been a horror to work under were it not for his wonderful character. Point was filled with love: he loved people, he loved nature, he loved the establishment he had built, he loved the good life it offered him and his clients, and he loved to laugh, as we will be seeing.

Probably most of all, he loved Marie-Louise Point, "Mado," the local hairdresser whom he married in 1930 and who more than fifty years later was still running the restaurant and maintaining its three-star standing, long after Point had gone to his reward. Shy but determined, working with the tools that he had at his disposal, Point had courted her with food, inventing succulent new dishes, or variations of dishes, for her each time she came to La Pyramide with her parents. After sending out *chef-d'oeuvres* like carrot soufflé or pike *au gratin* or Bressane chicken pregnant with truffles, he would peep longingly through a crack in the kitchen door to see if the girl of his fancy fancied them, and so, perchance, might fancy him as well. After they were married, she took over entire responsibility for the dining room, and anyone who has not seen Madame Point officiate over La Pyramide in her pearls and Chanel suits may know much, but most assuredly knows not the finest expression of the business of being a *maître-d'hôtel.*

History has left us a single image which forever will symbolize Fernand Point and the Point style: a marvelously clever photo taken in the early fifties by Robert Doisneau, a man who, coincidentally, is a part of the Holy Trinity of French photographers, the other two points of the triangle being Jacques-Henri Lartigue and Henri Cartier-Bresson. Doisneau arrived on a balmy summer day, walked along the red clay pathway to the terrace, which lay basking in the dappled light of the morning sun filtering through the leaves of the majestic plane trees which towered overhead. And there, seated in a comfortable armchair, Fernand Point was going through his morning ablutions. An immaculate white cloth was tied around his neck and, tentlike, spread out over his back and torso. The matutinal ritual was always the same: Point was being shaved by Vienne's preferred barber while his staff made kitchen and dining room ready for the day's clients. In a large stone mortar built into the terrace wall, lolling comfortably in a bath of cracked ice, a magnum of champagne was exhaling vapors of frigid stars from its round, green mouth. On the table next to Monsieur Point stood a crystal glass of tulip shape, silver-gray with condensation, which ever and anon he raised to his lips.

"Come in, young man, come in," said Point, and before Doisneau knew what was happening he had a glass of champagne in his hand. "You are here for the photo, is it not?"

It was, and as Point shook off his covering and straightened his polka-dot *lavalière* necktie, Doisneau was calculating. Pyramide, pyramide, hmmm, now lemme see.... There was the famous Roman vestige in town, just around the corner, a high, metronome-shaped pyramid that had marked the center point of the former Roman circus; there was the restaurant itself, named after the monument. And now he realized that there was Monsieur Point too, something of a monument himself at six foot three, perfectly pyramidal as he sat in the barber's chair with the white cloth around him, spreading regally outward over his magnificent tummy.

Doisneau selected a wide-angle lens and posed Monsieur Point standing with dignity in his black suit. Crouching low so that his subject's stomach occupied three-quarters of the frame, sloping downward from left to right, he snapped the picture that every photographer should have thought of before, but hadn't: Point the Pyramid. It was almost too good to be true, and Doisneau wanted to scram and develop his film, but he hadn't reckoned with the totalitarian generosity of this most famous of restaurateurs.

"On ne part pas de chez Point sans déjeuner," he declared, and that was that. Doisneau had the picture of his life and the meal of his life on the same morning, then, and he wasn't permitted to lay out a sou for either of them. That was Fernand Point.

"I was afraid they'd be mad at me when the picture came out," Doisneau remembered, "but no. They loved it. And Madame Point asked me for a blowup and told me to come back for another meal."

Doisneau's historical photograph pleased Point greatly because it offered him a new *bon mot* to inflict upon the curious who had the effrontery to ask him how much he weighed.

"My weight is confidential," he would reply gravely, "but if you wish to obtain my volume, you have only to multiply the surface of my base by my height and divide the result by three."

Point's ironclad rule was that La Pyramide had to begin every new day completely naked, with nothing in the fridges (there was no freezer) and nothing on the stoves: no meat, no vegetables, no sauces, no stocks, nothing. Even the *pâtissiers,* the most perfectionistic and nervous of kitchen craftsmen—atmospheric pressure, changes in humidity or the evil eye thrown by a tramp from across the street can cause a delicate pastry dough to go to hell—were obliged to live with this implacable rule, and Point took cruel pleasure in playing hide-and-seek with the smart alecs who thought they'd put something aside for the next morning. He was tall enough to see onto most shelves, and what he couldn't see he felt with his hands which he poked into every cranny of the kitchen every night before closing down shop. A lobster came back untouched, or someone had reduced too large a quantity of perfect, pellucid *glace de viande*, shimmering amber and delicious, just the thing for the kind of sauces that most people dream about? *Tant pis*—into the garbage with it! So it was with the dishes from which his customers ate and the vessels from which they drank. The slightest scratch on a Baccarat glass or the most modest chip on the edge of a Limoges porcelain plate condemned them to Point's vengeful hammer.

On most days, Point served a single menu, and every customer ate the same meal, prepared with fanatical care from the divine ingredients which had been brought to his door, like sacrificial offerings, by the local farmers, retailers and kids who knew precisely what the boss of La Pyramide wanted: nothing but the best. In this, his concern for the quality of the ingredients first and foremost, he laid down one of the golden rules of modern French cooking, and the result of his teachings is apparent today to anyone who takes the trouble to go early in the morning to Rungis, the wholesale market outside of Paris, to Les Halles of Lyon or to the open-air market on the embankment above the River Saône and watch the boys play the game of who-gets-the-best crayfish or sea bass or morels or whatever is coveted that day. Up as early as Dominican monks, slightly more bright-eyed after an atomic coffee at the bistrot across the street, the Bocuses, Chapels, Blancs, Lacombes and Bourillots vie with each other and with intransigent, ill-tempered old grannies for the pick of the crop, because it is there, in the market, only after the shopping has been done, that the day's menu can be planned: everything fresh and everything good; after that, cook it right.

"With good ingredients and a bad chef you can make a good cuisine," Point insisted. "But with bad products you will always make bad cuisine—even with a good chef."

Point's absolutism about taking his cuisine seriously was celebrated throughout France and, eventually, the rest of the world. The man simply would not compromise. Notoriety fairly leaped out at him in the early fifties when word got out that he had ejected, *manu militari*, a pair of Americans from La Pyramide because they wanted to drink Coke with their lunch. A genius of public relations,

Madame Point later told me that the event had never occurred, but I am not sure whether this isn't a bit of ex-post-facto diplomacy on her part. Point was fully capable of gestures like that. He was just as famous for the smoking trick. If he spied an unlucky customer lighting up between courses, he directed his waiters to follow standing instructions and bring coffee and the bill. "Ah, but I thought you had finished," Point would explain innocently when the evil gourmet protested. In 1940, after France had been defeated by the German war machine and the dreary occupation-time rationing came into effect, Point was hauled before a court in Vienne first for having sold meat dishes to customers who were lacking ration cards, and he confounded his judges with the purest Cartesian logic: "How do you expect me to ask for tickets from people who don't have any?" he demanded.

It was at another of these wartime disciplinary hearings that he made the famous historical pronouncement which in itself should have been enough for the *légion d'honneur* which he was eventually awarded. This time the accusation was that he had used cream—obviously procured from the black market—in his scalloped potatoes.

"No one has the right to betray a *gratin dauphinois*," roared Point.

"*La grande cuisine* should not wait for the customer," he instructed his pupils. "It is the customer who should wait for *la grande cuisine.*"

If his respect for women was old worldly, elegant and courtly, his attitude toward male customers was thoroughly cavalier, partly because of his dominating physical presence and partly because he was utterly unimpressed with rank and title. Most men, even those he was meeting for the first time, were simply *"mon petit,"* while those born to royalty were treated with all the profound deference of *"mon petit prince."*

Some people turn pale at the sight of spiders, snakes or mice; for Point, the horror of horrors was thin people.

"When I stop at a restaurant I don't know," he wrote, "I always ask to shake the cook's hand before the meal, because I know that if he is thin, I'm going to eat badly. If he is both thin and glum-faced, then I know that my only salvation is to flee."

Still, Point was Point, and the goodness of his heart led him to perceive qualities in almost anyone—even a thin man. "Check him out for me," he once instructed one of his staff after having turned away a suspiciously thin cook who had been seeking work in La Pyramide. "Perhaps he is a former fat man."

As simple as the day's menu at La Pyramide was the matter of the bill. Point had it presented elegantly, but hardly in the manner designed to please the race of people who become the accountants who check expense accounts. It contained a single figure for the amount due, with no detail of any sort beyond that. So towering was the restaurant's reputation and so intimidating the figure of The Master that hardly anyone ever dared to question him. One of the rare ones who did—a doctor, I believe—became the fall guy in yet another of the legendary Point gestures. Called to the man's table for the argument about the price, Point listened politely for a moment, then took the bill and tore it up. The doc had a free lunch that day, but he was requested never to return to La Pyramide. It was just the opposite that happened the day that a waiter mixed up his papers and gave to an American couple the bill for a neighboring party of eight. The Americans paid without a whimper and had departed when Point discovered the error. Telephoning frantically around town, he eventually managed to locate them to explain how they had been inadvertently swindled. And this time, for once in his life, it was Point who lost in the game of one-upmanship.

"That's okay," said the Yank. "The bill did seem a little high, but you gave us the meal of our lives. Keep the change."

This was a rare exception, though. Far more common were the freeloaders—broke or laden with money, it made no difference— who had their napkin rings *chez* Point, and who were never allowed to pick up a tab. They were friends, and Point was dictatorial about inviting friends to his board. Just as the young photographer Doisneau had lunched for free, so did the local notables, old cronies from his youth and a host of showbiz personalities who flocked to Vienne to pay court to *le roi Fernand* and to bask in the sun of his presence and the aroma of his truffles. At any time, it could be expected that up to a quarter of his guests would be eating for free, and Tuesday, theoretically the day of the weekly closing, was especially worrisome to apprentices and young cooks, because Point could be expected to turn up at any time of day or night with a hungry retinue in tow and provisions in hand.

"I don't go out to shows," he boasted. "The shows come to me."

Only once did he make an exception to this golden rule, when his friend Sacha Guitry, actor, playwright, moviemaker and aphorist *par excellence*, pleaded with him to come to Paris and make the birthday dinner for his fourth wife, the actress Jacqueline Delubac. Guitry was so eloquent that Point finally assented and, grumbling and sighing, boarded the train with his casseroles and assistants. That evening he whipped up a typical Point meal (seafood bisque, truffled chicken, foie gras, Pyramide salad, cheeses and desserts) washed down with typical Point drink (1906 Château-Chalon, 1921 Château Cheval Blanc and champagne, of course), for one hundred guests. When Guitry, who had the reputation of being tightfisted, asked him for the bill, Point answered with a lesson in diplomacy worthy of Dodin:

"I am not in my home here, so please allow me to consider myself one of your guests."

"You can't imagine the glory that Point enjoyed then," said Pierre Troisgros. "The man had an aura about him that was supernatural. Whenever he left Vienne I was the one he chose to be his chauffeur, and off we would go, at thirty-five miles an hour—he hated to go fast—in his Hotchkiss. And if we went to some place like La Mère Brazier in Lyon for lunch, the whole place panicked when they saw him walk into the room. He had a manner and a bearing that impressed even people who didn't know him. So you can guess what he represented for people who were in the trade. When he appeared it was as if Jesus had walked into the room."

If Point was the grandfather of the cuisine called *nouvelle*, he was nothing but *ancien* in his respect for the roots of French cooking. The very idea of anything even approaching *cuisine minceur*, would have inspired the most profound loathing within his august person. Other foreign fares might be interesting and even excellent, but the whole basis of French cuisine, he knew, was in the animal fats which doctors now tell us to avoid.

Butter was the banner under which he fought, and he repeated his war cry time after time to everyone who worked for him: *"Du beurre! Donnez-moi du beurre! Toujours du beurre!"*

As much as the cholesterol alarmists might like to think otherwise, you can't have French cooking without butter and cream. Their tastes, their magic qualities of liaison, their suave unctuosity are at the very heart of cuisine, both *grande* and *ménagère.* Even in Point's time it was known that too much animal fat cannot be good for you, but Point was convinced that butter was most dangerous and least digestible when it had been cooked to death, at which point it becomes black and sinister. His use of butter was generous, to be sure, but his touch was gentle; when he incorporated it into sauces or vegetables it was always at the last minute, barely melted, fresh and uncooked, and it gave that depth of taste that no margarine or miracle oil will ever be able to imitate. When he fried or sautéed in butter, he threw out the used, hot liquid and added new butter in its place. Following this line of thought, one of his preferred tests for an aspiring cook was to ask him to simply fry an egg. There may be dozens of approaches to this elementary classic of nourishment, but the Point system had to be the noblest and purest. There was only one way to fry an egg according to Point, and this was the mandatory procedure:

> Place a large portion of butter in a frying pan and let it melt white: that is, it should just barely spread over the pan. Naturally, it should not foam or crackle.
>
> Break your eggs into a saucer and slide them gently into the frying pan. Now they must cook so softly and gently that the white becomes just creamy and the yolk hot.
>
> In a separate saucepan, melt some butter white. Add a light touch of salt and pepper and pour the hot butter over the eggs, which have been removed from the frying pan to the serving dish.

Point treated his eggs with *respect*. How could it be otherwise, when he was in love with the lady *volailles* of Bresse, the satin-skinned *grandes dames* of the barnyard, white of feather, firm of flesh and ample of breast, the most desirable eating chickens anywhere in creation? If they, the ladies, deserved ruinously expensive necklaces of *T. melanosporum* and their late husbands were warranted long, hot baths of Chambertin wine, why should their unborn offspring not be deemed worthy of similarly noble treat ment?

Nobility was in every gesture and every dish of Fernand Point. Elephantine, he had the elephant's ponderous grace, gentility and intelligence. If it was partly because of all the free meals he so prodigally dispensed over his too-short career and partly because of all the tourist francs, dollars, pounds, crowns and other miscellaneous monies that he siphoned into the French economy that he was awarded the Legion of Honor, I suspect that it was nevertheless just as much for his practical jokes that the street outside the front door of La Pyramide now bears the name of Boulevard Fernand-Point. On top of all his other admirable qualities, Point loved to laugh and make people laugh, and his talent for practical jokes was diabolical and legendary. As we shall be seeing later in this book, it is an ancient and honorable tradition around Lyon to treat life as one continuing practical joke, and in this Fernand Point, enormous, dignified and poker-faced, was an artist among artists.

Postmen and delivery boys tooling up to La Pyramide on their bikes knew that they always had a glass of Beaujolais or two—or three or four—awaiting them as the reward for their efforts, an exact reflection of the French word for tip—*pourboire,* for a drink. What they didn't always know was that the solicitous attention of Monsieur Point, The Master Himself—How's the family? Looks like a good year for trout, doesn't it? Nice weather, too—could hide nefarious ulterior motives. Twenty minutes or half an hour later he would stride out the front entrance with a Beaujolais spring in his gait—and not find his bike. Or, rather, his bike would be where he had left it, but he couldn't recognize it because it had been magically transformed from black to brilliant pink, compliments of Paul Bocuse, Jean Troisgros, Maurice Coscuella or other members of the kitchen staff whom Point had dispatched posthaste to the sidewalk with pots and brushes.

As it still is today, Beaujolais was then the prime tool for the confection of absurdities, stunts and practical jokes of every manner. A bottle of Beaujolais was the obligatory balance—the weight in the other hand, as it were—to the broom when it came time for the monthly spider-web cleanup. Perfectionist down to the last detail, Point insisted that the ceiling of his dining room be swept clean of any nascent trace of cobwebs once a month, and the chore rotated around among the *commis* and *apprentis*. A broom in one hand, then, and the Beaujolais in the other, the lad worked his way from one end of the elegant room to the other, his head cocked upward in the requisite position for spider-spotting and Beaujolais-drinking, until all the webs had come off, and all the wine gone down.

It was a special honor for many a departing guest to be invited into the kitchen for a chat and a glass with the *patron*, and the honor was signalled to everyone in Vienne who knew Point's routines, because the poor fellow would leave the restaurant with renovated footwear. This was Paul Bocuse's specialty. Crouched low on the floor with a pot of whitewash, he would creep up under the anteroom table which Point had strategically placed there and carefully paint the man's heels white while Point engaged his attention with a discussion of the merits of the wine or a grave dissertation on the proper methodology behind the creation of a *fonds de volaille.* That very same guest might well have been taking his phaeton or his torpedo on down to the Côte d'Azur and might have asked Point to pack him up a picnic lunch fit for a gourmet. The picnic basket was something of a Point speciality, and historically might be seen as the first adumbration of the extra-restaurant commerce in which so many of the great chefs are engaged today. The Master invariably included thick slices of foie gras, cold Bresse chicken legs, several sorts of pastry delicacies and hard-boiled eggs—but he also made it a point of honor to insure that at least one of the eggs was still raw.

Louis Thomasi, the wonderful, modest sommelier who worked for fifty years *chez* Point until his recent, regrettable retirement, had the seniority and the shy good humor that made him the ideal victim for the young bloods of the kitchen staff. Every year poor

Louis looked forward to the opening of fishing season with an odd mixture of pleasure and apprehension, because he dreaded the *conneries* that the boys were surely planning to inflict on him and his boat.

We must open a parenthesis here for *connerie*. This is a fundamental notion that must be absorbed by anyone who wishes to understand the French, but most especially the French who live in Lyon and its environs. Most of them can manage to be serious from time to time, but their lives are guided by humor, and the broader, the bawdier and more Rabelaisian it is, all the better. For an existence perceived from this point of view, the operative word is *con* and its many important derivatives: *connard, conasse, connerie, déconner.* The class will come to order.

Con is a most unseemly word when taken literally, being a contemptuous slang substitute for "*vagin,*" but when taken figuratively it miraculously loses its grossness and becomes almost an everyday expression, used by ladies and gents alike, to signify dolt, fool or someone you really don't care for. If you make a silly mistake or a bad Monopoly move, you admit that you were *con*, in the adjectival form. If someone clowns around all the time, like Harpo Marx, *il fait le con*— he's making like a *con*; the term is amused now, even affectionate. A *connard* is a male dope, a *conasse* a female one; the terms are contemptuous. *Connerie* is perhaps the most important and versatile of all the derivatives of *con*: depending on how you employ it, it can signify a tragic mistake (*une grosse connerie*), a stupidity or a hilarious joke. And *déconner*, a multi-talented verb, means to make mistakes or pull off pranks. Have you got that now? Good.

It was definitely in that last sense that Louis the sommelier was regularly victimized *chez* Point. He had a nice boat for fishing on the swift cold waters of the Rhône, which passed only one hundred yards or so from La Pyramide. He kept it anchored along with a flock of similar green, flat-bottomed skiffs of his fellow fishermen, the kind that Monet used to paint, but the kitchen staff always knew which one was his, and the first day of each new fishing season represented a perpetual challenge for ingenuity and young muscles.

One year the skiff would be checked into the baggage room of the Vienne railroad station, another year onto the roof of Thomasi's house and another, near the tippy-top of a high chestnut tree.

"*Ah, les cons,*" Louis would sigh as he struggled to undo the deed and get on with his beloved fishing. The mayor of Vienne had exactly the same reaction when, on the morning of one 14th of July, he saw the official grandstand from which he and his fellow notables were scheduled to review the parade in honor of France's great national holiday: it was backwards. Point had directed the kitchen and dining room hands for the best part of the night to disassemble it and put it back together again turned around, facing the sidewalk.

"*Ah, les cons,*" Point himself had to say the day the firemen refused to answer his cry of distress. A fire had broken out in the cloakroom, but it was April first that day, and the firemen were certain that the call from La Pyramide was just another April Fool's Day imposture. By the time they finally saw the smoke and came running two rooms had been destroyed. But Point relished the irony of the situation and broke out champagne for the valiant *pompiers*.

"He was the *personnage* of my career," said Pierre Troisgros. "There was an atmosphere of joy at La Pyramide that I have never seen before or since. My time there was like being on vacation."

In March of 1956, worn out by too much good living, good eating and good drinking, Fernand Point breathed his last sigh, aged only fifty-six. So many doctors had eaten so many free meals at his table that he went to his reward under the eyes of a veritable *Nomenklatura* of France's most eminent specialists.

"I have been treated so well," Point whispered before checking out, "that I am sure to die cured."

"My master committed suicide by champagne," mourned his number-one chef, Paul Mercier. A few months later, Mercier, who exercised every day and never touched a drop of the stuff, dropped dead of a massive heart attack. Somewhere up there, someone must have been laughing.

V.
PAUL, PIERRE, MICHEL AND THE COOKING CALLED NEW

The meal began with a couple of small slices of foie gras, pink in the middle and surrounded by a ring of duck fat of that curious yellow-gold that Gothic painters brought to haloes above saints in the process of being martyred. Slices of lightly grilled *pain brioché*, still warm, served as toast. A pair of bright red *rouget* (cousin of our red mullet) followed: pan fried, in butter of course, their alabaster flesh so tender that you had to be careful when you attacked them with knife and fork, lest you make a mess of it, destroy the lovely, layered symmetry, break the bones and look like a clod. Lemon wedges, no sauce. A chilled bottle of Bâtard-Montrachet, the same color as the haloes but slightly more luminescent, helped it all along. Without question, it was the best breakfast I had ever had.

It was about ten o'clock of a warm May morning a few years ago, and I was sitting with my wife in the shade of a plane tree on the sun-drenched terrace of a restaurant near Lyon, but this time the place was not Vienne and the restaurant was not Point's. A few yards across on the other side of the road, the River Saône loafed along its idle course, accompanied now and then by a slow-gliding *péniche*, the big, diesel-powered barges from Lille or Le Havre or Conflans-Sainte-Honorine, with the little house at the stern and the skipper's car perched precariously on the deck up by the bow. Behind us, in the dining room and in the kitchen, the personnel, still in shirtsleeves, silently prepared the place for lunch with the same chores as were being repeated at the same time in thousands of other restaurants throughout France: laying out china and silverware, cutting and arranging flowers, cleaning fish, browning veal bones, peeling, turning and engineering vegetables into the properly disciplined shapes without which a *julienne* is not a *julienne* and a *mirepoix* not a *mirepoix*. Already the distinctive odors of *fumet de poisson* and *fonds de volaille*, the olfactory signatures of any good restaurant in the morning, were discernible in the richly scented spring air.

My wife and I had dropped by to say hello—we were on our way to another place for lunch—but we should have known that you don't just say hello and leave without breakfast, not here. The man sitting opposite us in his white chef's tunic was approaching fifty then (he's passed it now), and his black hair was just beginning to thin. At six feet or so, he was tall for a Frenchman, and although his frame and his easy, rapid gestures were those of an athlete, the discreet swelling amidships bore witness to the trade of the professional of food. Since he was not yet wearing his *toque*, the high, starched cotton bonnet invented by Carême as the badge of the business, his face emerged like a ruddy globe above the brilliant white of the tunic. An interesting face: craggily severe and sharp-featured, its centerpiece was the splendid beak of a Roman nose that imparted a roosterlike note; it was nonetheless liberally creased with laugh lines, and the bags under the eyes were the sure sign of the man who works (and plays) too much while sleeping not enough. Politely, he had taken a glass of wine himself, but he never touched it. Making breakfast was his job, not consuming it. Now he was devoting himself entirely to two things: watching with his intense black eyes to make sure we ate every last morsel, and talking.

A chef who sits with you watches you eat the way a comedian listens for laughs from the audience, but they don't all talk the way this one was doing that day: about the buying and preparation of food, the odd profession of restaurateur, gastronomic history, the clients who came to him from all corners of the world and how their tastes perhaps reflected national characteristics. But more than any of these subjects, he was talking about his fellow chefs, praising them boundlessly and recommending them to my urgent attention, insisting that I go visit them without delay and furnishing me with exact road directions, lest I be tempted to call off a trip through ignorance of geography. Alain Chapel is very nearby, he was saying; just don't forget to turn right and cross the river at Neuville. You've got to go to Illhaeusern, near Colmar, because the Auberge de l'Ill is probably the best restaurant in the world, and of course you can't forget Madame Point—I'll make the call and reserve if you like— and since you'll be passing by Vienne, you can take the route directly past Saint-Étienne and go on to Roanne to see Jean and Pierre Troisgros, who are much better cooks than I am.

Paul Bocuse was doing a number on me. And I, like everyone else who comes under the fire of his enthusiasm, humor and intelligence, was eating it up, figuratively and literally. I owe him a heavy debt of gratitude for it today, because it was through him and by him that I was introduced into the ancient and much misunderstood world of the brotherhood of practitioners of *haute cuisine*, became friendly with a large number of them and developed an affection and admiration that, with a few exceptions here and there, is pretty close to being absolute.

I feel almost guilty about devoting a chapter to Paul, because everyone else has already written so much about the man that there scarcely seems to be anything more you could add that hasn't already been said. He cultivates publicity, and journalists of all types and countries gallop in to Collonges-au-Mont-d'Or to eat his free meals and give him even more exposure, because he is colorful and outrageous and makes wonderful copy. He has been on the cover of *Newsweek, Paris Match, Stern,* the *London Sunday Times, The New York Times Magazine, Gault Millau Guide, El Pais* and God knows what other major publications. He is such a seasoned performer for TV and radio that by now he can offer expert advice to neophyte crews on the best lighting to use for the filming of truffle soup, *loup en croûte* or *poulet en vessie*. After so many years of being chased by foreign journalists and food writers (especially female ones, who are attracted to this unregenerate macho like moths to a 250-Watt bulb), he knows his lines by heart, and they all ask the same questions so often that he has to remind himself to let them finish before answering, in order to give at least the appearance of reflection.

"You know who the two most famous French persons in Japan are?" he asked me one day with the combination of self-satisfaction and wonderment that marks his character. "Alain Delon and me— more than Giscard or anyone else."

Occasionally, in spite of himself, he slips into the imperial third person when speaking of the Paul Bocuse phenomenon—because a phenomenon it is. Willy-nilly, half wanting it and half wondering how it all happened, he has become a *personage* and a first-rank international media personality, created in a 50/50 complicity with his friends the journalists. If you have already had your fill of Paul Bocuse prose, then, just skip the rest of this and go on to the next chapter, but even if you have decided that you hate him and that he is a discredit to the kitchen, you should know this: not only is he far and away the most famous cook of all time, but he is also the most important one to come along since Escoffier. By simply being Paul Bocuse, he has done more for the profession than all of his *confrères* put together. We all can name a few wizards who are probably greater creators than he and perhaps even some who know more about cooking (although I wouldn't like to give odds on that one). But in explaining why *la cuisine française* is at the summit it is today, one has to give a lot of the credit to Paul Bocuse.

Paul graduated from La Pyramide University under Professor Point at the top of the class, applied The Master's lessons of sophisticated simplicity, of generosity, humor and friendship, added a few touches of his own and ended up with the magic formula that eventually became known as *la nouvelle cuisine française*—which gimmicky slogan would better have been set aside and the cuisine described simply as the modern school of French cooking. Far more than any specific new ingredients—the green peppercorn, cabbage leaf, sweet-pepper mousse and kiwi follies that cyclically swept, like tidal currents, across French menus, leaving behind a driftwood of the bad taste of faddery—far more than the austere, Bauhaus presentations of filet and vegetable on enormous plates, the modern school of French cooking is a sociological phenomenon, a change in attitudes and approaches, a revolution in the role and situation in life of French chefs, and it is in this that Bocuse has been the most important of all of them. More than any of the others, he is the one who established once and for all that the chef was leaving the servant class at the same time as he was coming out of the kitchen, to appear in the dining room and sit down as an equal with the doctors, bankers and industrialists who were his clients: fellow entrepreneurs and fellow appreciators of the good things in life. If the idea of the owner-chef—the *patron-cuisinier*—took root with Point, Pic and Dumaine, it was Bocuse who established it as something very like a universal rule, one which British writer John Ardagh nicely referred to as "The Revolt of the Serfs."

The men of the Holy Trinity of Gastronomy were exceptional in their days. Today, their style has become generalized: now the chefs own the places where they cook, and the *maître d'hôtel* works for them. Or better yet, the *maître d'hôtel* is, to put it in bastardized French, a *maîtresse d'hôtel*. More and more, when young couples strike out on their own, they give the restaurant their own name to identify it as the personalized enterprise that Bocuse, Troisgros, Chapel and others of Point's students have championed—and it is the wife who does *la salle* while the husband takes care of *la cuisine*. This now includes the traditionally male domain of the wine steward. Stuck in your choice of wines? There are several excellent restaurants where you will now consult a *sommelière* instead of a *sommelier*. The word may not be in the dictionaries approved by the Académie Française, but the reality is there nonetheless. Today, twenty of the twenty-two restaurants that are generally conceded to be the best in France are chef-owned and run, and instead of hating each other and playing at the idiotic, druidical game of hide-the-secret-recipe, they band together in a brotherhood that resembles the medieval Compagnons du Devoir, the grouping of itinerant artisans that gave birth to the Freemasons. Like the Freemasons, they know each other well, and they exchange information, recipes and business tips, cooperating for the good of the guild, but, perhaps somewhat less like the Freemasons, they usually have a roaring good time while they are at it. This is the Bocuse influence that is most striking today. If cooks are no longer jealous of each other, it is largely due to the force of Bocuse's personality, his openness and his readiness to help. A born ringleader, he persuaded his fellows to scratch each others' backs, when natural inclinations until then had been more toward cutting throats.

"Il ne faut pas cracher dans la soupe," is a favorite expression of his:—don't spit in the soup—and it sums up as well as anything else his attitude toward the trade.

"You know, it's funny," Pierre Troisgros told me, wryly smiling as he said it: "A lot of us recoiled in horror the first time we saw Paul doing the things he did, but then a little while later we found that we were doing the same things ourselves. There's no doubt about it: he is a leader. All of us have followed Paul in one way or another."

"The profession ought to erect a monument to him," declared Madame Point. "Anyone who has a bad word to say about Paul will have to deal with me."

But of course she's prejudiced. She loves Paul like a son, and the feeling is reciprocal. Today still his voice becomes tender when he speaks of Fernand Point, and he is the first to admit that most of what he knows came from or through him. He learned the basics and the style in Vienne, then, but Paul did not become Bocuse until he returned to Collonges-au-Mont-d'Or, the village seven miles north of Lyon where Bocuses had been cooking ever since Paul's ancestor Michel opened a little *auberge* in an abandoned flour mill on the banks of the Saône in 1765. Passing boatmen, farmers, travelers and the local bourgeoisie were the clientèle, and what they preferred was simple country food, like rabbits from the hunt and tiny fish netted in the Saône, deep-fried and salted, accompanied by wines from the hills above Collonges or from a bit further north, in the Beaujolais country.

For the first few years, he was content to remain just Paul, the worker who had served at the stoves of a fancy restaurant but was now back with family tradition in the *guinguette*, the riverside bistrot he had inherited from his father: fishing, playing *pétanque* and serving the unpretentious country specialties that everyone dreams of finding in France, but which are becoming more and more rare. The influence of Fernand Point was too deep and too powerful to throw off, though, and almost in spite of himself he began enlarging his vocabulary, forsaking the *civet de lapin, coq au vin* and *blanquette de veau* in favor of the kind of dishes he had prepared in Vienne. Gradually, his style went from *cuisine de bistrot* toward *haute cuisine.* The word got out and the gourmet grapevine began buzzing that something extraordinary was happening at Collonges. In 1961 he won the cooking section of the national competition sponsored by the Ministry of Education to determine the year's Best Worker (Meilleur Ouvrier de France) and, concurrently, Michelin awarded him his first star. A year later the second one came. By 1965 he had his third star, the ultimate consecration, and he has never looked back since. At the time, his was the fastest rise to the top in Michelin history (his record was surpassed by Michel Guérard's one-two-three punch at Eugénie-les-Bains between 1974 and 1977), and eaters flooded in from all over Europe, America and Japan. In the days between his second and third star the rush of pilgrims was so insistent that he was reduced to bolting his front gate at 9 P.M. to bar the late arrivals whom his narrow kitchen and limited supplies of fresh provender could no longer accommodate.

"Those were the days when I made the most money," he said later. "The staff was small, I had my wife and my mother to help me, and we worked almost around the clock. I got rid of the paper napkins and stainless-steel knives and forks and started to buy proper china. But we still had the W.C. out in the courtyard while we had two stars. After that, I was able to buy back the old house and my name."

The man bought back his name. Bocuse tends to be like that:

all primary colors and archetypal story plots, just like in the movies, except that that's the way it really is. There are people who seem to be born for fiction, and Bocuse is one of them. Partly by his actions, partly by accident, and partly by a taste for provocation, he grew over the years into a kind of mythic figure, as much a symbol as an individual—which is precisely why so many adulate him and so many others heap odium upon him. Even without knowing him, people tend to assume a familiarity and assign him as the representative of something they like or dislike. His symbolic role in 1966, the year after his third star, was that of the avenging folk hero, returning to the field of battle to wreak vengeance upon a cruel destiny which had deprived the family of its very name. Paul's grandfather had been a fine cook, it seems, but such a wretched businessman that he had gone broke and found himself obliged to sell the ancestral inn and the name that went with it—Restaurant Bocuse—in 1921. His son, Paul's father, opened a more modest place in the shadow of the railroad bridge at Collonges and called it the Auberge du Pont de Collonges. It was to this that Paul returned after his six years with Point, still unable to use his name until he retrieved it in 1966 by buying back the original inn, a few hundred yards downstream from the present restaurant.

"My grandmother cried every time she saw the old place," Paul remembers. Just like in the movies.

Once he had the name well in hand, he never stopped using it. PAUL BOCUSE signs leap out at you all over the northern part of Lyon, especially along the banks of the Saône, and stand forth majestically in huge, white electric letters above his restaurant. The first time I went there I wondered if I might lose my way among the twisting lanes and hills around Collonges. What a silly idea: from one point to the next, as in a childhood treasure hunt or Boy Scout exercise, one bright red PAUL BOCUSE sign after the other leads inexorably downhill to the Saône, right-left, right-left, under the railroad bridge, until I was there, parked directly beneath the garden of delights.

"This guy isn't afraid of publicity," I remarked to my wife, and that turned out to be one of my better understatements.

Paul's reticence could perhaps be measured with a micrometer, but now that he has become a tourist attraction in France along the lines of the Eiffel Tower and Mona Lisa, he digs into even that supply with parsimony. And if we had to choose an architectural expression for this man-boy, man-symbol, it would not be his three-star restaurant, but rather the original Auberge Bocuse, now renamed l'Abbaye de Collonges and entirely rebuilt in Neo-Rustic—a huge, balconied hall with heavy beams, a walk-in fireplace (you ought to see an entire ox roasting on a spit there) and one of the world's finest collections of mechanical organs. L'Abbaye serves as Bocuse's venue for weddings, receptions and *prix-fixe* business functions, but what makes it truly different from any other similarly-oriented shop is *"Le plus grand orgue du monde,"* the world's biggest organ, as he (maybe optimistically) bills it on a picture postcard: a marvelously monstrous, baroque, polychrome mechanical organ by Gaudin, thirty-two feet wide and eighteen high. This handmade ancestor of the Moog synthesizer, all pipes and bells and articulated figurines, is said to replace one hundred ten musicians, and is designed to imitate the sounds of French horns, violins, clarinets, flutes, trumpets and trombones, castanets and virtually anything else you may desire. It runs electrically now—it was turned by steam power when it was built in 1912—but the organ is told what pipes to tootle by the same system of perforated cardboard cards that ran the spinning machines in Lyonnaise silk factories in the nineteenth century and IBM's first primitive computers just after World War II. Bocuse bought the machine as a ruin and spent a fortune to bring it to its present condition. He likes nothing better than to dart behind the monster, fire up the motor, compressor and bellows and play you a little *musique de circonstance:* "God Save the Queen" if you are a Brit, "The Star-Spangled Banner" for Americans or "Ain't She Sweet" for any woman under eighty. Then he steps down from the platform and poses for his customers in front of the clanging bells, thrashing drums and braying horns, basking in the Niagara of music roaring forth all around him. BOCUSE CIRCUS is written in bright red capital letters on the machine's gold and white pediment, and along the walls stand orderly rows of wooden merry-go-round horses, galloping in symmetrical parallax all the way to the north wall. He is happy.

"I love the circus as much as I love food," he says, in one of his movie-script lines, "and good red wine and women. But maybe you should reverse that order of priorities."

Bocuse's appreciation of women is as legendary in France as his *loup en croûte farci d'une mousse de homard*, the dish with which he won his M.O.F. title and which he and his kitchen staff are now stuck with for the rest of their natural lives, as is Pierre Troisgros with his *saumon à l'oseille*, Michel Guérard with his *pot-au-feu* and Claude Terrail of the Tour d'Argent in Paris with his *canard au sang*. Fanny Deschamps, a French writer who had the good fortune to come into the world as Alain Chapel's niece, theorizes in her wonderful *Croque en Bouche*, the book I wish I could have written, the way I wish Chapel were my uncle, that all serious cooks are sensual and sexual creatures by nature, and that if by chance they were not born that way they grow into it through years of obsessively seeking out the finest and most beautiful examples of fish, fowl, fruit and vegetable, of eyeballing them and then touching and squeezing them to test their freshness and firmness and then, when they are alone with them in the intimacy of their kitchens, fairly caressing them as they commune with their goodness to create beauty and pleasure. They're not intellectuals. When other kids were in prep schools absorbing the eternal verities of western culture by drinking beer and reading *The Nubian Slave*, the future stars of the gastronomic élite were peeling vegetables. It is natural for them to assess a beautiful woman the same way they would appreciate a beautiful sea bass or a plump woodcock. And if their hands stray from time to time, that's merely the force of professional habit. Cooks are obsessed with seduction: every time they send a dish out of the kitchen it is an act of seduction, and no matter how long they have been in the profession they notice what you have eaten and what you have not, just the way Bocuse's eyes were following the progress of my Breakfast of the Century a few years ago. If attractive women wish to be treated as intellectuals, let them go and discuss Schopenhauer in library stacks with philosophers. But if they run with cooks, they are likely to be approached somewhat less ethereally. Boys will be boys.

"Bocuse wouldn't have been Bocuse without his women," he

says, dropping into the third person once more. He was only rendering justice where justice was due. During the hardest years of establishing his presence on the gourmet scene and then working his way to the summit, he was tirelessly seconded by his wife, Raymonde, the beautiful and gracious blonde from l'Ile Barbe, the island in the Saône halfway between Lyon and Collonges, whom he married in 1946 and who functions, today as ever, as the absolute ruler of the dining room, like Madame Point in Vienne. Until recently, his mother, Irma, ran the *caisse* and wrote out the bills, while his daughter Françoise, who looks like she ought to be playing Carmen (she is as black-haired and piercing of gaze as the old man), was the receptionist. Irma is gone now, and Françoise married and occupied with her brood, but Raymonde carries on, the last active member of Bocuse's famous female mafia and by far the most important one. Paul is quite right: the restaurant could not function without her.

Curiously enough, it can function without him, and it does when he is off in Japan promoting his wines or the Paul Bocuse line of gourmet products, in America putting in an appearance at the Chefs de France restaurant in Epcot, which he shares with Gaston Lenôtre and Roger Vergé, or almost anywhere else in the world signing his cookbooks, presiding over an expensive meal for profligate millionaires, carrying out his historical role as a representative of France, the culinary trade and himself. Star of stage, screen, radio and TV, Bocuse travels a lot, and he gets a lot of heat from the gourmet establishment for his absences. A chef is supposed to stay in his kitchen, tradition says, lovingly preparing his specialities, devoting himself entirely and modestly to his clientèle, blushing at their praise.

Bocuse doesn't do things that way, and neither do the dozens of other great cooks who have followed his lead and branched out into other activities, creating a phenomenon known as *Le business de la grande cuisine française,* so real that it was featured in a cover story in *Fortune.* Just like Horatio Alger, just like the model provided in every American business school, Bocuse is a mountain climber at heart, and when there is another peak in his view, he has at it. Building his three Michelin stars was the first ascension, followed by the buying back of the old family inn and enlarging it, while also redecorating his restaurant into a place of sumptuous luxury. The enormous collection of music machines came next. And then one day he evidently looked around and decided that wasn't enough. As heretical as it sounds, maybe a man can want more than being admired as an *artiste* of the casserole. Bocuse did, and he left Collonges to go out and get it—in Paris, in Stuttgart, in Osaka and Tokyo, in New York, Dallas, Los Angeles, and Florida, wherever business people were falling all over themselves to thrust money at him and offer him deals that he couldn't refuse. Gaston Lenôtre soon was doing the same, and Michel Guérard and Roger Vergé and Jean-Paul Lacombe and a host of others, including many who had sniffed at his vulgarity in seeking money in the first place. An artist isn't supposed to be interested in filthy lucre, is he? Bocuse was the first to dare to take the step and become a businessman, too. God knows he saw plenty of them in his restaurant, and they weren't always overwhelmingly impressive. If talentless popinjays could make millions in real estate, insurance, hairdressing, psychoanalysis, advertising, the stock market or other such larcenous activities, why should a cook not be able to get a piece of the action, as well, in our world of free enterprise? Especially when he has spent twenty years or so proving his merit and building the staff that could keep the machine turning faultlessly in his absence? The answer seemed obvious. So is the wheel, but you've got to think of it.

Bocuse took to traveling, then, and almost instantly the chorus of enraged *oooh-lalas* began to reverberate around Collonges. The boss of Le Restaurant Paul Bocuse was an established star by then, and the customers figured they had a right to see him there in flesh and blood. Decidedly, mores had come full circle. A couple of generations earlier, their ancestors would have been outraged if a mere cook had had the cheek to leave his downstairs domain and come out and mingle with the gentry. Now they wanted to see Bocuse himself perform, and they didn't know and didn't care that Roger Jaloux, the chef whom Paul had hired at considerable expense to run his kitchen, was also a Meilleur Ouvrier de France, knew the Bocuse cooking by heart for having been his first apprentice, and was unquestionably a culinary genius himself. For years, clients had been eating food by Jaloux without noticing any difference in quality, but as soon as The Master was absent, the taste of ashes crept into the truffle soup. And the French, the world's best complainers when they put their minds to it, began complaining.

It became something of a gastronomic platitude to say that one had eaten badly at Bocuse's. I have heard the complaint many times, but whenever I pressed for details I drew a blank. The plaintiffs could not remember exactly what it was that displeased them, but they grumped even so. They liked to say they had eaten badly, I realized, because it was fashionable to say it. It is also nonsense. You can no more eat badly at Bocuse's—or Troisgros or Haeberlin or Vergé—than you can see ugly women onstage at Le Crazy Horse Saloon. It may not be what you like, or what you expected, but it ain't bad. Cheap-shot artists adore great restaurants, because they afford them the chance to shine. Or, rather, to appear to shine. Since they all know how to eat—the process is classical, consisting of taking aliments at Point A, placing them inside Point B and chewing until they descend to Point C—they feel themselves expert enough to judge their superiors. I play a little tennis, too, but not quite to the point where I figure I can whip that nasty little McEnroe. An American food critic made a laughing stock of herself a few years back by writing that she had eaten badly in just about every major restaurant in France, strewing the path of her chronicle with errors and complaining that liver at Bocuse's didn't taste like liver in New York. Bloody right it didn't, and still doesn't, and isn't likely to, either. Even with this performance, though, the most disgraceful exhibition of cheap-shooting I ever witnessed was at Pic—the wonderful, irreproachable, arch-serious Pic in Valence, the very temple of perfect eating founded by André and now lovingly tended by Jacques.

It was an aging starlet who was next to us, a false blonde, American—*hélas!*—sitting with a man she evidently felt she had to impress. Who knows what he was—a movie producer, maybe—but whatever his role in life, hers right then was to make a display of her knowledge of the French language and *la haute gastronomie* by systematically criticizing everything about her dinner, while picking at it the way dieters do. When, toward the end of the evening, Jacques Pic came from the kitchen to inquire if his guests were satisfied, she came out, in a loud, heavily accented voice, with the phrase she had been saving up all night:

"C'était ordinaire. Traytray zordinaire."

I hope she got indigestion that night. But I doubt it. The same kind of phenomenon obtains most often *chez* Bocuse, because he is such a star, and people love to measure themselves against stars, but there is an added complication with the male-female angle. I suspect that there may often be more than a little bit of sexual acrimony involved here: by far the greatest numbers of Bocuse revilers I have heard have been women, and I wonder whether what really displeases them is the continuing series of macho pronouncements that Paul has made to the press over the years, as a part of his permanent campaign of kidding and provocation. There is nothing a Lyonnais loves more than getting at people with a good joke, and Bocuse is the archetypal Lyonnais. The result of his provocations is that today half the women seem to love Bocuse and half seem to hate him. That's a pity, because his combat has been much the same as the one that western women have been waging of late, and it comes around to something like that big word, liberation. For some women, being a housewife isn't enough. For some cooks, being an *artiste* isn't either.

La belle Raymonde provides the continuity while Paul is out gallivanting around the world, and she effortlessly guides the staff which, as at most of the three-star establishments, numbers exactly forty-nine employees: fifty is the dreaded bureaucratic turning point, where French law obliges an employer to set up a *comité d'entreprise*, a kind of mini-union, within his shop, to sit regularly with its board to discuss working conditions and furnish its officers with an annual report on what he is doing to improve the lot of his personnel. In the French restaurant trade, the role of the *comité d'entreprise* has been traditionally handled by the chef's foot, dealing annual reports in the form of *coups de pied au cul*. Bocuse was never known for this form of discipline, but anyone who dined there in the days before the arrival of Roger Jaloux remembers with vivid clarity the stentorian sound of his tenor voice, *a capella*, giving orders one minute and bawling out (for once the expression is exactly right) some unfortunate *commis* the next. Mimesis works in the food trade just as it does everywhere else: during Jaloux's first year or so of service, the same piercing sounds that he had learned from his master came echoing from the kitchen, until Bocuse sat down and had a talk with his chef. Jaloux's blood pressure is as high as ever, but he has learned to speak softly now, the atmosphere in the Restaurant Bocuse is one of velvety calm and Raymonde no longer has to wince because the decibel count reaches saturation point.

"Paul was a self-willed boy, right from the start," I remember his mother saying with a sigh, several years ago. "He always had a mind of his own and knew exactly what he wanted."

What he wanted at age ten was mashed potatoes and sautéed veal kidneys, his favorite dish then, and the first one he mastered on his own. At age sixteen, after several years of working in the paternal kitchen, he was apprenticed out to an established restaurant in Lyon, for whatever it was possible to learn under wartime conditions of rationing and shortages of everything. One year later, when American troops liberated the Rhône Valley, he went to a recruiting office of the Free French forces, swore he was nineteen, and went off to campaign in Italy, eastern France and Germany. Within a year he came back home in a hospital train with a stitchery of machine-gun impacts across his chest, so artfully placed there by a German gunner that they somehow missed all vital organs. It was this improbable good luck as much as anything that persuaded him of the two principles that have guided him ever since: first, that he must have some kind of destiny in life, and second, that he'd better not take it too seriously.

He has seriously devoted himself to not taking life seriously ever since. "It's the best practical joke of all," he once commented, but the ones he has perpetrated in a long and distinguised career of clowning are enough to fill a small anthology. If it was Point who gave him the taste for the *canular*, he carried the art form to new heights, fired by a wild imagination, a gift for improvisation and an unbeatable supply of gall. When he joined Jean and Pierre Troisgros as a *commis* in the very proper, traditional Lucas-Carton in Paris, it was like adding potassium nitrate to sulfur and charcoal: instantaneously, the *conneries* began transforming the venerable surroundings into bedlam. The Bocuse boy trapped sparrows (with caviar as bait) in the Tuileries gardens and released them in the kitchen to do their air shows around the outraged head of Monsieur Richard, a chef of the old, hard, humorless school. Monsieur Richard was in the habit of arriving at work in coat and tie, then changing to his tunic and toque in the cloakroom, where he would slip into *espadrilles*, the canvas shoes in which he worked. Bocuse nailed the *espadrilles* to the floor. Monsieur Richard went to his caldron of chicken carcasses, boiling away to reduce to a *fonds de volaille*: Bocuse had slipped a human skull, copped from the catacombs, in with the fowl. Monsieur Richard looked at the provisions up on the shelves of the *garde-manger* and saw to his astonishment that the boxes of Camembert were moving: Bocuse had emptied them and replaced their contents with mice. Bocuse and the Troisgros boys went out strolling to the ritzy Place Vendôme on their day off, stationed themselves outside the august show window of Van Cleef & Arpels, jewelers to royalty and millionnaires the world over, and made a great show of coughing loudly, as if afflicted with acute catarrh, Pierre and Jean facing the window, Bocuse with his back turned. As soon as they had drawn the attention of the swells within, Bocuse turned around to display a huge *langue de veau*, a calf's tongue borrowed from Monsieur Richard, hanging from his mouth. *Ah, les cons.*

Left to his own devices when he returned to Collonges for good, Bocuse multiplied the *conneries* with profligate abandon. Invited to join an elegant duck hunting party, he spontaneously offered to bring along a picnic lunch, and how great was the celerity with which the bourgeois accepted the offer. When lunchtime rolled around, Bocuse searched the trunk of his car with ostensible panic and many oaths, emerging from his labor to admit that he was desolated, but apparently someone at the restaurant had made a mistake and packed only the cans of food for the dogs.

"Well, if it's good enough for them it's good enough for me," said the great chef, opening a can, spooning out a mouthful and ingesting the stuff. He had a friend in the canning business who provided the logistics of the joke: dog-food cans filled with foie gras. "Hey, you know," said Paul, offering the can around, "what those dogs eat isn't half bad."

Paul Lacombe, owner-chef of the famous restaurant Léon de Lyon, was a dear friend and hence a prime target for the Bocuse stunts. One of the most successful came when a target of opportunity, Christopher Soames, then British Minister of Transport, lunched in the elegance of Collonges and asked Bocuse if he could recommend a good Lyonnais bistrot for dinner. Why, yes, as a matter of fact, sez Paul, thinking quickly, I can. You go to Léon de Lyon tonight and see my good friend Paul Lacombe. I'll call him myself to make the reservation. Soames was well pleased with himself and with Bocuse, but at the appointed hour the pleasure rapidly palled at the arctic reception he found himself receiving from Lacombe. How could the poor man know that Bocuse had warned Lacombe about a foreign deadbeat who called himself an important politician, who had left Collonges without paying and was planning to do the same at Léon de Lyon?

"*Hallo*," said the victim, "I believe that Monsieur Bocuse called you about me."

"Yeah, he did," replied the second victim. "now buzz off."

Poor old Soames, trying to be polite and indignant at the same time in French, protested about the shabby treatment he was receiving and eventually was moved to make the fatal announcement that he was a minister of Her Gracious Majesty. That was the cue Lacombe had been waiting for.

"I know all about that. And I'm the Pope."

Lacombe felt the creeping horror of the man who begins to realize that he has been possessed when Soames's companion irrefutably identified himself as the British consul-general in Lyon and demanded to know what all this undignified nonsense was about. It was about Bocuse, Lacombe knew by then, but that was too complicated to explain. He sighed, made Soames a dinner that couldn't be beat, offered him champagne in expiation, and they finished the evening good friends. Paul Lacombe died, too young, a few years after the stunt, but his son, Jean-Paul, is there at Léon de Lyon in his place, cooking better than ever and keeping alive the Laurel and Hardy spirit that the Lyonnais appreciate so much. The next time you are there, ask Jean-Paul if you may test the force of your lungs by blowing the special bugle he keeps in the bar for that purpose. I got the pressure gauge almost up to two myself, but the record is well over three. The other customers don't mind the noise a bit—it's all part of the game.

As any practical joker knows, serendipity and circumstance can be seized at almost any moment to create havoc. Invited to a reception at the apartment of a champagne merchant, Bocuse found himself at the elevator at the same time as a delivery boy carrying an enormous bouquet of fresh-cut flowers. *"Tiens, petit,* I'll bring it up for you," he said, slipping the boy a 10-franc tip and taking the flowers from his arms, "I'm going to the reception myself."

After that it was child's play to remove the calling card of the fellow who had sent the flowers, insert his own in its place and arrive at the reception like a hero. But the joke didn't end there. After drinking a glass of champagne, Paul slipped away from the party and walked to a dime store, where he bought the cheapest and most hideous vase he could find, smashed it with a hammer and sent it along to the reception beautifully gift-wrapped—accompanied by the other fellow's card.

It is the dream of every cook, every food writer and every Lyonnais wise-guy to *faire marcher* Bocuse, to catch him in the net of some diabolical practical joke as monstrous as his own and make him bite. But he has ears like a rabbit, eyes like a bird of prey and a nose for jokes so finely tuned that he dodges all the traps strewn in his path. Certainly Pierre Troisgros did manage a good one in the days of their apprenticeship at Lucas-Carton, when he sewed a pair of pheasant wings on Paul's overcoat and helpfully slipped it over his shoulders as he was dashing out for a rendezvous with a girl-friend, but triumphs of that sort are excessively rare with *le grand Paul.* One of the most ambitious plans ever conceived in his honor came in 1975, when some unscrupulous Lyonnais, who knew that Bocuse was due to receive the Légion d'Honneur, laid his hands on a couple of sheets of stationery from the office of the *Président de la République* and sent a phony invitation to Collonges, asking Monsieur Bocuse to come and receive his medal from Monseiur le President Valéry Giscard d'Estaing personally, at the Elysée Palace.

Bocuse sniffed the air, caught the scent of something rotten and put in a call to one of the many influential friends who had been freeloading off him for years. Say, what if we arranged to have *Monsieur le Président* give me the medal, he suggested, and I show up with a bunch of cooks? We can make the meal for him and then sit down and eat it with him. It would be terrific publicity for him and us and France, wouldn't it? And that is precisely what happened: Giscard leaped at the idea, and Bocuse appeared in Paris with his foie gras, truffles and eight other top cooks in tow. The result was, just as he had predicted, one of the best publicity stunts of Giscard's reign. As a bonus to all the good press, Bocuse enriched his *carte* with the dish he created for the occasion, and which is now as renowned as his famous sea bass in puff pastry: truffle soup VGE.

"You've got to beat the drum in life," Paul said afterward, by way of explanation. "God is already famous, but that doesn't stop *Monsieur le Curé* from ringing the church bell."

Monsieur Paul, as his staff calls him in that mixture of formalism and intimacy which works so well in the French language, rings the bell a hundred times a day, but never more pleasingly than when he invites outsiders to join him in his morning marketing. Probably hundreds of foreigners have enjoyed this experience over the years, and it goes a long way toward explaining the extraordinarily favorable stories that result whenever writers take the trouble to go to Lyon and actually spend some time with their subject, rather than rewriting the mountain of clips already extant on the subject of Emperor Bocuse. I don't know when or how Paul got the inspiration of inviting people along on his shopping tours, but it was a first-rate idea: his time is so limited that he can rarely spare more than a few moments in the "normal" working hours of the day, and by taking his supplicants along with him on his matutinal food expeditions he kills two birds with one stone, getting his work done and handling interviews at the same time. Sitting on the floor of his panel truck amid a clashing chaos of aromas—here the fish, there the foie gras, over there the wild strawberries—takes a bit of getting used to, and it's not easy to take notes while he grinds his gears and makes the little Renault dart daringly through the Lyon traffic, but the experience has no counterpart.

The morning marketing of the chefs of Lyon and its environs is a ritual that contrasts completely with the style of Monsieur Point, who always had his food delivered to his door. All the world came to Point, but for Bocuse, Chapel, Blanc, Lacombe, Vettard, Nandron, Bouillot, Orsi, Bertoli, Léron and company—the top talent of the world's center of gastronomy that is Lyon—the market is like starting a school day with recess. It is a serious job to select the victuals for the day's menu, certainly, but when these men-boys meet over crates of asparagus or *chanterelles*, it is in an atmosphere of raillery and good humor that looks suspiciously like happiness. They are creators, they are their own bosses, their businesses are doing well, and they are friends. Whatever complications you wish to visit upon your life, how can you fail to survive with a start like that? Each *patron* does his own shopping for pleasure, then, but it is also a guarantee of quality and a badge of honor that they all wear with pride. They, too, could have everything brought to their doors, hoping that the merchants have selected the best for them, but the atmosphere wouldn't be there, and each chef would sit isolated in his own establishment, probably wondering what the other one was up to, and why. The result would be jealousy, suspicion and pettiness of the old mold, the one that Point cracked and that Bocuse and his friends smashed to smithereens.

There are two markets the chefs go to in Lyon: the *halles*, a vast and vastly ugly concrete structure in the modern section of town called *La Part Dieu* (God's Share) devoted mostly to whole-sale, but permitting retail activity as well; and the farmers' market on the Presqu'île, the peninsula between the Rhône and the Saône, where the sidewalk above the banks of the Saône is monopolized by the most astonishing collection of good things to eat that anyone can possibly imagine, and whose mere presence explains why there are so many great restaurants in and around Lyon. The raw materials they work with are unmatched anywhere in their quality and variety: the beef from Charolais, the poultry from Bresse, the winged game from the marshes of the Dombes, the freshwater fish from Alpine lakes and their feeder streams, and the fruits and vegetables from the Rhône Valley.

Paul wheels into the confusion of cars and trucks that reduces traffic to a single, slow-moving lane, triple-parks and starts on his rounds, checking out the produce available for the day, snapping a grean bean or breaking a peach apart between his thumbs to smell it, like a *tastevin* working on a Montrachet, copiously chaffing fellow cooks in his high-pitched Lyonnais drawl, and getting the same back, twice over. Once a week the *cuistots* get together in a bistrot near the *halles*, chip in to pay for a *mâchon*, the hefty Lyonnais equivalent of brunch. It is 10 A.M. or so when they sit down in a back room for solid portions of tripe, hot Lyonnaise sausage with a vinegary potato salad or ham hocks with lentils, wash them down with several *pots* of Beaujolais, laugh uproariously as they exchange news of the latest *conneries* within the profession and, for an hour or two, forget about *haute cuisine*.

Across the way, the gray concrete rectangular box of the *halles*, as distinguished a piece of architecture as any parking lot I have ever seen, sits there indifferently, waiting to surprise you, because the inside of the package is so infinitely more admirable than the outside. A visitor's first view of the *Halles de Lyon*—unless, on the way in, he crosses a mighty porter, a *fort*, tottering along at quick-step under two hundred pounds or so of beef carcass toward a delivery truck—is of the fruits and vegetables: row upon disciplined row of Breton artichokes, Picard potatoes, Provençal tomatoes and squash, carrots, peas and beans of all sorts, picked in their prime and washed, brushed, combed and laid out at attention, all of them screaming out the secret little ultra-high-frequency message that only cooks can hear: cook me cook me cook me. And preferably with lots of that delicious Normandy butter from *la mère Richard* over on the other side of the aisle, standing in bright yellow *mottes* the shape of artillery shells, fairly bursting with the seductive shrapnel of cholesterol, and so what, you wanna fight about it?

Renée Richard is great. If Chaucer had not already invented her, the Wife of Bath incarnate, Rabelais would have given it a try one hundred years or so after. Blonde, handsome and queenly in her white smock, she presides over her B.O.F. (*beurre-oeufs-fromage*) shop with a grace and assurance that would be authoritarian were it not for her agile mind and the ironic hint of a smile that is always at the corner of her mouth, ready to break into a laugh or throw out a torrent of needling *persiflage*. Paul is her favorite, and hence her favorite victim, and if there is a photographer or film crew present, she will throw her arms around him with monumental abandon, to give the magazine or TV public an unbeatable image of *la belle vie* in the markets of Lyon.

There may be some cheese specialties that *la mère Richard* doesn't have on her counters, but I haven't met them yet. Great bulky wheels of Edam, Gouda, Emmenthal and Tomme, as heavy as a man, stand next to little fresh goat cheeses, so youthful that they are still soft and oozing whey, while white, virginal Fontainebleaus, as delicate and fluffy as soufflés, avert their eyes in the presence of the tough guys of the trade, the Époisses and *fromages forts* that pop their muscles under sweaty shirts, ready to carry away your senses of smell and taste. They are serenely ignored by the aristocrats, the blue-veined cheeses of Roquefort and Ambert. Renée wraps Paul's lavish order of the day (his cheese platter has to be seen to be believed) in the company of her daughter, young Renée, who has the same blond hair, quick smile, alert eyes and white smock, although a couple of sizes smaller. Little Renée was a good girl who went away to college and got her law degree, but then she thought about it and returned to the *halles*, a chip off the old block. Thank God for her intelligence: lawyers are a dime a dozen, but cheese shops of this quality can be counted on the fingers of two hands, with maybe the addition of a toe or two.

On both sides of Renée's B.O.F., the *charcuterie* stalls explode with the goodness of the pig, in every possible shape and form, salted, smoked and herbed, exuding a heavy, suave, appetite-whipping aroma that catches the stroller a few yards before he gets there and then, like a good host after a party, accompanies him all the way down to the door at the other end. The butchers, unanimously assumed to be millionnaires, handle their steaks and chops the way Yves Saint Laurent handles silk, while the *tripiers* lay out their snouts and ears and brains and feet and intestines and lungs and hearts and testicles and other rare delights with such loving care that if you look at their stalls with the proper squint you could take the composition for a cubo-surrealistic painting. I developed the *tripier* squint many years ago. It is somewhat akin to the slaughter-house gulp.

Monsieur Pupier, the *poissonier*, wears a permanent scowl as he patrols his damp domain in blue shirt and rubber boots, garden hose at the ready. Beneath him, at kneecap level, are wide, bubbling aquariums in which lobsters, crabs and sea bass take their last swims while, waist-high, fields of chipped ice glisten white, bearing a polychrome harvest of sea creatures laid out in apple-pie order. Monsieur Pupier, whose shop is approximately 250 miles from the nearest salt water, manages to have a better selection of irreproachably fresh fish than you could find in Saint-Malo, Concarneau or Marseille, a bit of commercial magic that is owed to polystyrene packaging, superhighways, night-driven trucks and money: you want the best fish from the dockside auctions held in the morning darkness when the boats come in? You can have them if you pay the price, and Monsieur Pupier pays it, because he knows who wants what—and what their customers expect.

Neither Paul nor any of the other cooks asks about the price. They'll take care of that later—or, rather, *la patronne* will take care of it when she pays the bills. What counts now is to get the best stuff. After a quick check of a scribbled shopping list, Paul strides over to the little café inside the building and bellies up to the bar for a snarling cup of puissant black coffee while the boys fill his truck with the morning's purchases. A fast visit to Bobosse's shop across the street for foie gras and the artisanal *saucisson de Lyon* which he serves to his guests *en brioche* as a little appetizer to pass the time while waiting for the first course, and it is already time to get back to Collonges.

Paul's constant and continuing campaign of education and propagation benefits Bocuse, of course, but, far more than any of the other great cooks, he feels a duty to work for the larger good of the trade. History, accident and his own powerful personality have given him the leader's role—or did he just assume it? Either way, the result is that he beats the drum tirelessly for his *confrères*, sending journalists around from restaurant to restaurant, making arrangements and phone calls himself, arranging business lunches in which the press's only duty is to eat, assessing characters with his fine, complicated, Byzantine intelligence and placing people together who will find points of common interest that, one way or another, can redound to the good of restaurants, tourism and France. It was not a mere public relations scam when Jacques Médecin, mayor of Nice and secretary of state for tourism under President Giscard d'Estaing, officially took him into his ministry as a part-time counselor a few years ago. Michel Guérard (Eugénie-les-Bains), Georges Blanc (Vonnas) and Roger Vergé (Mougins), all of them masters among masters in the business, doubtless have risen to their present summits of three Michelin stars on their own merits, but Bocuse was behind them from the start, big brother and cheerleader, making sure that no one could forget their merits. He personally introduced me to all three of them and to a host of other, younger cooks who are working their way up the rungs.

This instinct to help is so solidly ingrained now that the best of the pros occasionally suffer from their own generosity. Not long ago, I was having a glass of something refreshing with Pierre Troisgros at the round family table in a corner of his kitchen in Roanne, where he, his wife, Olympe, and his son, Michel, take their meals while keeping a professional eye on the various apprentices, *commis* and *chefs de partie* who keep the machine turning the way it has to turn when you are at that level of quality.

"Hey, the cowboy," shouted Pierre in the direction of the far wall, where an uninterrupted picture window runs the length of the room, letting in a flood of light and giving the boys a great view of the parking lot. A dozen or so figures in white were whipping and snipping and cutting and carrying on. "Come over here and say hello to your compatriot."

The man who approached, smiling hugely and beaming behind large, black Barry Goldwater specs, looked about as much like a cowboy as Leonard Bernstein or Henry Kissinger do, and he was clearly in some kind of seventh heaven to be there, working and learning in the shadow of the Luciano Pavarotti of restaurateurs. He was, I learned, a psychoanalyst from Los Angeles (where else?) who had earned enough money to take a year off and pursue his hobby of cooking—and what better place to start than *chez* Troisgros? What, indeed. But Pierre's overpowering need to have a resident shrink inside his kitchen didn't seem quite as clear. How, I wondered, did he happen to get help like that?

"Well, you know," said Pierre with a rueful smile, "friends of friends and the things you say at night when you're sitting with nice clients. Sometimes, somehow, with all the back and forth talk, people get the idea that you could hardly make your place work without them. So one day they show up, and what do you do then?"

Pierre has had an enormous number of Americans in and out of his kitchen over the years, most of them because he is a man who has trouble saying no, and sometimes the thanks he receives in return are as gracious as a kick in the shins. One of his more distinguished alumni, a professional cook this time, followed up his stay in Roanne by writing an article in which he suggested that Troisgros kitchen personnel were not only overworked but underfed as well, and fought like stray dogs over bits of steak returning uneaten on clients' plates. Pierre sighs philosophically and rolls his eyes. What can you do with people like that? Gaston Lenôtre, Normandy's Mozart of pastry and a close friend of both Troisgros and Bocuse, solved the dilemma of the inability to say no by founding a school for *pâtissiers*. Now, if you want to come and spend a few days or a few weeks *chez* Lenôtre, you sign up on an enrollment form and you pay tuition fees.

It might be a good idea for Bocuse to try something of the same, because he has a problem pronouncing the magic negative himself. I was afforded a striking demonstration of this combination of presumption on one side and generosity on the other one morning when I was taking my ease on the very same terrace at Collonges where I had experienced my unforgettable breakfast. Lucien, one of Bocuse's *maîtres d'hôtel,* emerged from the restaurant to ask me to come in and have a word with the *patron.* There was something he was having a problem with. The problem was that the person standing with Paul, a young, elegant and refined American with brushed blond hair, didn't speak any French, and could I translate please?

"Tell Mr. Bocuse," the American explained, "that I am a fellow cook of French food, and that I have come here to spend a few days in his kitchen. I'll help out for free—naturally I don't expect him to pay me—and just do odd jobs and lend a hand here and there, so I can observe how he works."

"Does he realize," Paul asked me, "that I get a dozen letters a week from guys like him asking to come and work for free in my kitchen, and that I turn them all down, systematically? Does he know I don't need any extra help, and that another person in the kitchen—especially an untrained outsider who doesn't even speak French—is nothing but a bother to me?"

I started to translate, but Paul cut me off with a wave of the hand. "We'll see about that," he said. "Tell him to sit down and have lunch."

Paul not only offered the stranger lunch—and me, too, as payment for the two-minute translation job—but the full-dress lunch, with champagne cocktail, *foie gras, loup en croûte, suprêmes de volaille* and the entire mad parade of cheeses and desserts, and the wine with it all, too. The young man picked at his lunch with all the delectation of a housemaid going through dirty laundry, pushing his plate aside after a few mouthfuls and explaining that he had to watch his weight. I could have wrung his neck. When you get a free lunch from Bocuse, you eat it all, goddammit. Your figure is irrelevant. And yet, even with that performance, Paul did take the character into his kitchen for three or four days, and he sent him on to Troisgros afterward, too—although I suspect that this was more in way of a practical joke than a favor.

What the young man had been hoping to learn from Mr. Bocuse was something that everyone was calling *nouvelle cuisine* in those days. *Nouvelle cuisine* was all the rage, and everywhere in the world chefs of every age and persuasion were plunging into it with the fervor of Moonies who had discovered that God was alive and well in South Korea. *Nouvelle cuisine* was exciting and different and a true revolution, and it meant that you could eat all the food you wanted and not gain weight—better yet, you could even lose weight with *nouvelle cuisine.* It was dietary!

Of course, all of this was, and remains, nonsense. The Great Nouvelle Cuisine Soufflé has pretty much fallen by now, leaving a trail of old press releases, shattered illusions, unused purée machines and scraps of kiwi peels. And, above all, confusion. Hardly anyone knows how it all happened, or where French cuisine stands today in its aftermath. It was changed, to be sure, but how, and how much? The simplest way to find the answer is to go to Roanne or Collonges or Illhaeusern or Vonnas and see and appreciate classical cuisine that has been intelligently updated, moderately lightened, stripped of pomp, served *à l'assiette* (that is, the plate filled and arranged in the kitchen rather than served from trolleys by waiters) and given names that are understandable. Contrary to popular fable, stocks (*fonds*) are used in this modern style of cooking, and butter and cream and, yes, even flour, too, within reasonable measure. But so much agitprop and misinformation has circulated about *nouvelle cuisine* that you could be forgiven if you came to the conclusion that its component parts were air and water and pretty herbs. You wouldn't be entirely wrong, either, if you specified that most of the air was hot.

As we have seen, it all began with Point, Pic and Dumaine, who passed their style on to Bocuse and his friends, who in turn adapted it to their own age. It was for these disciples of the Holy Trinity—and most especially Bocuse and the Troisgros brothers— that the fateful phrase was coined for the first time, around 1970. The deed was done by a couple of smart Parisian journalists who caused a revolution in their own profession by being the first food critics who knew how to write well and entertainingly. Henri Gault and Christian Millau, who had started writing feature columns for *Candide*, a rather trashy weekly, continued onward with the now-defunct daily *Paris-Presse l'Intransigeant*, and then founded their own gastronomic monthly called, simply, *Gault Millau*. They became the popes of *nouvelle cuisine*, because they were the ones who invented the phrase in the first place and then, in a very crafty, tremendously successful marketing campaign, identified their very persons, and hence their magazine, with the concept and the style. In the explosion of publicity that followed, Gault and Millau prospered mightily for several years, and their magazine along with them, a fact which served to blow the phenomenon ridiculously out of proportion. What ought to have been the theme for a few articles and then more or less forgotten, struck a sensitive chord, and the vibrations went flying through the gourmet establishment. Those two fate-charged words became an all-encompassing smokescreen, a rallying cry for sated, novelty-hungry food writers and a terrific gimmick for a host of entrepreneurs who may not have known much about cooking, but recognized a great opportunity for profits when they saw one: minuscule portions of half-cooked food, with hardly any preparation involved beyond sculpting carrots into Japanese shapes, served on big plates and sold at prodigious prices.

The best of the professionals did not need any sloganeering to perfect their modern style of cooking, but masses of other, lesser talents put French cooking through a long, tiresome phase of cutesiness. These were the ones who took a craft that had always had its roots in peasant traditions and the good, rich products of the fat land, and sent it into a silly sideways tack toward precious Parisianism, one of western mankind's most dangerous maladies. People who called themselves restaurateurs displayed much more zeal in interior decorating than in cooking, and French cuisine stumbled into a period of confusion and sterility. Most of the fault lay with the food critics—an extraordinarily influential lobby in France—not so much because they had created the movement in the first place, but because too many of them cheered it on even when it fell into caricature and excess.

Why? Much of their misplaced zeal might be attributed to the force of novelty and the good old mortal failing of hubris, which persuades human beings that they have invented something that no one had ever thought of before. But there is another explanation for the almost fanatical behavior of the food critics during this curious period, one that is rarely invoked but probably of deeper importance than all the others: *they weren't hungry.* Professional eaters, they had to confront the table at least twice a day, week in and week out. As unbelievable or even as laughable as this may sound to the non-initiate, eating two sophisticated French meals a day, which starts as fun and delectation, rapidly becomes a horrifyingly taxing marathon whose inevitable result is satiety and a kind of desperation bordering on claustrophobia. Too much food, too much cream, too much butter, too much wine and fine alcohols, constitute a regimen that few can bear for any length of time—see the chapter on my friend Jean Didier—and the liver, head, stomach and bowels are soon crying for surcease in the face of yet another onslaught of nourishment. Let the moralists draw what conclusions they wish, but that's how it is, and it can be truly close to torture. Add to this the vanities that happen to obtain in our day and age—everyone's supposed to be thin now—and you have a situation that is ripe for revolution. Well, the revolution came, and it was called *nouvelle cuisine.* But it was based on a fallacious assumption: that the general public felt the same way toward food as the professionals did, that is to say with a mixture of detached curiosity and foreboding that can, on the most trying of days, become downright revulsion. The point is that the general public doesn't eat in great restaurants twice a day. Even for those who are gastronomically inclined, the frequency would be more like, say, twice a month. For these occasional eaters, such a meal is a rare and festive occasion, and if it is rich, well, so what? A feast is supposed to be rich. For the men and women who do it for a career, though, food is their means of livelihood, but it is also a kind of enemy, and the table is an examination, a trial and an obstacle course. Might as well make the exam as easy and light as possible. Hence, the enthusiasm that greeted the birth of the *nouvelle cuisine* soufflé: fundamentally, it was food for professionals:

"Light, light, light, I want to eat light. I've got a dinner tonight, *miséricorde.*"

As if all of this were not complicated enough, Michel Guérard had to come along at about that time. Oh, dear.

If anyone in the world is responsible for giving *nouvelle cuisine* its *lettres de noblesse,* it is this short, puckish and fiendishly intelligent renegade baker who vaguely resembles Roman Polanski and whom no less an authority than Bocuse, The Great Helmsman Himself, has called "the most formidable type I know in cooking." He is the magician and the prophet, the one whom Gault and Millau increasingly associated with their idea of what modern cooking should be (they are close friends) and the one whom all the minor-leaguers imitated the most—a development that, with a few exceptions, was most baneful for French cuisine, because imitating Michel Guérard is approximately as fruitful as trying to imitate Shakespeare, Cervantes or Red Smith. When, in the sixties, he ran his doll-house-size restaurant, Le Pot-au-Feu, in the Parisian working-class suburb of Asnières, he was unanimously considered the best cook in the capital, but the place's tiny dimensions and modest appearance limited it to two Michelin stars. Combining a pastry cook's exactitude—every ingredient has to be measured and weighed with precision—with a true inventor's creativity and pronounced taste for surprise (which he attributes to the short man's need to distinguish himself), he reeled off such a string of astounding creations, one after the other, that the Pot-au-Feu became virtually a closed club. Finding a table there was perhaps the greatest challenge facing the concièrges of the Ritz, Bristol, Plaza-Athénée and other similarly distinguished flophouses. From the world over flocked the rich and the curious and the beautiful, to marvel at the aerial lightness of Guérard's *feuilletées* of asparagus tips, prawns and truffles, the nose-thumbing attack on convention with foie gras in salad—*vinaigrette* on foie gras!—or, *justement,* the unheard of, feminine delicacy of his *pot-au-feu,* the very dish with which Dodin had destroyed the pretentions of the gourmand prince. Bocuse, the Troisgros brothers and Jean Delaveyne, of the great Camélia in Bougival, all encouraged the *Wunderkind* and sent the gastronomic press stampeding to Asnières, and Guérard responded with a fire-works display of inventiveness, taking the base materials of food and spinning gossamer out of them. If anyone's cuisine was *nouvelle*, it was Michel Guérard's. It was light the way Debussy's music is light, but it was definitely not dietetic. Michel is no fool: he knows that the best way to make dishes taste wonderful is to use plenty of butter and cream in their creation.

Then, in 1972, an urban renewal project condemned the Pot-au-Feu to be bulldozed into history. Michel was so thrown off balance that he wandered off, goggle-eyed, and got married. The lady of his choice, Christine Barthélémy, was a tall, cool Parisienne with the face of a model and the mind of the business school graduate that she was. Christine's father, a man of many activities, had given her a spa, or health resort, at the foot of the Pyrénées, near Biarritz. Eugénie-les-Bains, the place was called, and its specialty was treating skin problems and obesity. Eugénie was a pleasant enough place, but its reputation on the gastronomic circuit was roughly on the level of a HoJo's in Paterson, New Jersey, so when The Wizard himself decided to move in with his casseroles, it had nowhere to go but up. Parisian gourmets briefly mourned the passing of a great talent—Guérard had buried himself in the Landes, a million kilometers away, and no one was going to take the trouble to go there for lunch—and turned their attentions to sauerkraut with figs, or whatever other *nouvelle* fads were catching their fickle eyes at the moment.

Down in his huge barn of a white elephant at Eugénie, Guérard was forgotten—but not for long. The fiend was thinking hard, and he had long been in the the habit of turning out surprises. He already knew how to cook; that was no problem. What he decided to work on was something much more striking and potentially commercial: a new way to feed fat people. I visited Michel during his first year of residence at Eugénie, when he was still feeling his way, and I remember his excitement when he spoke of his latest discoveries. The food that professional dieticians had been feeding fat people was *triste à mourir*, he had found, so sad it was enough to make you want to die: boiled carrots, boiled beef and boiled potatoes. What a challenge: surely there must be something better. Michel had turned his kitchen into a laboratory and was working on ways to make food that was low in calories but still tasted good. The project was coming along very nicely, and he passed me photocopies of a week of the menus that he had worked up for his patients at the spa. He was calling his new approach *cuisine minceur*. He had his patients in mind, of course, but he was also aiming his experiment straight at the hearts and minds and stomachs of the French gourmet establishment, the Parisians and the all-powerful food guides.

"I had to do something dramatic and different to draw attention to Eugénie," he admits today. "*Cuisine minceur* was just the thing."

Thus was born the greatest single source of confusion about the modern school of French cooking. *Cuisine minceur* was never meant to be considered as an integral part of normal French cooking, even of the modern school. It has nothing to do with *nouvelle cuisine*, and even less to do with *cuisine classique*. It is, as Pierre Troisgros described it, an excrescence, a little branch growing out of the main tree. It is food for sick people. But such is the genius of Michel Guérard that he managed to make food for sick people taste good. At the expense, I might add, of unbelievable complication. Anyone who thinks he might whip up a little *cuisine minceur* on his own, even with Michel's excellent cookbook in front of his eyes, would do well to take on something easy, like reading Hegel.

"People got *cuisine minceur* mixed up with *nouvelle cuisine*," Michel said. "But the two are very different, technically and philosophically. Even today, people still confuse them, like old francs and new francs."

Anyone can make a non-fattening diet, even a doctor, and any cook can boil vegetables and sprinkle them with herbs, but to make slimming meals with the variety, subtlety and excitement that spring out at you from the menus at Eugénie is a bit of legerdemain that only Guérard and a handful of other conjurers have mastered. When he began his perilous enterprise, he had nothing more than his *idée directrice* and food composition charts for bookish research.

It was from this point zero that he worked up the inspired and un-expected combinations that could give taste to otherwise bland dishes and developed the cooking techniques that imparted sub-stance and the appearance of heartiness to the lightest and thinnest of concoctions.

His best allies, he discovered as his research continued, were the vegetables and herbs from his kitchen garden, but he was far too smart to go for the gastronomic inanity of vegetarianism: vegetables are made for accompanying and enhancing, a fact that has been ob-vious since prehistory, when mankind and dogkind and Tyranno-saurus Rexkind first noticed that a grub or a possum tasted better with wild mint or thyme than with mud. A steamed chicken leg, Michel realized, even when stuffed with non-fattening sweetbreads and mushrooms and truffles, was still bland and uninteresting just like that, but assumed astonishing depth and character when served with a thick green sauce composed of marjoram, watercress, spinach and mushrooms, cooked together in a bouillon, blended into a smooth emulsion and then reduced over direct flame. *Gigot de pou-lette*, he called the creation, and most first-time tasters were con-vinced that somewhere along the line Michel had sneaked in a good chunk of Normandy butter or a heaping tablespoon of *crème fraîche*. And yet the little masterpiece "cost" no more than 500 calories.

And so it went, into a whole new syllabus of gastronomic mar-vels executed like a Fred Astaire solo. From magic trick to magic trick Michel pulled low-cal gastronomy out of his hat and made fat people jump though hoops, but he never had the pretention of rein-venting French gastronomy with *cuisine minceur*. It was some-thing different, a sideline that was part medical, part publicity stunt and part challenge, just for the hell of it, just to see if it could be done. It could, because he is a rare and most talented bird, but let us not fall into the trap that has claimed so many others. *Cuisine min-ceur* is not the be-all to end all: when Michel cooks for pure eating pleasure, he dives joyfully into the larder of forbidden fruits and up go the calories.

"Butter, cream, and egg yolks are the base of French cooking," he says, sounding very like Bocuse, "and it strikes me as difficult to do without them, for the classical, rich cuisine, anyway. The Chinese do it, but that is another cuisine entirely. This being said, I think French cooking has never been as good as it is today, and this is mostly because of the *nouvelle cuisine* movement. Without *nouvelle cuisine*, nothing would have happened, but we have to agree on what we mean by the term. For me, *nouvelle cuisine* is simply a freer way of doing the old one."

With his record-breaking rise into Michelin's orbit—one star in 1974, two stars in 1975 and three stars in 1977—Michel definitely put Eugénie-les-Bains on the map and had the pleasure of seeing the Parisian gourmets who had written him off come crawling down to him in the sticks, whining for a taste. If he is forever established now as the living symbol of the sleight of hand characteristic of the modern school of cooking, he is the first to agree that the razzle-dazzle is nothing more than a minor part of the whole: Magic Johnson's ball handling, after all, is only a preliminary to scoring. Bocuse, Troisgros, Chapel and the others who were in on the start of the modern movement, when Michel was still laboring more or less anonymously, have drawn the lines of their own departures from Escoffier perhaps less dramatically than Guérard, but the sum of the parts at Collonges, Roanne or Mionnay is altogether as impressive as at Eugénie. If Michel is playing Debussy on his stove, Troisgros is into Shubert, Chapel Chopin and Bocuse Beethoven. Modern cooking is much more an attitude than a method or an ingredient.

"A new spirit of restauration," is the way Pierre Troisgros explains it, "away from excesses and in the direction of simplicity and friendship. You could even call it democratization, if you're not afraid of big words. The cooks are in charge now, and the barriers between them and the public are down. Thank God we had *papa* to teach us about that."

For those travelers who had the good luck to know Le Restaurant Troisgros in the sixties and early seventies, there are two images that stick in the memory as vividly as the first taste of eggs scrambled with sea urchins, that unlikely but perfectly oracular combination: the little old kitchen and the little old father. The kitchen, like the restaurant, has been enlarged to grandiose, red-laquered proportions now, but for the first twenty years or so, Jean and Pierre and their growing army of assistants tended their pots and pans in the modest galley which had served their mother as the cooking place when their restaurant was simply a bistrot opposite the Roanne railroad station. It was both comical and impressive to realize that so much food of such incredible quality came from the overheated, overcrowded back room, where the cooks had to walk with their elbows in, lest they bonk into a passing *entrecôte* or pigeon making its last flight on a silver platter, with a bellyful of garlic.

Papa Troisgros, Jean-Baptiste, was small, too, but he more than made up for his size by the smarts which had driven him to send both his boys away to Monsieur Point in Vienne and the apparently bottomless supply of humor and *joie de vivre* with which he presided over the dining room while the kids labored in the kitchen. A Burgundian down to his deep ready laughter and up to the bright sparkling eyes behind his glasses, Jean-Baptiste knew and appreciated the things of the table so well that he had sensed right from the start that his two sons would turn the place into just the kind of restaurant he loved. How right he was, and with what pleasure did he undertake his tours of the tables in the old restaurant, describing dishes about to arrive and accepting compliments for dishes already consumed, with all the modesty of the father who had sired prodigies, no less. If, from time to time, Jean-Baptiste deigned to yield to a client's entreaties and join him for a sip of Volnay or Corton-Charlemagne, he insisted on drawing up a chair and sitting down, because it was uncivilized to drink standing up, as in a vulgar bar. If Jean and Pierre were the heart of the restaurant, Jean-Baptiste was its soul, and it could not have been more fitting that when he finally decided to yield to the pressing entreaties of Le Seigneur up in the great restaurant in the sky, he did so while he was at table, with a glass of fine Burgundy in his hand.

Pierre smiles tenderly at the memory now, but is quick to point out that *papa* wasn't always as easy as the indulgent *bon vivant* who showed his face to customers. The same intransigeance that moved through the veins of Point, Pic and Dumaine was in his, too, and it was largely because of his uncompromising nature that the brothers took Point's cuisine, looked at it (and themselves) again, and made it *nouvelle*.

"*Papa* was the chance of our lifetime," said Pierre. "When we came back to Roanne from *chez* Point, we thought we were the world champions. There wasn't anyone who could teach us a thing. But then when we turned out a *selle de veau Orloff* for him, or the other classic dishes we had done at Point and Lucas-Carton, *papa* put us in our places, but fast.

" 'You spent your time learning stuff like that?' he asked us. 'That's *de la merde*—that's not worth anything!'

"We were outraged, Jean and I, but papa stayed on in the kitchen with us, and he waited by the dishwasher's sink to see what was coming back uneaten. '*Les enfants*,' he said, 'you've got to stop making that right away. *C'est zéro, ça*. It's the client who decides, not you. Just taste it and try. You'll see.'

"I was so angry and hurt that I spent a whole month without speaking to him. We communicated by notes—we actually wrote each other. But he was right. We had not tasted what we cooked. In those days cooks didn't do that. They just kept on turning out the same old *merde*. Papa made us taste our dishes and finally understand what we were doing. He made us take the point of view of the clients, and then he took us by the hand and led us out into the dining room to talk with them. And that was the start of nouvelle cuisine."

Fashions change and the names of the players change. In a few years, every name in this book will be out of date, some entirely forgotten, and food writers will be chattering about open cuisine or mystic cuisine or neorenaissance cuisine or whatever. The term *nouvelle cuisine* has virtually passed away, and so much the better. What will stay is infinitely more important than any such pettifoggery—an art that has spread its fascination well beyond the borders of France, to the point that the originators are being emulated with admirable skill all around the world. The Germans, the Scandinavians, the English, the Japanese, the Americans, the Australians and probably plenty of others whom I am forgetting have assimilated the lessons, so sedulously, that the best of them are now head-to-head with the masters of the land where it all began. The French have the home-team advantage of history and eating habit on their side, plus the enormously important patrimony of butter and cream and vegetables that are unequalled anywhere else, but these physical factors are not necessarily enough to insure that France will always be better than the others, come what may. That difference is, as Pierre Troisgros said it, in the spirit. For Michel Guérard, the spirit transcends any technical aptitude and becomes almost sacred, like a mission with which he and his *confrères* have been invested.

"I firmly believe," he told me one day in Eugénie, "that there will always be a specificity to French cuisine, and that we French cooks have a role in history: to be the creators for western cooking."

Let a hundred flowers bloom, then, and let all the other countries learn to enhance the table as well as the French do. And, while we're at it, down with ethnic snobbery: if these creators can teach the Germans and Americans and Japanese and all the others to steal their expertise and bring their own cooking up to the level of the French, we will own both the thieves and the stolen-from a standing ovation. But I'm not counting on it happening the day after tomorrow.

VI.
THE DEVOTION OF THE
LONG-DISTANCE EATER

Ever since Grimod de la Reynière, the brilliant gourmet with the warped humor, decided that the pursuit of excellence in esculence was a subject as worthy of a cultivated man's time as law, science or theology, there have been Frenchmen who have built their livelihoods at the table, eating to live and living to eat. Today, the profession of food criticism is practiced full time by only a handful, mostly for the major restaurant guides (*Michelin, Bottin Gourmand, Gault Millau, Auto Journal*) and various newspapers and magazines. But the numbers of nationally known critics and, by consequence, the problems posed to restaurateurs, are heavily increased by the freelancers and occasionals working for the more obscure regional publications. The charlatans, too, complicate matters by representing themselves as food writers in order to get a better table or—who knows?—a bottle of wine or a free meal.

Grimod did his eating at home simply because restaurants did not exist then, in the sense that we know them today. Since him, though, the critics have been eating out, and their influence is tremendous. A good review, or even a simple mention without further commentary, can fill an unknown restaurant overnight, while a bad one can cause such anguish and loss of patronage that threats, lawsuits and, on one occasion at least, suicide can follow. Occasionally women can be found in the ranks of the critics, but as a general rule they don't hold up well—the physical exhaustion is appalling—and in general the club is reserved for men. The professional eaters try to maintain a cruising speed of about ten restaurant meals a week, which makes, with time off for weekends and vacation and just plain recuperation, for a total of about five hundred serious meals a year—and some of them manage even more. But no matter how many places they visit, there are always more beckoning out there on the gastronomic landscape, tantalizing and torturing at the same time: new talents waiting to be discovered, or old talents wondering why no one loves them anymore. There are literally thousands of restaurants that can be classified as very good, and it is beyond the capacities of any single critic to eat in all of them.

These sheer numbers, then, explain the need for the inspector system used by the guides. Since the *Michelin*, the *Bottin* and the others have the ambition of covering the entire landscape of quality restauration, they need teams of critics who split up the work, sector by sector. Michelin's inspectors are by far the most numerous, but even this, the mighty red national institution, has recourse to the same kind of help that the other guides use, honorable correspondents (notably the Club des Cent in Michelin's case) in the form of journeyman gourmets who send in tips on discoveries, confirmations on places already known and rockets of odium if they feel they have been treated badly. After all, they reason, they are only following, in their own way, the same mystical role which Michel Guérard assigns to the brotherhood of cooks, guaranteeing that the ancient notions of quality persist, and that, in this field without fail, France remains Number One.

There are two kinds of professional critics: the anonymous and the personal. The anonymous, the monks of gastronomy, are pretty much limited to the guides, but even within the ranks of the guides, the top forks are as familiar to restaurateurs as rock stars are to teenagers. Much of this was the doing of Gault and Millau, who from the start gave their enterprises a swinging, fashionable Parisian image that directly reflected their own lively personalities. The tendency today is toward the personal, then, and it would be a foolish receptionist, *maître d'hôtel* or chef who has not committed to memory the unlovely visages of Henri Gault, Christian Millau, Robert Courtine, Philippe Couderc, Georges Prades, Paul de Montaignac, Henri Viard, Jean Ferniot, Claude Jolly and the few others who can make or break them with their commentaries.

There are so many good restaurants in France, and the competition for customers so intense, that the critics are courted with an energy and sycophancy that infinitely surpasses their innate merits as persons. Eager restaurateurs fall all over themselves to heap blandishments upon them, and the least of these is a free meal: rare bottles, fine foodstuffs and even, on occasion, money represent the frankincense and myrrh that the poor *patrons* too often feel they have to bear as tribute to these latter-day Caesars, in the hope that they will deign to turn their thumbs up in print. Often, alas, it works: it requires an individual of rare force of character and lucidity to bear in mind throughout his career that he is only a modest human being, after all, and not succumb to the delusions of grandeur that are so insistently encouraged by the power he wields through his publication and the flattery washing around his ears as he gets to work, chomp chomp.

Refreshingly, it is sometimes the opposite that happens. When a chef has a hard head and self-confidence and is utterly convinced that he is right and the critic wrong, the results can be a pleasure to contemplate. Jacques Manière, one of the most creative and influential cooks of his generation, went for years, first in a bistrot in a Parisian suburb and then in his two successive Paris restaurants, Le Pactole and Dodin Bouffant, virtually ignored by the *Guide Michelin* while everyone else was hailing him as one of the rare geniuses of his generation. Why? The story was that he had bodily ejected a Michelin inspector into the street because he seemed more interested in the state of his toilets than his cuisine. Like a president of a multinational who decides to go off to the country and raise goats, Manière eventually retired from the deluxe treadmill of *haute cuisine* and opened an admirable little bistrot in the village of Granges-les-Valence, across the river from Pic. Manière swore he was going to do only simple, family-style cooking from then on, but his creativity caught up with him, and little by little his Auberge des Trois Canards turned into the same kind of sorcerer's den that all his other places had been. His *auberge* is now one of the most extraordinary—and reasonable—eating places south of Lyon. Manière has just as much force of invention as before, but fewer tables, fewer complications, fewer food critics and fewer worries.

Michel Guérard went into rustication, as we have seen, out of love rather than disgust with Parisianism, but even down in the impenetrable *paysage* around Eugénie-les-Bains, unjust criticism caught up with him, from the acid pen of Philippe Couderc, the critic for *Minute*, a right-wing weekly. Michel, who is one tough little cookie beneath his smiley exterior, left standing orders with his staff at Eugénie to politely show Monsieur Couderc the door if he should have the effrontery to show up again.

The quarrel has been patched up now, and Guérard diplomatically praises Couderc's grand qualities, but one who will not call for a truce is Gilbert Le Coze. Gilbert is a stubborn Breton with a face that recalls Robert Redford and a mind as obdurate as the rocks of Portsall, which reached out and grabbed the supertanker *Amoco Cadiz* a few years ago, much to the discomfiture of Standard Oil of Indiana. Gilbert and his gorgeous sister Maguy (that's Breton for Maggie) came to Paris in the late sixties from the coastal village of Port-Navalo, founded a small restaurant in the shadow of the Tour d'Argent, went through the traditional starvation for a couple of years, but finally, by dint of ridiculously hard work, built Le Bernardin into the best fish restaurant in Paris. When they were small and little known, the food critic for the daily *Le Monde*, Robert Courtine, wrote a commentary which Gilbert found to be waspy, unjust and stupid. Rather than working politely through his staff, as Guérard had done, Gilbert signified to Courtine that if he ever showed his face in Le Bernardin again, he, Gilbert, would personally kick him out on his distinguished ass. Today Le Bernardin has moved to a posh location next to the Arc de Triomphe, is big and successful and boasts two stars in the Michelin. But the offer of the rapid expedition onto the sidewalk still stands, and Courtine does not show his face there. He retaliates by pretending in his columns that the restaurant does not exist.

I had always viewed the singular trade of food criticism with a conflicting mixture of sentiments: envy for these characters being paid to do so much wonderful eating and meet so many interesting creators of *haute cuisine,* but also a kind of scorn—or impatience, at any rate—with the bitchy quarreling and one-upmanship that are so endemic within the brotherhood and, finally, a vague dubiousness about how serious it all was in the first place. It was to straighten out my thoughts that I briefly joined the profession a few years ago, in the company of Jean Didier, then editor in chief of the *Guide Kléber.* The Kléber at the time was the single greatest rival to the Michelin and, like the Michelin, it was sponsored by a tire company in view of propaganda for the marque. Unfortunately for Jean and the Kléber, the Michelin company eventually bought a controlling interest in Kléber and phased out the guide. Jean went to work for another company and founded the marvelous *Bottin Gourmand,* a guide that is even better than the Kléber and, once again, he is challenging Michelin. Whatever his employer, though, Jean has a solid reputation within the trade as a middle-of-the-roader, neither ultra-personalized and fad-prone like Gault and Millau nor anonymous *apparatchiki* like the Michelin inspectors, and, in any case, vastly knowledgeable, conscientious and hard working: in short, a gentleman. When I joined him for a week of professional eating, I had the redoubtable good luck to strike again right into the heartland of *la haute gastronomie:* Lyon and its environs. It was quite an experience.

It happened to be in Valence, halfway between Lyon and Avignon, that I was struck by the importance of the Seraglio Metaphor. Jean Didier was sitting at the wheel of his bright orange Lancia, resting, composing his mind and stomach. It was noon Thursday. To his right were the immaculate stucco walls and the big oaken front door of Pic, the wonderful Pic, the very one which had been one of the pillars of the Holy Trinity. Jean had been eating all week long. Now, duty called again, but he wasn't hungry. It was day five of the tournée.

Jean said, yes, he often suffered the Seraglio Metaphor, *oh oui, oh oui*, he whose job brought him several hundred times a year into the temples of dining which most ordinary mortals only dream about. They were the stuff of routine for Jean, like middle-income houses for Fuller Brush salesmen. He not only had the opportunity to eat like a prince every day; he was expected to. It was his responsibility to ingest exquisite creations day in and day out, almost without respite. The Seraglio Metaphor struck him when he faced an important meal—duty calls!—but was totally and irretrievably not hungry. In moments like that, the ancient male fantasy of the harem begins to appear more like a nightmare than a delectation. The Seraglio Metaphor is the underlying truth behind the food critic's imperative to perform, even without appetite.

Jean felt the numbing anguish of satiety as he sat in his parked car. He'd already been spotted, he knew. The Alfa Spider isn't exactly a discreet car in the first place, and when it is bright orange, the top restaurateurs in France instinctively snapped to attention, because it was a likely sign that the *Guide Kléber* had arrived. In the course of his three decades in the profession Jean has eaten so much, and so hard, that his teeth have literally spread apart. At the august age of fifty-one he had to have teenage-style braces installed to bring them back together again. If that's not devotion to duty I should like to know what is. Jean has the company spirit and isn't afraid of heavy symbolism, either: the Michelin's cover is fire-engine red, but the Kléber's was bright orange—exactly the same color as his car.

Jean sighed, slid out from behind the wheel, carefully locked up, squared his shoulders and marched into the restaurant. And within seconds, there came that goddamn champagne again.

It sounds ridiculous—it *is* ridiculous—that a gourmet can become so jaded, so surfeited by good things that he inwardly winces at the appearance of a bottle of fine champagne, but such are the dynamics of the Seraglio Metaphor. Jean had been drinking fine champagne, great Burgundies, rare Côtes du Rhône, magnificent Bordeaux and sublime *digestifs* ever since Monday morning. Not to mention all the food that had accompanied them. Now, as he walked into the beautiful, flower-laden dining room, past the respectfully smiling *maître d'hôtel* and the respectfully inclining waiters, into the welcoming arms of Jacques and Suzanne Pic— "*Mais, quelle surprise, Monsieur Didier, et quel plaisir*"—his athletic digestive tract was stalled, his appetite extinguished. Pic made a quick, imperious gesture, muttered a few words *sotto voce* to Alex, his sommelier, and within seconds a bottle of Billecart-Salmon had appeared on the corner table by the picture window, nestling snugly in a silver bucket, surrounded by a crackling sea of tiny ice chips. A man of impulse, Pic had thrown caution to the winds: he had chosen a *rosé* champagne, knowing full well that most gourmets and food snobs disdain *rosés* of all sorts. But he knew his wine, had confidence in Billecart-Salmon's magic. Jean smiled graciously, sipped—it was chilly, dry, refreshing, the color of an onion's outer skin—and almost immediately fell to discussing with Monsieur Pic the composition of his lunch menu. It was the professional reflex of the eating trade. As the moments passed, as the delectable possibilities flashed past his mind's eye—a young guinea hen, perhaps, or an orgy of truffles in a flaky pastry shell, or a lobster, or maybe a stuffed pigeon, or a saddle of lamb—the champagne began its subversive work, tickling his guts, building the base of yet another nascent euphoria. Jean felt his stomach juices coursing again. His appetite was coming to life. At length, after much scholarly examination and comparison, Monsieur Pic and he agreed on a *menu dégustation* which would offer him the chance to judge small portions of a wide range of the specialties which, naturally, Pic himself would prepare:

Fisherman's salad (lobster, scallops, crayfish tails and green beans in a vinegary mayonnaise)

Feuilleté bohémienne (truffles and foie gras in a flaky pastry shell, topped by a Périgeux sauce)

Filet of sea bass, with caviar and a champagne-based sauce

Artichoke hearts with baby asparagus tips, accompanied by a light hollandaise sauce

Saffroned veal sweetbreads on a bed of fresh spinach

Cold breast of duckling cooked with raspberry vinegar, served with fresh peas and cucumber mousse

Turbot with fresh morels

Salmon filet with leeks

Fricassée of lamb with basil

Cheeses and desserts

Pic suggested that a small filet steak might be indicated after lamb, but Jean didn't feel he needed any beef. The menu seemed good enough as it was. He took a sip of champagne, nibbled on a grilled almond, and waited. He was feeling better. Luckily, that's the way it usually happens.

Jean had begun his eating trip, or *tournée*, at 6:30 in the morning of the previous Monday, wheeling south out of Paris on the Autoroute du Sud, heading toward Lyon, France's third largest city, which is, as the ancient joke goes, washed by three rivers: the Rhône, the Saône and the Beaujolais. As he prepares each year's edition of a guide, Jean arranges his *tournées* by regions and subregions, following a preestablished calendar which by year's end will have brought him into virtually every corner of the country The point of each trip, and each meal, is to double-check the quality of the restaurants on his route against the rating he has given them in the previous edition of the guide: for the Kléber, a crowned red rooster (The Best Restaurants in France); a crowned black rooster (Great Restaurants, Comfortable Surroundings); a crowned stew pot (Great Restaurants, Simpler Surroundings); and uncrowned roosters or stew pots (Fine Restaurants). If he finds them better, or worse, he changed the symbol in the next year's edition. Naturally, he had neither the time nor the stomach to try all the restaurants of a given area (he had regional correspondents and inspectors for that), but Jean feels duty-bound to visit the best ones every year. This time he was striking at the center, the best of the best. As always, his secret hope was to find a chef so serious, a meal so superb, that he could make another promotion to his top category, the *coq rouge couronné*, Kléber's equivalent of Michelin's three stars. The recital that follows is the story of one week of work for a professional eater.

DAY ONE

Darting south on the freeway, Jean was holding the Lancia back, keeping a nervous eye on the speedometer. Watching speed is new to the French. For decades, the country's laissez-faire approach to traffic regulation had made them the world's most lead-footed and undisciplined drivers. On freeways, one drove as fast as one's car could go, which made for some jolly touring, a lot of spontaneous *grand prix* action at over 100 m.p.h. and some of the most creative smashups this side of a train wreck. The shocking, immoral and probably unconstitutional imposition of a *limitation de vitesse* radically changed their automotive habits: now the game is to see for how long you can stay at exactly 130 kilometers per hour, or slightly above 80 m.p.h. Jean drove on, occasionally making a temerarious push up to 132.

Cramped in his little car, his bald pate just barely clearing the roof, his eyes large and liquid behind his oversize horn rims, he bore no resemblance whatsoever to the cartoon image we all carry in our heads of a full-time trencherman. Taller than most Frenchmen (6'1"), he was also remarkably trim, almost slender at 170 pounds. There was a certain vague similarity to former President Giscard d'Estaing. Jean was happy to attribute his freedom from obesity to a nervous character and a fast-acting digestive tract which Dame Nature was kind enough to give him at birth. Smoking a pack of Stuyvesants a day also helped keep his weight down, he admitted. It is a curious quirk of history that many French professional gourmets are heavy smokers, in spite of the presumable damage to their palates.

They hold on to cigarettes by a kind of desperate instinct, for fear of ballooning into uncontrolled bloatation without them. Times have changed. The terrorism of fashion spares no one, and now even career eaters want to appear svelte. Reassuringly, though, the other side of the barrier is still holding fast: none of the great French chefs are smokers, and few of the lesser ones.

"I like cooks," Jean was saying. "They are artisans. They work with their hearts." Jean enjoys talking and is clearly proud of his deep, sonorous, radio announcer's voice. Like many Frenchmen, he falls easily into long and involved exposition of his reflections, presented in didactic, schoolmaster fashion.

"Cooks are not commercial people," he went on. "They are respectable. They are people with roots in the peasantry, just like the food they prepare. Contrary to what most people believe, French cooking is for people with modest purses. Or should be, anyway. It is the cooking of shepherds and vineyard laborers. French cooking is simple. Once it becomes a *cuisine de spectacle*, I am against it. It is a waste of money and it is false."

It was 11:45. Jean left the freeway at the wine town of Mâcon and struck off southeast toward his first stop, the hamlet of Thoissey. For several days he had been eating lightly in Paris. Now, as he approached the restaurant called Le Chapon Fin (crowned black rooster, two stars in the Michelin), his gastric juices were flowing in anticipation. He was starving.

"It's decided, though," he intoned. "No overindulging. No drinking too much. Everything balanced. No mixing."

He pulled over to the side of the country road to adjust his tie, put his jacket on and dropped the car's convertible top, in order to arrive at the Chapon Fin in the sporty and relaxed "American" manner which he admires.

"This being said," he added, "I really could use a little drink right now."

He meant wine, naturally, which the French look upon as a food and a tonic for the body. "I never drink alcohol—only wine," they will say, and then go on to consume two or three liters in a single day.

As the Lancia crunched over the gravel, a white-coated waiter peered curiously out through the glass door, then abruptly disappeared into the depths of the building.

"We've been spotted," said Jean with a deep bass grunt. He reached into the pocket of his blazer and popped two Sulfarlems. These tiny pills, hardly bigger than match heads, are one of the secret weapons of the eating establishment. Acting on the liver, they excite and advance the flow of bile, as an aid to quick digestion. Jean and his colleagues swallow Sulfarlems the way split ends guzzle Gatorade. He locked up and strolled into the Chapon Fin. He was eager to start. He was feeling good.

He was met at the threshold by Pierre Maringue, the sommelier and second authority in the restaurant's chain of command, who was smiling the quizzical, half-apprehensive smile common to most restaurateurs at the arrival (always unannounced) of the Kléber. Maringue regretted that his father-in-law and boss, Paul Blanc, who had founded the inn back in 1932, was away in Spain for a short vacation. He was desolated. But he still knew where to find the champagne. With a swift, practiced hand he twisted the cork off a bottle of Laurent-Perrier Cremant, and the champagne announced itself with a polite, almost noiseless exhalation of carbon dioxide. (It goes without saying that no French sommelier will ever allow the cork to explode out of the bottle; that is considered bad form and vulgar showmanship—and besides, it is bad for the wine.) As if on cue, Jean and Maringue fell into learned discourse about the quality of last year's crop of Beaujolais. It was already good, they concluded, and was quickly getting better. For the ritual analysis of the menu, Maringue sent a waiter to fetch the chef, Gilbert Broyer. Broyer appeared in his white blouse, white apron and white chef's hat, looking apprehensive. He refused a glass of champagne ("I'm working") and immediately began ticking off what he considered most recommendable that day. At length Jean and he agreed on a plan of attack: *quenelles de brochet* (a mousse of pike with a creamy white-wine sauce), frogs' legs, a sophisticated "stew" of freshwater fish filets with vegetables, an assortment of cold pâtés, cheeses and dessert. Jean liked the simplicity of the composition. It was like a little country picnic.

"The reason for the frogs' legs," he explained, "is that the herbs and garlic in the butter will cut the richness of the cream sauce on the *quenelles.*

He tasted his Beaujolais with the great chewing, sucking and smacking of lips characteristic of expert *tastevins,* then instantly ordered the waiter to put the bottle in a pitcher of ice water: it was still too warm. As for the meal, almost anyone else in the world would have considered it fabulous, but Jean felt impelled to make some criticisms: the pike's sauce was too thick, too sticky and too salty; evidently it had reduced too much. Jean imagined that Broyer had become flustered ("He's trembling"), but forgave him with the arrival of the big, luscious heap of buttery frogs' legs and the even better stew of fish filets. When the trolley of cold delicacies rolled up to the table, he exiled the potted hare and the foie gras out of hand—too big and too rich. Instead, he opted for small portions of duck *galantine* and a goose liver *terrine.*

"Too much laurel! Too much thyme!" he cried in an urgent whisper. "The herbs completely dominate the meat. That's the third error he's made." Jean chewed a bit longer, sipped some Beaujolais, chewed again, reflected, then felt himself ready for another statement. "And there's too much fat in the goose *terrine.*"

He sighed, made a few quick jots in his notebook. There would be no promotion this year for the Chapon Fin. When it was over, when the cheese and desserts had been consumed, Jean ordered a toothpick and called the waiter over. It was lecture time. Jean likes lecture time.

"Young man," he said, "I thank you very much for your help, but I permit myself to make you a few observations. First, you didn't ask me how I wanted my salad seasoned. The *vinaigrette* was good, but you could have asked me what kind of vinegar I wanted. You could have given me a choice of perhaps six oils. Secondly, you should have asked me before serving the coffee: did I want it short and concentrated, or long and weak? Did I want it from the espresso machine, or did I want it in a *filtre?* I beg of you, young man—always ask the clients such things. People come to a beautiful restaurant like this and spend money. You mustn't betray them."

The waiter smiled and nodded, like a chastised schoolboy.

"*Bon,*" said Jean with a smile. "I feel in form." He was content to have delivered himself of his criticisms. "Let's go taste the wine."

While taking champagne with Maringue he had met an old acquaintance from a newspaper in Lyon. He and his colleagues had been delegated to choose a barrel of Beaujolais, to be bottled and used for the paper's promotional campaigns. Jean and his friends spent the rest of that afternoon in the salon of wine merchant Georges Duboeuf at the nearby town of Romanèche-Thorins. In all, each man tasted seventeen samples. After the wine-tasting there was a modest feast: country sausage, ham, pork chops and spareribs, cheeses and country bread, apple tart and . . . more Beaujolais. Jean was beginning to feel the old familiar dread: too much good stuff, too much good stuff. The Seraglio Metaphor.

At seven o'clock he was in Vonnas, home town of the La Mère Blanc (crowned black rooster), where Georges Blanc, the now famous nephew of the Chapon Fin's owner, does his own cooking. Georges was just over thirty then, dark, intent, serious and ambitious. He was not hiding the fact that he was shooting for the top ranking in both the Kléber and the Michelin. He had taken measure of the target, and he was calmly making his way toward it. Most observers thought he would make it soon. (He did—the following year.) But his serious nature tended to incite Lyonnais wags toward their beloved practical jokes. One of the most spectacular recent stunts had occurred spontaneously the year before, when a wicked friend of Georges's dared the two young ladies with whom he was dining in Le Mère Blanc's sumptuous décor to remove their clothes. They did, with studied deliberate calm, and consumed the rest of their meal *au naturel* except for the fine linen napkins posed over their thighs. Great French restaurants can be jolly places.

"A little refreshment, Monsieur Didier?" inquired Georges deferentially. "A little champagne?"

"No thank you, Monsieur Blanc," Jean instantly replied, shuddering inwardly. "But if you could send a cold bottle of mineral water up to my room?"

At dinnertime, Georges was eager for the Kléber to make the acquaintance of some of his latest creations. The menu he worked out with Jean was considerably more complex than the lunch at his uncle's place had been: salad of watercress and duck liver with *vinaigrette* and truffle dressing; grilled filet of salmon; a creamy-winy stew of lobster and crayfish tails with young vegetables; casserole of chicken with vegetables, basil, garlic and scattered truffles; Georges's own special potato pancakes; cheeses, sherbets and desserts. The white wine was a 1974 Meursault-Charmes, followed by a 1969 Grand Échézeaux. Georges was bringing out a bottle of Sauternes to accompany the dessert when Jean held up his hand and waved it off.

"Too much is too much," he said, almost desperately. But that didn't stop Georges from popping open a bottle of champagne after the meal was finished—"just for a friendly drink together."

By the time the champagne ceremony was finished it was nearly midnight. Jean clambered up to bed with the leaden legs all Frenchmen recognize as the sure sign of too much wine. He crashed into a deep slumber and slept right through his breakfast call.

DAY TWO

"Georges has made progress," he concluded the next morning, en route south again. "His restaurant is better than his uncle's. But I'm not sure he's ready for the top yet. It's tough, to be at the top."

In midmorning Jean dropped in to say hello to an old friend, Georges Berger, the owner and chef of La Mère Bourgeois, a superb little restaurant in the nearby village of Priay. He regretted that he couldn't stay to eat, but he compromised by tasting the lobster which Berger was cooking. Madame Berger cracked open a bottle of Beaujolais. Jean had a drink with them and he was on his way again.

By half past noon he was comfortably installed on the sunny terrace of La Mère Charles in Mionnay, drinking a cocktail of champagne and raspberry syrup. Formerly a modest family bistrot (it was painted by Utrillo in 1929), La Mère Charles is now a monument to the cooking talent of Alain Chapel, who is generally considered one of the half dozen or so greatest chefs in the world. Naturally, his restaurant sported a crowned red rooster in the Kléber and three stars in the Michelin. Antoine, the headwaiter, suggested a series of several entrées, making it sound as simple and easy as a hostess serving up stuffed celery and Ritz crackers. Antoine is a master of understatement. Jean agreed with his idea.

"Good," he said. "That way we'll be able to work."

Some work. It began while he was still out on the terrace with the champagne: deep-fried whitefish and baby sole hardly bigger than artichoke leaves. It was what the French call an *amuse-gueule,* or palate tickler. He moved inside for the serious business, opening the hostilities with a salad of sautéed fresh morels (the season is only two or three weeks long, and he was in luck with his timing) over crayfish tails with a buttery sauce accented by a tiny point of anise. With it he drank a cold Brouilly, one of the best of the Beaujolais growths. A ragout of sea bass and red mullet followed, the two filets sitting on a bed of chervil, spinach and Swiss chard. The sauce on the sea bass was based on white wine, and on the mullet, red. Chapel was having fun playing with colors. Jean devoured them with a flat spoon, making little gutteral noises of contentment.

At a table to his left, and at another behind him, some serious sexual electricity was crackling. For the couple behind, the formalities of courtship had obviously been terminated several nights earlier. They were enjoying a duckling as much as they enjoyed each other, their lunch resembled an erotic feast. The girl was as soft and humid and warm as an oyster poached in champagne. To the left, the relationshp apparently hadn't been consummated yet, but it clearly was about to be. He was a middle-aged business type with a wallet full of money, a belly full of champagne and a head full of self-confidence; she looked remarkably young, hardly more than seventeen or eighteen, but the deft, fleeting touch of her hand on his cheek and her knowledgeable use of the lingering smile were masterful demonstrations of the art of seduction as practiced by what the French call a *fausse vièrge.* She was in control, and she was doing fine. If anyone was going to be had that afternoon, it was the businessman.

Jean continued chewing. Now it was tender, white asparagus, lukewarm, between delicate rectangles of flaky pastry, with rooster kidneys and thick slices of truffles. At this moment his entire world, his person, his aspirations, his life, were concentrated upon this *feuilleté d'asperges* and its hollandaise sauce, upon each savory explosion of taste when he bit through another rooster kidney. You take your sensual pleasures as they come.

Gérard, the sommelier, poured a Bonnes-Mares 1971 into his oversize snifter-style Burgundy glass, taking care not to agitate or bruise the wine. Jean destroyed a filet of duck foie gras with sweet turnips. When the cheese table rolled up, he opted for his sophisticated-peasant number, ordering a plate of green leeks to accompany fresh goat cheese. He ate them crunch crunch under the bemused gaze of the Mexican Interior Minister, who was lunching with his family at a table by the window. Jean's meal ended with a simple lemon sherbet and a coffee. But not, of course, just any coffee. It should be a *filtre*, he specified, and a mix of Columbia, Mocha and Costa Rica: "Colombia for fullness, Mocha for the color, Costa Rica for the perfume."

In the Royal Sofitel, the hotel he had chosen for the night in Lyon, Manager Jean-Pierre Anquetin offered him a late afternoon whiskey and asked him to taste his *terrine* of calves' feet. By the time the ceremonial was over (the calves' feet were an interesting idea, but they lacked depth), the earth had inexorably revolved around to dinnertime. It was only Day Two, and he had only three meals under his belt. But he wasn't hungry.

"The foie gras is passing badly," he muttered. "I'm stalled."

He was sitting in the crowded, *sympathique* second-floor dining room of Léon de Lyon, which is probably the best bistrot on the face of the earth. Jean-Paul Lacombe, the young proprietor and chef, whose daddy had been the boon companion in clowning of Paul Bocuse, and who isn't above the occasional *connerie* himself, was trying to talk him into some of the *spécialités de la maison*, but Jean and his digestive tubes were adamant. With the grimace of a man in acute discomfort, he ordered nothing but a dish of creamed leeks. Although not meant as such, it was an affront to the artistry of Lacombe, who is an extraordinary, inventive and passionate cook. (In other similar moments of distress, Jean has been known to order soft-boiled eggs and toast for dinner in internationally renowned restaurants.) Lacombe disappeared back into his kitchen, but he was determined to have the last word: he sent out an unrequested *salade Léon de Lyon* to keep Jean company while he waited for his leeks. The salad was a delicious little creation of foie gras, a duck filet, mushrooms and green beans. Jean picked at it desultorily.

"Ah, foie gras," he said, his deep voice edged with polite disgust.

Since he arrived he had been sipping at the bottle of Pouilly-Fuissé which Jean-Paul had sent to his table. Now, as he pushed the mushrooms around his plate, the cold, fruity wine began to accomplish its mission. Almost imperceptibly, Jean found his disgust giving way to professional interest.

"Hmm," he said. "There must be some truffle juice in the dressing."

A few moments passed. He ate a bean, then reflected, stared around the room—and stabbed his fork into the foie gras.

"*Ça y est!*" he announced with a triumphant smile. "It's happened! I'm hungry again." He quickly devoured the rest of the salad.

"It's just like a horseman who's fallen at a jump," he said. "You have to get right back into the saddle and attack the jump again." (In France, the word saddle is frought with digestive double meaning.)

Jean polished off his leeks, and the cheese and dessert, too. The only truly eventful moment of the evening occurred when the waiter poured out the red Burgundy accompanying the leeks. Jean found it too warm, ordered a bucket of ice and plunked a big cube into his glass, to the utter astonishment of the young and perhaps dogmatic waiter.

"That's what I think about the rules," he said, giving the vulgar high sign known in France as *le bras d'honneur*. "There are no rules."

DAY THREE

The big project of the day was lunch at La Pyramide in Vienne. The temple. The museum. Point's place. Jean repeated all the old stories about Point's unyielding severity and admitted that when he was a young cub in the business he had been so awed that he had never dared to smoke at all in Point's presence. Now, with his widow, Mado, in charge, he had the courage to do so at the end of the meal—but he requested her permission first.

When he arrived at La Pyramide's big white gate, he had already checked out another restaurant a few miles south of Vienne, the Bellevue, which, he had heard, was trying hard. He had appeared incognito to look over the dining room and peruse the menu while having a glass of Côtes du Rhône at the bar. *"Une maison sérieuse,"* he concluded from his quick once-over, but he would reserve detailed judgment for another time. Now, he was thinking only of Fernand Point, of Mado and of Guy Thivard, the chef who was in charge of the kitchen and whose reason for existing was to scrupulously respect the recipes and style of his dead master. In case he ever forgot, Mado was ever-present, with her piercing eye and subtle palate, ready to call him back to order. And now she was there: elegant and assured, she greeted Jean as soon as he passed from the legendary terrace into the little vestibule where she watched television between *services.*

"A bottle of Dom Pérignon, Louis," she told the white-haired but still boyish sommelier. She took a symbolic splash in her own glass and sat down to talk with Jean as he planned his lunch. It was a rare honor. Many were the wealthy food fanatics who would have paid dearly for the honor of Madame Point joining them for a drink. Jean liked the idea of fresh morels, the same that had been so good at La Mère Charles, but Madame Point raised an eyebrow.

"I'm afraid you'll have to have them *en casserole,*" she said. "We had problems this morning with the *pâte feuilletée,* so there is no *croustade.*"

The pastry chef must certainly have caught some considerable heat for that. Jean stuck with the morels nonetheless, but prepared the ground first with an old Point specialty, pâté of thrush flavored with juniper berries. After the mushrooms, Madame Point sent over a tart pear sherbet to clear mouth and stomach for the rich, creamy *cassolette* of veal kidneys that followed. Through it all, some big-league wine one-upmanship was going on between Jean and the 69-

year-old sommelier. "The Dom Pérignon stands up to the pâté, I think," observed Louis.

"A great champagne stands up to anything," said Jean, winning one point.

Shortly after, Jean allowed that it was his birthday that very day. "I would be tempted to order a vintage from my birth year," he said, "but then of course that would have to be a Bordeaux, wouldn't it?"

"If you're fatigued, you can call for a Bordeaux," said Louis with feigned innocence. "One likes Bordeaux after a certain age." One point for Louis, a true-blue Burgundian by birth. Jean compromised and asked him to choose a good Côtes du Rhône for the main course. Meanwhile, he took a flinty, fruity Condrieu white to accompany the mushrooms.

Louis uncorked the red wine without going through the ritual display of the label. Jean immediately recognized that he had been challenged. Louis filled his glass and placed the bottle at the far end of the table, its label facing outward. Jean sipped.

"Goddam!" he fairly shouted. "That's a truck! That's a bulldozer!"

The powerful, sun-nourished wine was of a red so deep that it bordered on blue. Jean had to think for several moments before making a pronouncement.

"I think it's a Côte Rôtie," he ventured, "but I'm not sure." He did not even try to estimate an age.

Louis turned the bottle around: Côte Rôtie. Tie score, 2 to 2.

After lunch Jean joined a friend at another table for a glass of ancient vintage cognac offered by Madame Point. Their conversation turned to Marc Fournier, Europe's number-one collector and restorer of fairground organs and mechanical music machines and who, among other notables, counted Paul Bocuse as a client; it was Fournier, whose house was just down the street from La Pyramide, who had done the restoration of Paul's huge Gaudin. The two men decided to drop by and pay him a quick visit. Fournier was delighted to see them. He cracked open a bottle of champagne for the occasion.

By dinnertime, Jean had only half regained his appetite. The attractive redhead who waited on him in La Renaissance in the industrial burg of Rive-de-Gier, across the river from Vienne on the road to Saint-Étienne, was the wife of the owner and chef, Gilbert Laurent. It was his first trip to the establishment, and Jean didn't identify himself as the man from Kléber. Madame seemed troubled by his appearance and his expertise, but she obviously couldn't place him. Jean consumed a plate of smoked country ham and a lake salmon poached over a bed of garden herbs, accompanied by a bottle of white Côtes du Rhône. As he was eating the fish he noted that the waiter had left the alcohol flame burning under the chafing dish, in which the remainder was reposing. He grumbled, even though the tarragon-laced sauce was delicious. When the waiter proposed a second serving (there was a whole, plump filet still untouched) he haughtily refused it without even a taste, maintaining that by then the salmon had been ruined by the continuing heat.

"I just meant to keep it warm," the luckless waiter protested. Jean sent for the headwaitress and politely but firmly scolded her for the waiter's misplaced good intentions. Madame was desolated. Would monsieur like something else to replace it? No thank you, said Jean. He had had a very full day. Somehow, in the long interlocution that ensued, it came out that he was Jean Didier of the Kléber. Madame was more desolated than ever. She instantly sent for her husband, who appeared from the kitchen in his full chef's regalia, looking wretchedly unhappy. He sat down to explain his policy on lake salmon, snapped his fingers and sent for a bottle of champagne.

DAY FOUR

Driving out of town the next morning, Jean was expatiating on the tribulations and trade secrets of the long-distance eater. Luckily, hangovers were rare for him, although he often had a hard time waking up in the morning. He had never known any of the various hangover pills to do any good. Aspirin for the head, maybe, but that was bad for the stomach. Several of the gastronomic critics walk as much as possible to help their digestion, but there wasn't any miracle remedy for that, either. Some of his *confrères* have been known to make themselves vomit, in the style of the ancient Romans, but he was not prepared to go that far. There are limits to gastronomic dedication.

Today's lunch was to be another high point of the trip—Troisgros in Roanne. Roanne is an undistinguished and not particularly gracious city on the banks of the Loire whose only attraction, unless you are a military buff interested in the tanks that are built there, is Le Restaurant Troisgros. When Jean entered the restaurant, he took the professionals' route—up from the parking lot through the back door and directly into the kitchen—the little old kitchen on this occasion, because the brothers had not yet done their reconstruction and expansion. There, amid the bubbling pots, the heaps of mushrooms and raspberries and the enormous slabs of Charolais beef, Pierre was holding court and keeping things in order. As massively built as a bull, but also gifted with the fine and subtle intelligence of a scholar of human nature, Pierre is possessed of the magic power of speeding-up: one glance from him at an appretice or *commis* and the work suddenly goes twenty percent faster. Jean lifted a few lids off pots, stuck his finger into a *glace de viande*, then followed Pierre into the bar for a *kir maison*, white Burgundy with a shot of black-currant syrup. Jean Troisgros wasn't around that day; he had gone down to Pauillac to do a little party cooking for Philippe de Rothschild, who owns some vines there. Over in a corner booth, Pierre's wife and daughter were just finishing their lunch of soft-shelled lobster, beasts that had been trapped just after shedding last year's carapace.

"If you had come half an hour earlier, I would have given them to you," Pierre said. "You don't see many of them."

Jean consoled himself with an appetizer that was a little invention of Pierre's: *a salad of civelles*, transparent baby eels smothered in crushed tomato, oil and vinegar. To his thorough satisfaction, he found that he was starving. He raced happily through the famous Troisgros *mosaic* of vegetables (artichoke hearts, green beans, celery, carrots, asparagus tips and truffles bonded together by a mousse of pork,) thrush pâté with a spinach and potato salad, oysters lightly poached in champagne and filets of John Dory on a bed of green vegetables, washing them all down with cool red Burgundy. For the main course, a pigeon cooked with whole garlic cloves, the choice of the wine was both more important and more tricky.

"I'm more Burgundy than Bordeaux," said Jean, "and more Côtes de Nuits than Côtes de Beaune," spontaneously coining a vintage maxim for the vocabulary of future wine snobs.

"Why don't I give you a 1973 Bonnes-Mares?" suggested Gilbert, the sommelier.

"Bravo!" cried Jean. "He remembered—my favorite!"

Tie score once again. Shortly after the arrival of the lusciously plump pigeon and its side order of sautéed mushrooms, Pierre sauntered out of the kitchen to see how things were going.

"I'm working," said Jean between mastications, "I'm working."

When the waiter, Michel, proposed the vast Troisgros cheese platter, Jean came forth with some more didactic discourse, lightly brushed with naughtiness this time. "Young man," he said, "I'm drinking the Bonnes-Mares '73, so I will choose my cheese in consequence. I will take one goat cheese only, and not too young. Never two women in my bed at the same time, and never two cheeses on my plate."

A little champagne with dessert, a long professional chat with Pierre over coffee, and it was a good afternoon's labor for the *Guide Kléber*. At 5:30 P.M., the two men rose and went to the bar, where Pierre opened a bottle of fine Pommard and brought out a little munching material of hot tripe sausages, slathered with explosive mustard. It brought tears to Jean's eyes.

That night, back in Lyon, he had his first true breakdown: he cancelled a restaurant and stayed in the hotel. He consumed a bowl of onion soup and a glass of Beaujolais in the snack bar. For shame.

DAY FIVE

Jean didn't want to admit it, but he had trouble going through Monsieur Pic's monumental menu. Naturally, Pic meant well: by nature he is as generous as he is shy, expressing himself through the profusion of delicacies which he sends forth from his kitchen. But Jean wasn't feeling in form. After a brief reawakening of desire with the pink champagne and the fisherman's salad, he found himself bogged down with the salmon filets. He plugged on through a sense of duty, but his heart wasn't in it. He was paying the ransom of the late twentieth century, where men just don't know how to eat the way their ancestors did. As he sat there in Pic, surrounded by luxury, attention and food, Jean would have passed for a sparrow had he been in the company of any one of the Big Stomachs. Today, there were three wines with the lunch: a white Condrieu and a Saint-Joseph and a Cornas, both red, of course. When Monsieur Pic joined him after dessert and coffee, he brought another bottle of champagne with him—Pol Roger Brut this time. Jean took one look and one sip, then sent the bottle back. It was off color, he said; the cork must have been bad. Everyone was desolated. The sommelier trotted out with another bottle. This one met his approval.

Driving back to Lyon late that afternoon, he had to fight off the waves of drowsiness generated by the wine and the overwhelmingly generous menu. This time, he held the Lancia well under the speed limit, and everyone passed him. It was rather a dishonor for the owner of a bright orange Spyder, but one makes one's concessions where one has to. Jean knew that he wasn't out of the woods yet, not by a long shot. Tonight's dinner was at Paul Bocuse's.

The problem yet again was, Jean wasn't hungry. And that was a big problem. They were waiting for him at Restaurant Bocuse, of course. Once the word got around that the Kléber was in the region, they knew very well he had to drop by the Emperor's place sooner or later. They were ready. It was the lovely Françoise, Paul's smoky-eyed daughter, who greeted him at the door and a few seconds later, in the dining room, he received the second half of the double-whammy in the person of Raymonde, Paul's equally attractive wife. Bocuse himself was out of town, as it happened, doing a little business in Tokyo, but with the female mafia watching the shop (his mother was just arriving at the *caisse*) while Chef Roger Jaloux barked his orders in the kitchen, things were under admirable control.

As soon as Jean took a seat, a champagne pinkened with *crème de framboise* appeared before him, along with a plate of *amuse-gueules*. Secretly, he wished he could just have a salad and go to bed, but when you are the *Guide Kléber* you don't play the wilting virgin. You are expected to eat. Bocuse's famous truffle soup was a must for starters; it was then a fairly recent creation, and Jean had never eaten it. He followed it with a hot pâté in a pastry shell and a lukewarm salad of lobster with garden vegetables and herbs. The accompanying Beaujolais came from the cellars of Georges Duboeuf, where Jean had gone wine-tasting what now seemed like a couple of centuries ago.

In spite of his protestations, Luigi, the waiter gave Jean a second helping of *pâté chaud*. Luigi, known to the staff as Kiki and who bore a startling resemblance to a young Jerry Louis, had been serving Jean for fifteen years. He knew that Monsieur Didier had a particular weakness for *pâté chaud* and *sauce poivrade*. At 9:20 P.M. Jean popped another bile pill. He felt hot and uncomfortable.

The lobster was fabulous, of course, but now Jean was truly laboring. He felt as if he were on stage—which wasn't too far from the truth, ensconced as he was at *table numero un*. By an act of sheer will he chawed mechanically through the lobster, enjoying it as much as if it were cardboard.

"One is full up, huh," he remarked. He went on chewing, but the pernicious combination of too much food and no exercise was having its fatal effect. Jean was bloated. He had heartburn. His stomach was churning. He hurt.

"I have gas," he said.

He passed up the cheeses and barely managed to do justice to Bocuse's trollies of desserts, probably the lushest and most generous in France.

DAY SIX

"I've been born again! I'm brand new this morning."

Jean was feeling good. He had digested well and slept well. The optimism had returned. He felt ready for anything.

"The dinner last night was of great finesse and elegance," he said, now remembering what had been a trial as a treat. "That *pâté chaud* was sublime."

He was heading north out of Lyon, on the last leg of his *tournée.* Only one meal remained. The little Lancia ate up the kilometers as if it, too, were optimistic. Almost before Jean knew it, he was off the freeway and on the twisting country road leading toward Saulieu, home of the grand old Côte d'Or, Alexandre Dumaine's place. The Côte d'Or had had an irregular record since Dumaine's departure, and had slipped off the main line of the gourmet establishment's migratory path. Now it was owned by Claude Verger, a terrible-tempered terrier of a man who had made a comfortable fortune selling kitchen equipment to cooks and had learned so much about the trade that he had decided to become a restaurateur himself. Verger had brought his young protegé, Bernard Loiseau, down with him from Paris to run the kitchen. Chef of the Côte d'Or at only twenty-six, Loiseau shouldered a responsibility that was heavy with history, but in his youthful enthusiasm he was utterly unfazed—he was aiming for the top: three Michelin stars and a red-crowned Kléber rooster.

Loiseau was so eager for Jean's visit that he was literally watching the road, because this time the Kléber had telephone ahead. When he arrived in the parking lot, Loiseau came out to greet him before he had even squeezed out of the car. Within minutes, Jean had a *kir* in his hand. He and Loiseau walked down the hill to say hello to Gérard Houssaie, a young cook from Normandy who had taken over the neighboring Vieille Auberge. Houssaie was about Loiseau's age, but he had the advantage of having his wife with him. Loiseau was a bachelor, in the prime of life with the sap running hard, but he had no diversion beyond food in Saulieu.

"There's nothing here," he sighed. "No girls, no action, nothing. I'm just devoting myself to bringing the Côte d'Or back to the top. Other than that, I'm bored stiff."

Jean rewarded Louiseau's monklike fealty to *haute cuisine* by destroying his lunch with undisguised pleasure. Loiseau watched every plate as it came back to the kitchen. If Jean had left the least scrap uneaten, he probably would have rushed out demanding to know what had displeased him. He was hell-bent for gastronomic seduction, and he could not hide it. The lobster *terrine*, the poached oysters and the ragout of fish with red peppers disappeared into Kléber's maw with the help of a delicious 1971 Puligny-Montrachet, bright yellow, fat and full of flowers and honey. The red that followed, with the thin, rare duck steaks, was a vigorous Latricières-Chambertin. Louiseau's lunch was light, imaginative and easy to eat. Jean told him so, and for a few minutes the young bachelor didn't even care that there were no girls in Saulieu.

With the desserts, Claude Verger himself appeared, just down from Paris at one hundred miles an hour, not bothering to watch for cops, and he had gotten away with it, too. As sharp and aggressive as a gamecock and as outrageous as a standup comedian, Verger has always adored shocking people with his patent generalizations, expressly designed for provocation. He called for a bottle of champagne (Perrier-Jouët) and railed on, finding almost everything bad in the profession. Ninety-five or even ninety-nine percent of the cooks in France were lousy, he shouted, and only two or three of them were capable of putting together a decent *steak marchand de vin*. The only guy who knew how to make sauces was Pierre Troisgros—but then most sauces were no damn good, anyway.

Failing to get a rise from his audience with generalities, Verger tried to make Jean put up his dukes by turning his sarcasms to the guides and the food critics. You're all whores, he shouted, but Jean wasn't reacting. He felt euphoric and benign. He was thinking about taking it easy back in Paris, and drinking mineral water for several days. His *tournée* was over. He had made it. He could feel his digestion synchronizing. He took another sip of champagne and smiled.

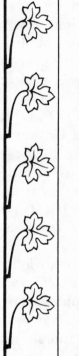

VII.
REACHING FOR
THE STARS

It was seven years after Didier's epic *tournée* that I saw Bernard Loiseau in Saulieu again. The boy was thirty-three now, and there had been some important changes in his life: he was thinner, having lost twenty-five pounds on his own cooking; he had less hair, more worries, but the same amount of enthusiasm, which means a lot; and he had a wife, now, so his monkish days were finally over. The lovely Chantal, with her blond hair, her movie star smile and her hysterical poodle, was now in charge of the *réception*, the dining-room personnel, the interior decoration and keeping Bernard warm at night, none of which duties he had been able to perform satisfactorily as a bachelor. His domain was the cuisine and The Big Picture.

For the cuisine, no problem. He had begun as a seventeen-year-old apprentice—rather old, that, but these things can happen—to Jean Troisgros in 1968, the very year that Jean and Pierre won their third Michelin star. There had been rough moments, like the time that Jean had bellowed, in front of all the other kitchen

personnel: "If this kid becomes a cook, I'll be an archbishop!" But
Bernard the Bird, as his name translates from the French, kept flail-
ing onward with that indefatigable supply of ardent optimism with
which he was born, not fearing to ask the dumb questions, smiling
when he goofed and picking himself up when he fell. In his own
way he, too, became a *Wunderkind*, and Claude Verger, a talent
scout if there ever was one, made him chef in one of his Paris restaurants, La Barrière Poquelin, at only age twenty-two. Chef at
twenty-two! Usually, that's as dangerous as bringing a kid into a
major-league ballpark to hit sliders at fifteen, but occasionally it can
work. It did with Bernard, and he quickly made a mark in the capital with a manner of cooking that was as Verger liked it: very fresh,
very rare and very light. The style was futuristic then, but it was
only a start: the kid was beginning to find his own way, and presently he would be going further—a lot further.

In 1975, Verger did the French equivalent of buying Mount
Vernon, Penn Station or Old Faithful: he heard that La Côte d'Or
was for sale, and instinct told him he had to make the plunge, fast,
before some unspeakable developer did. Dumaine's place was truly
a national monument, with its cool, shadowy salons, its murals and
its handcrafted woodwork, mellowed and darkened with the unique
patina that only half a century of direct exposure to perfumed
shoulders, prehistoric Armagnac, expensive Burgundies and Cuban
cigars can create. But the Philistines gladly would have bulldozed it
all away in favor of a supermarket or a drive-in bank.

"Pack your bags," he said to Bernard. "You're going to Saulieu."

That was where The Big Picture came in. When you are appointed chef at La Côte d'Or (now only age twenty-four), it is a
thousand times more daunting than taking over a little-known restaurant in Paris, as he had done at twenty-two. Bernard was walking on hallowed ground, saying mass in Saint Peter's, batting lefty
at Ebbett's Field, looking up through the gloom to the right field
screen where Dixie Walker used to lob them over into Flatbush. He
walked into Dumaine's kitchen on a cloud of emotion and with a
lump in his throat. Golly.

The personnel of kitchen and dining room gave him the once-over. They were all gruff old salts formed in the grand tradition, truculent of manner and economical of smiles, but underneath the harsh exterior, they proved to have their hearts in the right place as far as Bernard was concerned: they hated him.

"I used to work my ass off all day long," he recalled, "and then go up to my room and cry for most of the night, I was so sad and frustrated. Finally it got to be too much. One morning I came down and called them all together. 'Take a good look at my face,' I told them, 'because it's here to stay, so you'd better get used to it. Now either do that or get out.' And you know what? They got out. None of them are here anymore."

Bernard had his new personnel in place when I met him with Jean Didier, and he had just won his first star in the Michelin, two years after his arrival. Even then, at twenty-six, a mere stripling, he was aiming for the top. He wanted three stars, and he was going to get them, come hell or high water. That was The Big Picture and he had pursued it from the moment he crossed the threshold of La Côte d'Or.

The second star came in March of 1981, and in October of the same year the hopes of winning the third suddenly appeared more realizable, when Chantal and Fifi (hideous cur) consented to come to the country and share their destinies with a *cuistot*. Now he had a person—and a decorative person, too, which couldn't do any harm—to take care of all the aspects of the business that a cook has neither the time nor the talent for. The formula fell into place when Verger made the best wedding present of all, by agreeing to sell him La Côte d'Or, interest-free, at a price he could pay over several years. Now he was the *patron*, and Chantal the *patronne*. There were two of them to reach for the stars.

The stars which every French cook aspires to are not stars at all, but what the French call *macarons*, the bumpy round symbols in the Michelin which resemble the insignia of a major in the United States Army. When they are awarded, they come in packages of one, two or three, and the authority that does the awarding is the guide division of the Michelin tire company. Sticking with our military analogy for a moment, we can say that one star means you have made the grade from enlisted man to officer in the army of cooks. Two stars means a high-ranking officer, the commander of a restaruant that "merits a detour," as the Michelin puts its. Three stars, limited to the generals of the profession—in 1985 there were only nineteen of them in all of France—signifies that your establishment "is worth a voyage." A separate trip, from Paris to Lyon or the Côte d'Azur or the Pyrénées or wherever, just to eat? But yes, *mon cher*. This is France, after all, and the Michelin is the Michelin.

There is nothing else like it. The food critics come and go, the fashions change and different restaurant and hotel guides are published from time to time with an eye on that huge market of eaters out there, but they all risk falling by the wayside eventually; only the Michelin always remains, the majestic red Bible of gastronomy, steaming along at its own measured pace, crushing the opposition and depressing its most fervid detractors by its quality and inevitability. It has its irritating faults, it has a tendency to appear smug, it occasionally makes mistakes, but it is *the* book of reference, it outsells all the others, and it is the one, more than all the others combined, in which cooks dream of seeing their names, preferably garnished with those cute little *macarons*. The impact of the Michelin on restaurants' destinies is direct, dramatic and usually immediate. Careers are made and broken by the Michelin's judgments; restaurants prosper or go broke; cooks become members of an envied élite or founder into blank anonymity. The power of the Michelin is terrifying and not to be taken lightly.

"*C'est Waterloo!*" wept the new chef at Lapérouse, one of Paris's great traditional restaurants, upon learning several years ago that his establishment had been demoted from three stars to two.

Alain Zick reacted in a rather more percussive manner. Chef of the fashionable Paris restaurant Relais des Porquerolles, Zick was horrified to learn in March, 1966, that he had been demoted from one star to none. In October, he blew his brains out. Understandably, Michelin spokesmen deny a direct link between the two events (Zick had been having personal problems as well), but the Parisian press saw it clearly as cause and effect.

On the other hand, approval by Michelin inevitably has happy results, and merely being mentioned in the guide without further distinction is generally enough to insure a steady flow of customers. And if stars appear, the flow begins to resemble a torrent.

"All the out-of-town customers come because of Michelin," said Jean-Paul Lacombe of Léon de Lyon. "A friend of mine spent an enormous amount of money building up his restaurant in Pont d'Isère, but he just wasn't getting enough customers. He was about to put the key under the door mat when—*toc!*—he got a star in the Michelin. Suddenly the customers started coming and he got over the hump."

The *Guide Michelin* began with our century. André Michelin, the Auvergnat inventor who founded the tire company that is now the second largest in the world, dedicated himself to promoting the use of the private automobile and shrewdly guessed that drivers would appreciate a brief catalogue of addresses for eating, sleeping and having their machines repaired. In 1900 he brought out his first edition, a little red booklet measuring 10 by 15 cm, bright red and numbering 399 pages. (And, incidentally, filled with ads for hotels and garages, a bit of vulgar commercialism that Michelin haughtily eschews now that it has ample budget to do without. Other guides swallow hard and accept ads.) He gave it away free, thinking of all the tires it would help sell. How right he was. In 1901 the circulation had risen to 54,000, and it has been going up ever since. Today, the Great Red Book is France's best bestseller, with the possible exception of the Bible, although not necessarily even that, if we look at sales on a yearly basis. Its 1984 edition sold almost 700,000 copies and, although it gives information on thousands of hotels and restaurants, the starred eating places are extremely limited: 534 with one star, 90 with two, and 18 with three.

After 1900, two dates marked significant changes in the Michelin: 1920 and 1926. It was only in 1920 that the company began charging for the guide instead of giving it away. This decision is said to have come after Monsieur Michelin visited a provincial garage and spotted a copy of his precious red book jammed under a gimpy table to shim up a short leg.

"If that's the way they treat my guides," he grumped, "then they're going to have to pay for them."

But it is the second date, 1926, that is most venerated in the eating trade: Michelin initiated the system of awarding stars to judge the excellence of an establishment's cooking. For the business of *haute cuisine*, it was like the creation of the Legion of Honor.

"There's nothing better. It's the top. It means you are number one," said Pierre Troisgros. "When we got our third star, our turnover went way up—it was absolutely flagrant. But the Michelin also forces us to hold the standards up. Those three stars are like the sword of Damocles over our heads. It is a service to the public."

"A light to guide us," Alain Chapel, a man with a lyric penchant, was not afraid to say. "The Michelin spirit means quality in the tiniest details."

Chapel and I were sitting in a corner of the bar of his celebrated restaurant in Mionnay, sharing a breakfast as we spoke. Suddenly his eyes narrowed and he leaned forward to examine the floral design of a beautiful china jam pot. Apparently he had spotted a minuscule scratch, invisible to the common of mortals.

"Take this away and break it!" he roared to the waiter. "I'll buy another. I won't have chipped china in my house."

Better than with any words of explanation, he had illustrated the Michelin spirit. This dedication to uncompromising excellence that is required for the winning of something that has no intrinsic value whatsoever, but an enormous potential for profit, makes a nicely moralistic metaphor for the trials and rewards inherent in many phases of human activity. Politicians can strut and posture and change their images according to the latest advice from their PR men, ill-tempered louts can corner the market in silver or sowbelly futures and the rich can get richer in any one of a million ways, but the intelligence, character and devotion required for a third Michelin star are found in few.

It was to follow up on the metaphor, then, that I spent some time with a couple of chefs whom I count as friends, Bernard Loiseau and Georges Blanc. Georges has already made it and, as I write this, Bernard is still trying. In effect, I gave myself a private audition with each of them and then watched and listened as they launched into Shakespeare's great soliliquy, "What dost it take to get Three Stars in The Michelin, forsooth?"

For Georges, I will always have two symbolic images in mind. The first is of a lunch which he made for a select group of his peers, and the second, years later, his dramatic arrival—*coquus ex machina*—by helicopter. I was standing on a boardwalk above the grassy banks of the River Veyle in the little town of Vonnas, halfway between Mâcon and Bourg-en-Bresse, when I heard the helicopter thudding in the distance and watched it, sleek in its green and beige paint, as it whistled in over the farmland, banked smartly to the right and softly settled, paws extended, onto the bull's-eye of the landing pad, halfway between the tennis court and the swimming pool. Nice job. A door flew open and a trim, black-haired young man in slacks and cashmere cardigan sprang down and dashed free of the prop wash. Hardly breaking stride, he waved a quick goodbye and hustled across the sun deck onto a flowered walkway hugging the side of the building, turned into a glass door and entered his domain: an ultra-modern stainless-steel and tile kitchen. Almost immediately he began giving orders to the five or six assistants who were already at work.

Georges Blanc had arrived.

It was late spring of 1981, a few weeks after the fourth most momentous event of his life, roughly equal in importance to his birth, his marriage and the birth of his two sons: the acquisition of his third Michelin star. Georges's elegant hotel-restaurant installation in Vonnas, La Mère Blanc, was the only one to be so promoted in 1981. It represented a personal achievement that had hardly seemed likely ten years earlier, when I first met him, thanks to Paul Bocuse.

Georges was the kid then, twenty-eight years old and as shy as he was reserved. As he has done so often with so many other of his younger *confrères*, Bocuse had more or less ordered Georges to set up a lunch and then had convoked friends, and myself, to it. This was the first time I had seen the Veyle and the picture-postcard park of Vonnas. As I strolled through, whom should I come upon but Jean-Paul Haeberlin, he of the lilting Alsatian accent and the fabulous Auberge de l'Ill in Illhaeusern, doing a watercolor of a weeping willow reflecting in the stream, with the red tile roof of La Mère Blanc bang center in the background. Gaston Lenôtre joined us a bit later, and we sat down with Bocuse and a few others at a large corner table which Georges had laid for us on this, his normal closing day.

The menu was all traditional that day. Either Georges hadn't yet learned to do differently or he didn't dare, and preferred not to take any chances. There was a hugely generous presentation of crayfish, scarlet and steaming, which we picked off the "bush" one by one and ate with the peppery, eye-watering *nage* in which they had been cooked, cracking them open with our teeth and making a great, sloppy, Sybaritic mess of juice and carapaces all around us; frogs' legs with enough butter to build a dozen birthday cakes and enough garlic to make a Neapolitan smile; and *volaille de Bresse à la crème*, the timeless chicken in cream sauce with a flavor of such depth and power that I am still convinced that Georges is hiding something from me, although he has explained the recipe a dozen times. The lunch was regional food at its finest, the traditional dishes which three generations of women had been cooking in the same place before him: his mother, his grandmother and his great-grandmother.

It was this constant feminine presence in the kitchen that had earned the inn its name—Mother Blanc—and Georges had just taken over the restaurant, the eight-room hotel and the account books when the third "mother" (his own, this time) hung up her apron and retired. As the first male heir after an illustrious succession of females, he was something of a professional curiosity. The Blanc women were firmly enshrined in local legend as Michelin aristocrats. Great-grandmother Virginie had been cooking since 1872, long before the guide existed, feeding farmers and fowl merchants who came to the Vonnas marketplace, but grandmother Elisa won her first star in 1926 and the second in 1931. George's mother, Paulette, took over in 1936 when she married into the family and began the long, hard apprenticeship to Elisa, cheerfully accepting the sixteen-hour days and maintaining the two-star quality until she, in turn, stepped down in 1968.

Theirs had been a very special and especially wonderful branch of the main tree of French gastronomy, a phenomenon that flourished in the provinces, especially in Lyon and its environs, but was much less prevalent in Paris: *la cuisine des mères*. "Mothers' cooking" was both a culinary style and a philosophical attitude toward life. It was done exclusively in modest but comfortable country *auberges* or unpretentious city bistrots. As a rule, they were small mom and pop operations, with mom in the *cuisine* and pop in the *salle* (or perhaps, more often, outside with his friends, playing *pétanque* and drinking Beaujolais while *la mère* worked). The customers, in those days before the automobile culture, were locals, the traveling salemen known as *commis-voyageurs*, and, on weekends, big-city people who took the train for a Sunday lunch in the country. The food was not expensive, and the wines were from the area, often drawn from barrels in the *cave* and served in carafes. There were always stockpots murmuring gently on the back of the coal stoves, and the *spécialités* were the traditional, slow-cooking *plats mijotés: pot-au-feu, blanquette de veau, boeuf mode, poulet à la crème, civet de lapin* and all the other magical creations that are usually dismissed in English as stews. The French regard them with a veneration that is almost mystical, now that they are becoming harder and harder to find in anything approaching the quality of the great old tradition. If, in season, a hunter happened to tramp in with a fat hare or a fisherman with a glistening pike, *la mère* saw no reason why she shouldn't cook it for him, and just charge for her time. That was her job. It was hard but she loved it.

Mothers' cooking is virtually gone now, as the notions of society, regions and the family have undergone their own sea changes. If you are of a mind to shed a tear for its demise, though, take care not to confuse it with its successor, women's cooking. There are some points of similarity, to be sure, beginning with the sex of the executants, but the lines are not as clear as they used to be. Women's cooking, which became tremendously fashionable in the wake of the *nouvelle cuisine* rage and continues to flourish today, is less specifically female than *la cuisine des mères*, being, in most cases, simply another, rather androgynous, branch of the modern school of cooking. There are distinctions, but in cooking as in everything else, the trend today is for the women to do as the men do. Whether that is a good thing or a bad thing, I leave for my intellectual superiors to judge. In her *Croque en Bouche*, Fanny Deschamps theorizes that since modern women learned how to make love they have forgotten how to cook, but I reject this arrant and intolerable sexism out of hand. There is room for both. I can think of several successful women cooks in whom I would place my entire confidence as to their love-making capacities.

But I digress. Back to Georges. *Le petit Blanc*, they called him in those days, because he hadn't made a first name for himself yet. *Maman* was Madame Blanc, mightily honored, and his uncle at the Chapon Fin in Thoissey was Paul Blanc, one of the regional notables, but Georges was still on trial. At lunch that day with Bocuse and his friends, I can scarcely remember him saying a word. The silence was not all timidity, though: Georges was watching and listening and learning. The smile was reserved, but he listened very carefully, and his deceptively soft brown eyes did not miss a thing.

"Around then my only concern was holding on to the second star," he told me later. "It was years before the thought of a third one even crossed my mind."

They were trying times, and Georges looks back on them today with a kind of bittersweet fondness. Within the Blanc family it had been understood that he would eventually be taking over the eight-room hotel and restaurant, ever since his fourteenth birthday, when his father had called him to his office and spoken to him man to man. Monsieur Blanc *père* had developed a nicely prosperous bottling and distributing business for wines, beer and lemonade, while his wife ran the *auberge* with the help of a couple of local ladies. Now it was time to make the decisions about his next several years of schooling. Which one would it be: the kitchen or the bottling business? Georges thought gravely about it for a few seconds and then made the announcement that would determine his entire future existence.

"I'm going to work with *maman*," he said.

The route was traced: a technical high school for an accounting certificate, then the hotel management school at Thonon-les-Bains, on the shores of Lake Geneva, gave him the academic foundation which is common for the trade today, but was utterly unknown only a generation earlier, with the Bocuses, Troisgros, Ducloux and company, whose only academies had been basement rooms with coal-fed stoves where the professors delivered lectures with their booted feet. A couple of years of military service (in the Navy, where he cooked for an admiral aboard an aircraft carrier) brought him to full manhood, but nothing of all this had prepared him for the hard reality of being apprenticed at twenty-two to his own mother.

"For the last two years before she retired, I was the employee and she was the boss," he recalled. "It wasn't easy. She made life tough for me."

Paulette, the tender tyrant, implacably broke her boy into the immutable routine of a workday that began at seven-thirty or eight and didn't finish until midnight, and wrung the hotel-school book learning out of him, in much the same way that *papa* Troisgros had done with his two self-confident sons, replacing it with *maman's* way: boning ten thousand frogs' legs; mashing pike meat in a mortar as the first step of the incomprehensible alchemy whose end product is the lighter-than-air miracle called *quenelles de brochet;* reducing, skimming and seasoning the crayfish stock for the *sauce Nantua* that would accompany the *quenelles;* learning the right temperature of the butter so that the famous Vonnas potato pancakes will remain as fluffy as they are fat; browning the beef cubes just so, before confiding them to the Beaujolais which would transform them into *boeuf bourguignon;* and giving himself over to the alchemy by which three generations of Blanc women had developed the unimaginably superior taste of their family's *poulet à la crème.*

"We've always been severe for work in the family," said Paulette, who is now the dynasty's senior citizen, and who acts as a reception-desk hostess, benign and ladylike, with nary a trace of the black cape and Dracula teeth with which she terrorized her son during his apprenticeship in her kitchen, "I made Georges work, that's true—and work well, *comme il faut.* I formed him, just the way my mother-in-law formed me in my youth. It was a favor she did me, and I did the same for him."

Thanks, mom.

"Yes, I had a hard time in those years," Georges can admit today, "but she is right: It was for my own good. When I took over the business, I had to show everyone that I was up to the level of the place. The critics were ready to ambush me if I slipped up."

The critics were the industrialists from Bourg, Mâcon and Lyon, the seasoned travelers who had found that Vonnas was the ideal stopover point for the car trip from Paris to Geneva, and the legions of serious gourmets, who remembered the classical masterpieces of *cuisine de mère* in Vonnas the way Proust remembered *madeleines,* and who were prepared to humiliate any young whippersnapper who might dare change the least syllable of their renditions.

In 1966, just the way it happens in love stories, Georges met a vivacious and willowy blonde at a ball in Bourg, married her and brought her home to mother. Jacqueline, his new wife, was undoubtedly bright, and the prettiest new girl in Vonnas, but she had everything to learn about gastronomy and hotelkeeping. So what do you do in a case like that? You put the girl to work, that's what. Jacqueline and Georges did their apprenticeships side by side, then, and in spite of the tension at the start, their marriage is all the stronger for it. Sorry for the platitudes, but that's how it is. Sometimes these things can't be avoided.

"Jacqueline was with me all the way on this," said Georges. "She never complained. I couldn't have done it without her."

Slowly and timidly, Georges began suggesting changes. For the old-line traditionalists who had been in love with three generations of Blanc women, altering the wonderful old menu was equivalent to touching up the stained glass at Chartres, but *maman* let him give it a try—very, very carefully. The veal scallop with a sauce based on butter and sorrel which he added to the menu was not too dangerous, since it was a variation on a theme already made famous by the Troisgros, who had done roughly the same thing with their thin salmon filets. The *escalope à l'oseille* met with veiled surprise, but it was successful all the same, and it encouraged him to continue. Georges began experimenting with seafood, a specialty that the Blanc women had virtually ignored, since transport had been too slow in the old days, and the rivers and lakes were teaming with pike and char and trout and crayfish, anyway, so why bother? *Le petit Blanc* seemed to have ideas, which, everything considered, was probably dangerous. He would bear watching.

Watching is what Michelin is there for. The guide's twelve full-time inspectors crisscross the country 365 days a year according to a schedule established in Paris headquarters, looking for interesting new restaurants and watching old ones for the signs of laxity which can lead to demotion or the excellence which might add a star. Unlike Jean Didier, Gault and Millau and the other "personalized" food critics, the Michelin men are always incognito, drive ordinary middle-price cars, dress conservatively and cultivate a faceless image of bourgeois nondescriptness. The fact that intelligence agents do the same thing is lost on no one, least of all the restaurateurs on whom they are always snooping. Gastronomic KGB operatives, they visit restaurants sometimes alone, sometimes in pairs, sometimes with their wives—but they are always unrecognizable.

"You can never tell when Michelin is there," said Jacqueline, "so there's no way you can warn the personnel to pay special attention to such and such a guest. All you can do is try to be as good as you can for everyone."

Which is exactly what Pierre Troisgros means when he refers to Michelin as a public service and a Damocles sword. The inspectors make mental notes on the reception, the service, the decoration, the tableware, the cleanliness of the toilets—and, of course, what is on their plates. Certainly, more than all the other elements, the food is what counts, but no backsliding of any kind goes unnoticed. One week out of three the inspectors are back in Paris, filling out forms and writing up the finely detailed reports that go in, with customers' letters, to form each establishment's dossier. The dossiers grow fat with the years, unlike the inspectors, who eat carefully. The editors of the *Guide* collate the "objective" details of price, compare the value judgments, then make their most important decisions *en collège:* the vote to take away or to add a third star must be the unanimous agreement of all the inspectors and top editors. They watched Georges for a decade and a half before making the decision.

"Of course you need *savoir-faire* for this business," said Georges, "but even more than that, you've got to have enthusiasm and sincerity. You can't cheat when you're at the three-star level— even if you know that only one client in ten could possibly notice the cheating. In fact those are the ones who keep you honest. Those are the ones you work for." He reflected a moment, and then burst out with another of those atrocious platitudes that spontaneously spring to the lips of three-star chefs. Along with children, the mentally deficient and perhaps a few reclusive preachers, they are probably the only human beings who actually believe such awful bromides when they say them. "Money's not what counts for me," he went on, further aggravating his case. "What I'm looking for is to be the best in my trade. There are other values in life than money."

Appalling, isn't it? We were driving through the rich Bressane countryside to a tiny hamlet near Mâcon, where the object of our visit was Louis Chevenet, a gentle, smiling man in his forties with graying hair and the soft eyes of a mystic. Chevenet is an artisan, a maker of goat cheeses of such perfection that Georges has to compete with Bocuse and Chapel for his share of the paragons of the art that Louis creates from the two hundred fifty whiskey-colored lovelies whom he knows individually by name and who come running up like children when he approaches, their little milk bags swinging gaily between their hind legs.

"You know," confided Chevenet, patting a small brown head, "you can raise cows and pigs without love, but with goats it won't work."

One of them was so pleased to be in our presence that she reached nimbly upward and, quick as a wink, tore a page from my writing pad. Chevenet watched with avuncular pride as she munched through my prose, a born editor if there ever was one. We negotiated a short but perilous passage down a slippery, rusting and nearly vertical iron ladder, into the dank murk of an earthen cellar, where hundreds of cheeses were aging in moist repose.

"An incomparable product," said Georges reverently, tasting one after the other. "I wonder if . . ." His voice trailed off momentarily as he pursued his line of thought. "I wonder if it might be possible to serve this as a first course, instead of at the end of the meal."

Chevenet nodded his enthusiastic approval. "In a salad, maybe," Georges mused. "With fresh herbs and a hint of olive oil."

I didn't know it at the time, but I was living a privileged moment: the birth of a three-star creation. Two weeks later Georges had added his goat cheese salad to the menu of La Mère Blanc.

It took Georges years to learn this kind of inventive spirit which is so typical of the great chefs. Or perhaps it would be fairer to say it took him years to dare to apply it. Taking charge of a monument like La Mère Blanc at such a young age, he first had to placate the traditionalists before taking their toys away from them and offering them newer and perhaps better ones in their places. Nor could he have succeeded in transforming his *cuisine de mère* into *haute cuisine* if he had stayed within the hallowed old walls that he had inherited. Everything had to come together at the right time; going for the third star is appallingly tricky. Get one element just a little bit wrong, and the whole damn thing goes blooey. "Harmony" is a word the editors of the *Guide Michelin* use over and again when they speak of Vonnas: the delicate balance between food, service, comfort and the surroundings.

As sole master of La Mère Blanc, Georges introduced his inventions with utmost caution, taking care not to offend the old clientèle, but he had already made the decision to go for the top. By the early seventies, he had become convinced that the family *auberge* was stuck forever at the two-star level unless he changed its character dramatically. It was *sympathique*, all right, but it was not three-star class. Borrowing and mortgaging, he embarked on an audacious building and redecorating program that utterly changed the style of La Mère Blanc. When he was done with it, his family's friendly little country inn was gone, finished. What had taken its place was beautiful, but unfamiliar. It was a dangrous step, an expensive one and a gamble. His ambition was showing.

"My father was against it," he recalls. "We had a good, steady two-star business that the family had built up over the years. It was a risk to change it."

Georges put his head down and ploughed on anyway. If, for the sake of history, he suspended sentence on the *poulet à la crème*, he guillotined *quenelles de brochet* and *boeuf bourguignon* from his menu in favor of sophisticated creations of lobster, sea bass, sole, scallops, foie gras and duck, ingredients previously foreign to Vonnas. The wine cellar, which the Blanc women had been content to leave as a summary accompaniment to the kitchen, grew apace with Georges's forays into the vineyards of Burgundy and Beaujolais and Bordeaux until he had built it into one of the most impressive in France, now counting more than 50,000 bottles.

Devouring his savings and borrowing what to lesser men would have seemed like terrifying sums of money, he designed a vast new wing which grew at the back of the hotel, supported on one side by piles driven into the mud of the Veyle, down to bedrock. The hotel's eight small rooms became fifteen large ones of luxurious comfort, and he furnished them with regional antiques. The old dining room disappeared and a gleaming, stainless-steel kitchen took its place, while an entirely new dining room large enough for one hundred guests, all stone and tile and tapestries and walk-in fireplaces, appeared behind it. For good measure, Georges threw in a swimming pool, a tennis court equipped for night games and the one and only helicopter landing pad in Vonnas.

"Everyone laughed at me when I had that helipad built," he says now with undisguised pleasure. "But there have been days when I've had up to three helicopters parked out there. They're not laughing anymore. It's the same thing with the prestige suite."

The prestige suite was a hunch he played, an idea that seemed to fly in the face of reason, but which turned out to be a stroke of genius: a single accommodation of two-hundred-fifty square meters, on two levels and with three private terraces. It costs a lot more than the other rooms—about $250 a night, depending on what exchange rate you use for the franc—but it has already become famous in the trade and is permanently booked months is advance.

As he passed his thirty-fifth birthday, it was rapidly becoming apparent that *le petit Blanc* was going to become *le grand Blanc*, whether or not the traditionalists liked it. Now Georges carried a telephone beeper around in his shirt pocket, and if cooking was still central to his preoccupations, he was also concerned with interest rates, amortizations, cash flow and profit margins. On the three-star level, at least, the days of navigating by poetical genius alone are finished. It's a shame, but that's the way it has to be: a great restaurant is a kind of dream factory, but it is also a business. When Georges returned to Vonnas from the navy, La Mère Blanc's personnel had consisted of his mother and four employees. Now the staff is 49—that magic union-free number—plus himself.

By the late seventies, word was beginning to circulate within the rarefied world of the gastronomic establishment that Georges Blanc—he had a first name now—was making a push for the third star. It was around then that Jean Troisgros visited Vonnas and took a long, appraising walk through Georges's new installations. He came back to Roanne shaking his head with admiration.

"George is the one who's doing the most these days," he told me at the time. "You've got to go take a look at what he's done there. He's got more guts than all the rest of us."

When the heavy construction work was finished, Georges worked on the details: more period furniture for the rooms, replacement of the old red and white road signs with new ones in more reserved, classy tones of beige, white and brown. Jacqueline changed the silverware and glasses, bought new and more expensive tablecloths and napkins. A closed-circuit TV monitor between kitchen and reception hall allowed Georges to watch guests arrive, lest he miss an important one who merited a personal greeting. Georges instituted a new policy of having his waiters announce the title and composition of each dish as it was presented at the table, a tactful reminder for those—it is a fairly common fact of restaurant life— who have forgotten what they have ordered.

The gastronomic rumor mill spoke more and more insistently of a third star for La Mère Blanc as the decade changed, but when the 1980 edition of the *Guide Michelin* appeared, Vonnas bore the same two stars that had been there, immutably, for close to fifty years. If Georges felt any disappointment, he didn't show it. It is not his nature to make a display of his emotions. He returned to his kitchen and worked on more new ideas. His installation was impeccable, he knew. Apparently Michelin had not been convinced by the cooking yet. He would have to try harder. He knew very well that the inspectors would be back throughout 1980, checking in on him for 1981.

They came, all right. In all, eight of the twelve full-time inspectors dropped by Vonnas during 1980. Now there was general agreement that La Mère Blanc seemed to merit the third star; what was needed was a final double-checking to make certain that none of the eight felt he was judging too hastily: were there seasonal variations in quality? Did Blanc express himself as well in the autumn, when the wild game season was on, as he did in the springtime, when the last of the winter oysters were meeting the first tender young vegetables?

Eight times, then, Georges passed the exam for his doctoral thesis, but, unlike other students, he was never able to know when or on what point he was being examined. Nor was this anywhere near a record: when Michelin gave its first three-star rating to a restaurant outside of France (Villa Lorraine in Brussels), it inspected the place no less than seventeen times.

At year's end, at a plenary meeting of inspectors and editors in Paris, Michelin voted unanimously to promote La Mère Blanc to the top. The 1981 guide was laid out and made ready for printing in the almost paranoid secrecy that characterizes the entire Michelin operation. Georges sat and waited. The guide officially went on sale on March 3, 1981, and that was the day when he finally heard the good news. It is an absolute rule throughout the trade that every cook remembers the exact time and circumstances marking his Annunciation.

"It was 11:30 in the morning," he recalled. "Jacqueline and I were sitting in the kitchen cutting the birthday cake for our little son, Frédéric, who had just turned six that day. A woman from the

Associated Press called for an interview. Jacqueline made her repeat it to make sure it wasn't some kind of joke."

Presently, messages began appearing on the telex, and the phone rang all that day and the next. The messages were not only from Europe, but from the Americas as well, and Japan and Australia and New Zealand. Literally overnight, Georges has become an international celebrity. He and Jacqueline put in an order for a dozen copies of the Michelin.

Almost immediately, La Mère Blanc began experiencing The Michelin Effect, a phenomenon that occurs whenever a restaurant is awarded a third star and translates into a mob of new customers. Everyone who had been thinking of trying Vonnas some day wanted to go there right then, and others who had never even heard of La Mère Blanc found themselves inexplicably seized by a ravenous hungering for *marinade de blanc de poularde* or *aiguillettes de canard beaujolaise*. Business rose by 50 percent, and perhaps half of the new arrivals were foreigners, who found Georges's menus at 140 and 250 francs miraculously cheap for a three-star establishment. (They've gone up a bit since, but then, what hasn't?) More than any advertisement or signposts could do, Michelin had put La Mère Blanc on the map.

"In a way, things are worse now," said Jacqueline. "Now that we have the three stars, we have to work harder than ever to prove we deserve them."

Frankly, though, she didn't seem to be as unhappy as all that.

Georges had been a notable; now he became a regional VIP The *département* of the Ain, which now could claim two three-star establishments (the other one is Alain Chapel), adopted a chef's hat as its official emblem. The prefect, the highest governmental official in the region, wrote Georges a warm personal letter of congratulations and, not long afterward, made him a Knight of the National Order of Merit.

Today *le petit Blanc*, not so *petit* anymore, basks in the same kind of magical aura which surrounds movie actors and football stars. Diners routinely ask him for his autograph and consult him as gravely as if he were a high priest, while his boyish countenance regularly appears in articles and ads from one end of the country to the other. Nor is the business world immune to his suddenly acquired charm: the day I watched him alight from the helicopter, a champagne company had deemed it worth its while to hasten its corporate flying machine to Vonnas and fetch Georges between his lunch and dinner services to carry him 150 kilometers away for a personal appearance.

Those are the kinds of perks that danced before Bernard the Bird's eyes when he came to Saulieu and realized that the tool which had been placed in his hands could carry him, too, all the way to the top. Let's be fair, though: it is not for the perks alone that a young cook makes the exhausting and potentially ruinous push for three Michelin stars, any more than you can be absolutely sure to eat better in a three-star place than in a two-star one. The three-star restaurant is an exercise whose execution is as complicated as a decathlon, and which is not suited to every cook. Some of them simply say to hell with it, concentrate on their table alone and stay happy with one star or two. (The occasional stories you hear about eccentric geniuses making three-star cuisine in out-of-the-way villages, unbeknownst to the guides is, alas, utter wishful thinking. The French gastronomic grapevine works infinitely better than any anti-missile early-warning system.) For those who are not afraid of hassles, though (the French word is *enmerdements*, a fine, straightforward scatological image of central importance to the language), the prospect of going for the three Michelin stars is the same kind of challenge that fascinated and possessed Lee Iacocca when he first signed on with Ford. Such a one is Bernard Loiseau.

"Schlaak! Toc! Vlan! Clack! Paf!"

Bernard was describing his cooking. The onomatopoeia isn't written quite the same way in French as in English (dogs go *ouaf* instead of woof, guns go *pan* instead of bang and people who stub their toes cry *ai* instead of ouch), but the energy-charged sincerity which led him to these verbal explosions was the universal sign of the man who had something very special to say, and was determined to put it across, even if he had to play charades to do it. We were charging at quick-time around his domain, from salon to salon, into the ladies' room, luckily empty at the moment ("Look at that wallpaper, pretty good, huh?"), across the ringing, oil-stained cement slab of the hotel garage, destined to be his future dining room when the loans come through, out to the gaping vacant lot where he had torn down some useless sheds and, some day soon, a soothing, green garden would be growing, over to the *pension de famille* next to the Côte d'Or, which he had just acquired and through the renovation of which he was going to increase the count of his rooms from the eighteen small ones which Dumaine had left to thirty large, comfortable and expensive ones. Bernard had it all blocked out, step by step, and he and Chantal were advancing on the master plan as fast as the banks sprang the money free. The rooms will be here and here, facing out onto the park, and the dining room will be here, so the clients don't have to listen to the trucks on the *nationale* anymore, and the new kitchen will be right in front, where the main entrance is now, with the windows facing out on the road.

The road is the Nationale 6, *la Six*, as renowed in French folklore as Route 66 in the States, although not celebrated in song quite so winningly. The main artery from Paris to Lyon since before medieval times, *la Six* is strewn along its entire length with inns and post houses, and Saulieu is one of the towns most richly furnished. It is amazing, and a little sad, to see the plethora of large hotels and restaurants lined up along the main drag of this overgrown provincial town, whose total population can hardly number more than 4,000, a reminder of the old days of leisurely travel. The old clientèle is gone now, because the superhighway south, the *autoroute A6*, completed in the early seventies, followed another track, leaving Saulieu in the middle of nowhere as far as most drivers are concerned. Now they go southward like lemmings, in four lanes, stopping to nourish themselves, if we may use that expression, at vile gas-station caravanseries along the way, where they fight each other for space to get overcharged for loathsome *steak-frites*. There is no longer enough traffic on *la Six* to support the traditional eating and sleeping places in Saulieu, and not enough locals to make up for the damage done by the *autoroute*. The only way, in fact, that a restaurateur can be certain that people will go out of their way to come to him is to possess three Michelin stars. For that, the French (and a lot of British and Dutch and Germans, too, and of course Americans) are happy to wander off to the middle of nowhere.

That's what Bernard was counting on as he gleefully plunged deeper and deeper into debt. Nor, he realized, did the name of the grand old institution called La Côte d'Or inspire any brand-loyalty within the bosooms of the Pepsi Generation, which was beginning to flirt with gastronomy, and that explained why he decided to personalize his operation in the same way that Bocuse and Troisgros and Chapel and others have done. Now there was a black, scripted signature with letters a yard high hanging on the stone of the Côte d'Or's historic façade. BERNARD LOISEAU, it reads, while above it, untouched since the old days but definitely of secondary importance, stands the trace of history: LA CÔTE D'OR. The symbolic message could not be clearer. The Côte d'Or is Bernard Loiseau now, and he is doing things his way. The times have changed. It was no accident that he had decided to knock the place topsy-turvy, because he had been doing a lot of looking and a lot of thinking, and he had concluded that a program like this was his only hope of winning the third star. And someone else had already shown the way.

"My model is Georges Blanc," he was saying. "He's the one who understood the future better than anyone else. Straight cuisine isn't enough anymore. You've got to go up to a higher level, where you give the client peace and calm along with the food. People want to get away from the cities and come spend a weekend in an atmosphere of refinement and relaxation. They want to wake up to see trees and grass and hear birds singing. The future is in *hôtellerie*, so I've got to expand. Georges is the one who showed the way. Even if his guests forget what they have eaten after a while, they will remember La Mère Blanc because of the beauty of the place. That's marketing. That's what I have to do here if I'm going to make it."

From the Bocuse generation to Georges Blanc to Loiseau, progressively younger, the cooks march to Michelin's drum, tramping up to the guide's headquarters on Avenue de Breteuil in Paris, just behind the Invalides, to pay the tribute of their persons at least once a year, inquiring as to the state of their dossiers and respectfully wondering if perhaps *ces messieurs-dames* might have some advice for them on how they could improve their food and their service. Jean-Paul Lacombe, he of the Léon de Lyon dynasty, a devil of a cook with his two stars anchored in bedrock, still lowers his voice with something very much like awe when he tells of the first trips he made there as a beginner, after his father had died and he had to take over the place much earlier than he had thought to. There is Kafka in the air when he describes the stuffy, windowless and barren meeting room to which he was led, the simple, prison-style table and the wooden chairs, and finally the appearance of the high priestess, a vestal virgin of indeterminate age with a tone as welcoming as a nineteenth-century schoolmarm and a manner as dry as the Gobi. Jean-Paul could feel the palms of his hands sweating, and he stumbled away from the meeting shaking, with the horrible feeling in the pit of his stomach that he had somehow failed an obscure and unspecified inquisition. Michelin is no joking matter, and you'd better get that into your cook's head once and for all. For Bernard, Georges Blanc's model was the goal that he was aiming at, but the message from the sky ordaining him to make a go for it was a word from Michelin.

"Fill out your *hôtellerie*, Monsieur Trichot told me, and you'll have the place full every night," he said, recalling one of his recent meetings with Michelin, his voice tinged with the same reverence as Jean-Paul Lacombe. Monsieur Trichot is the boss of the guide, a position that makes him in his sector roughly equivalent in influence to Ayatollah Khomeini in his. On his advice alone, without any promise whatsoever of reward, Bernard indebted himself up to his ears at high interest rates for the expansion program, while paying out his own salary one hundred percent to Verger for the sale of the commerce in the first place, and only wishing that the intractable constraints of mathematics would permit him to borrow even more.

"I don't give a goddam," he said. "I'm thirty. I'd rather be in debt now, while I'm young. I've still got one of the most rotten kitchens in France, because I'm spending all the money on the hotel side, but that's all right: you don't need a $300,000 kitchen to cook a good red mullet."

He wasn't joking. Dumaine's famous old kitchen must have

been fairly tired already when he left it, but now, twenty years later, it was a shambles on two levels, with holes in the ceiling, pre-Cambrian equipment held together with wire and chewing gum and a dandy view out over the concrete slab of the garage. This, a three-star joint? Well, why not? Bernard's assistants down below in the black hole of the pastry section, standing on the wobbly tiles by the stoves, worked just as assiduously as the boys in the Troisgros culinary paradise, and the dishes they cooked were borne with proper pomp to a dining room that was as elegant as ever, where the customers didn't have to know about the wire and chewing gum. And what dishes! That is the subject, the only subject, that has the power to make Bernard wax onomatopoetic.

"*Schlaack!*" as he had been saying when we left him. "*Vlan!* That's what it should be each time you take a mouthful. It's the taste—the real taste. Each time it should be like an explosion in your mouth. *Paf! Clack!*"

Bernard was seated in the *petit salon* now, so brimming with enthusiasm that he fairly trembled from the excitement of it all, smacking his fist into his palm for emphasis, waving his arms, rising and then sitting down several times again during his exposition, the words tumbling forth so fast that it was all I could do to keep the pace. With his soft brown eyes and his white chef's tunic, he was making a personal display of the colors of the Charolais cattle, famed for their good natures and even better steaks, who thrive in the region and in honor of whom a sculptor with the ever-so-French name of Pompon had erected a life-size bronze statue on the main square. But there was nothing bovine about his drive and ambition. If anyone was seeking to initiate a cultural revolution in French *haute cuisine*, it was Bernard the Bird: the lad had invented Maoist cooking, purer than the pure.

"We've got a new style of cooking here. I'm going off the beaten path—no more thickening of sauces with egg yolk, no more *déglaçage* with alcohol. No cream, no *fonds*, no *fumet de poisson*, no *demi-glace*, no fats and only enough butter so that the food I'm cooking won't stick on a Teflon pan, and even then I'll pat the food dry with a paper towel. I'll deglaze a pan with water or lemon juice or vinegar, and all you'll have for a sauce are the essences at the bottom of the pan. This is a cuisine of essences, of infusions. I'll thicken a red-wine sauce with a purée of carrots and a white-wine sauce with a purée of onions. You know what you're eating! You finally get the real taste of salsify or cabbage or *langoustine*. They have the taste of what they are. They explode in your mouth— *Vlan! Schlack!* It's a splendor in your mouth!"

Loiseau's *cuisine à l'eau*—water cooking—has created a great and often acrimonious debate within French gastronomic circles, because he has gone miles beyond mere *nouvelle cuisine* to another planet of his own creating—one which, he is convinced, will be the norm within a decade. For now, as he invents and then steps forward to present his latest composition, he basks in the outrage as much as in the hosannahs, like a young composer who has just put on his first *pièce à scandale*. If Bocuse is Beethoven and Guérard Debussy, Loiseau is Stravinsky, Schoenberg or perhaps even Stockhausen. I haven't made up my mind. What I need to help me along the road toward judgment are a few more meals like the extraordinary lunch he fired up for me the other day.

It began with a filet of red mullet, cooked on the skin side only, in a Teflon skillet with only a touch of olive oil. By the time it reached me, the filet had cooked through to its other side by the heat of the plate on which it was served, and it reposed, red against white, on a bed of sweet garlic purée. This purée, a masterpiece in itself, was concocted of fresh cloves that had been cooked for half an hour, in water which Bernard had changed three times in order to eliminate their muscular punch. Soft and ready for the table, the garlic had been blended into a suave purée, then thinned with milk to the consistency of mashed potatoes. Over it all was spread a thin and yet rich sauce of chervil infused in water.

A filet of salmon followed, cooked on one side only like the mullet. It was accompanied by asparagus tips cooked in water, and the sauce, although watery in appearance, was deep and potent, because it was made of truffle juice. The next course was diminutive pink *langoustines*, shelled raw and cooked in olive oil over low heat, and sauced with the essences of their own carcasses, which had been infusing in the water with which Bernard deglazed the frying pan. No butter, no cream, and they lay on a bed of steamed, yellow-green cabbage. There was a curiously unexpected hint of sweetness, the same light sugary taste which occurs in some creatures of the sea, and most strongly in scallops. I could have eaten more, but I was saved from starvation by the arrival of veal sweetbreads, braised in next to no butter until light tan and served with a colorful troop of garden vegetables: green beans, fingernail-size onions, zucchini, peas, carrots and broad beans, cooked in water. The sauce, once again, was simply the water, reduced, which had deglazed the pot in which the sweetbreads had been braised.

An Époisse from right next door and two creations of the goat, a *claque-bitou* and a Sainte-Maure, took care of the cheese course, and a "terrine" of orange and bitter chocolate with fresh mint sauce ended the meal as surprisingly and edifyingly as it had begun. The whole experience was delicious, disconcerting and utterly original, and it raised much conjecture within my fevered brow. For one thing, it struck me, this was not food for beginners. Dispensing entirely with the depth of taste, the smoothness and richness that butter and the concentrated *fonds* impart, which had been the signature and the specificity of *la cuisine française* since the days of Carême and earlier, seemed an enterprise of the most perilous sort. Food experts were certainly amazed and charmed by Bernard's wizardry, but they looked at it as technicians, like the professors who know what polythyroid Gottlieb centrifugal switchover network to look for when your TV set breaks down. Henri Gault, for example, the very man who had invented the term *nouvelle cuisine*, has gone on a French radio station to call it "perhaps the best cuisine in the world," but I wondered, and still do, how the ordinary weekend gourmet would go for this super-refined variant of *cuisine minceur*.

Do the day-by-day customers want to flirt with Bernard's culinary Maoism, or do they finally prefer to wallow in the comfortable old bourgeois sins of the classical cooking? Do they really *want* to have the real taste of salsify? The question remained open in my mind as I quit Saulieu and drove past the *étangs* of the Argentallais. It was there, by this fish-filled marshland, that I had heard a wisecrack of Bocuse's which had been making the rounds of the cooking brotherhood. Paul, who had been weaned on Point's absolutist *"du beurre, du beurre et encore du beurre,"* was a good friend of Bernard's and, as usual, was doing his best to help him along the road toward the top, but this didn't stop him from being a Lyonnais and being Bocuse. The inspiration for his wisecrack came as he and some friends were standing on a little stone bridge after a meal at Bernard's table, gazing down at the flow of water, gurgling away to some distant lake.

"You know, it's a shame," he had said with a sigh, "to see all that good sauce go to waste."

As I drove along the twisting rural road toward the *autoroute,* the same superhighway which had dealt such a heavy blow to Saulieu by curling around it to the east, I gradually left behind me the stubby, second-growth forests of the Morvan region, and now the lush pasture land of the Auxois, dotted everywhere with farmhouses, ponds, copses and cattle, spread out before me like a travel poster for the most beautiful countryside imaginable. In every direction, men, women and beasts were engaged in producing milk, butter, cream and eggs in lavish profusion and of a quality that is envied the world over. But right there, in the very middle of this caloric cornucopia, an enthusiastic young Savonarola of the casserole was turning his back on the traditional, to produce a cuisine that was brilliant, delicate, austere and iconoclastic. He was convinced that it was the cuisine of the future, and that all the other serious cooks would soon be doing the same thing.

I wasn't sure. I didn't know. If you have invented a style of cooking that eschews the products and techniques that are specifically French, it may be astounding—and Bernard's is—but is it *la cuisine française*? Can you make three-star cooking without butter and cream? Point would have been both amused and horrified, but times do change. It remains to be seen whether or not Michelin believes it. It is the authority that Bernard the Bird is trying to convince. If he succeeds, he knows, the others will come around. They always do.

VIII.
FLOUR POWER

Although I don't quite approve of the maneuver, I know
that professionals of the restaurant circuit occasionally
like to throw knuckleballs at chefs to test their powers of adaptation
and their willingness to please the clientèle. Thus, one Parisian food
critic stirred up a memorable row a few years ago by swaggering
into a dozen or so of the city's finest eating places and ordering a
salade de tomates and then writing an article on the reaction of the
personnel to his special request and the quality of the dish that followed. A Michelin inspector whom a friend of mine once had the
singularly rare privilege of meeting (they are usually as reclusive as
those white bugs that hide under rocks) admitted that he did the
same from time to time with a plain omelet: was it just the right
golden color on the outside? Was it the right shape, plump in the
middle and tapered at the extremities? Was it *baveuse* (drooling)
inside, as every self-respecting omelet must be?

I say I don't approve of this kind of stunt because I find it irritating and presumptuous. The chef is a professional who has
learned his stuff one way or another and has planned his day's menu

in function of his experience, his personal preferences and the goodies which he has found in the market that day. Asking him to jump out of his program and make something special for you—especially something on the elementary level—is, I find, like asking Yehudi Menuhin to drop everything and play you *"Frère Jacques"* or "How Much Is That Doggie in the Window?" However, I have to admit that I am guilty of something of the same kind of behavior when it comes to bakers and *pâtissiers:* I tend to judge them not on their most complex *tours de force*, but on their croissants. I have this thing for croissants.

I'm not even sure when it began, but it may have been aboard the old S.S. *Flandre* (affectionately known to us steerage passengers as the Flounder) when I was a student, coursing across the briny deep on my way to France for the advanced studies which would bring me to my present exalted station in life. Although we kids were separated from the swells above us by the class system, the kitchen cooked for everyone, and the bakers and *pâtissiers* turned out the same continental breakfasts from the same *pâte levée*, which gave us the same wonderful croissants as the demigods upstairs in the first-class cabins. Taken that way, early in the morning, still soft and warm and exhaling the fumes of Normandy butter released by the heat of the ovens, they were milestones, as important for marking the change of civilization which we were undergoing as were the incomprehensible philosophers whose boring books we occasionally drove ourselves to crack open. With the years of residence in this country and in my travels from France throughout Europe, I have continued to use croissants as a measuring stick for the quality of life in each place and the gustatory intelligence of the persons who seek to persuade me to break my fast with their comestibles. The stick measures as well with hotels and bars and trains and airlines as it does with the pastry shops of the cities where I happen to be wandering. It was with this background in mind, then, that I was thunderstruck—but not altogether surprised, come to think of it—a couple of years ago when I realized that I was eating the finest croissant of my life in a factory, of all places.

It had come out of a basket that was placed on the coffee table separating me from a little man who looked like an adverstisement for France. With his white hair, rubicund face and piercing blue eyes, exactly the same color as Paul Newman's, he was as *tricolore* as the French flag. We were sitting in his office at one edge of his factory in Plaisir, a nicely named but otherwise undistinguished town near Versailles, having breakfast with the products of his assembly lines as we talked. I say assembly line the same way I say factory: Neither of these words come close to doing justice to the extraordinary operation which I was about to see, as soon as I finished my coffee and this, umm, *these* delicious croissants, and, yes, I think I *will* have another, thanks. I was going into my breakfast reverie again, starting the day right with a croissant by Gaston Lenôtre, the funny little man with the *tricolore* face, the true successor to Carême, the granddaddy of all of today's bakers and pastry makers. Like Carême, he is the absolute leader in his field—flour power, indeed—not only the best-known *pâtissier* in the world but probably the most important, too, a man who is changing the codifications of his ancient trade and making new ones, who comes up with new ideas the way a cow comes up with milk, who has multiplied his influence many times over by his three books and the thousands of professional *confrères* whom he has taught in his school. What Bocuse, Troisgros, Guérard and company did for cuisine and Georges Duboeuf for the wine trade he has done for pastry-making, and if there is today a *nouvelle pâtisserie*, its father is Gaston Albert Célestin Lenôtre.

As I destroyed yet another of his masterpieces, I gazed at Gaston with the kind of gratitude that Labradors reserve for the guy who opens the can of dog food for them, and was suddenly suffused with a powerful image, a memory of something that Georges Simenon had once spoken to me about. We had been talking about foreigners arriving in Paris for the first time, predisposed to liking it, but nervous as well, put on edge by the sharp aggression of the inhabitants and the cool indifference of the city's beauty. Simenon was only nineteen when he came to Paris in 1922 from his native Liège, sitting up on an overnight train, and the memory he retained was of breakfast that instantly redeemed a cold, wet and heartless city. He was an ambitious Belgian kid who had all of the Inspector Maigret series ahead of him, all the 1,500 short stories and the more

than 400 novels which were to make him rich and famous and envied, but at the moment he felt lost and small. Suitcase in hand, he
walked the gray streets until he found a cheap hotel. Then he did
what any sensible person would do: he had breakfast. I had been
pleased to hear that his reaction to croissants had been just about
the same as mine. Us literary geniuses gotta stick together. Many
years later, he wrote about the experience in his memoirs.

When he leaves the hotel, the décor already strikes him as
less grim. He has a roof over his head. Now he is hungry. For
breakfast, he is accustomed to bacon and eggs, bread and butter, cheese.

He enters a bar and orders a coffee. He peers hungrily toward a basket on the counter, filled with crisp croissants.

"Could you give me one, please?"

"Help yourself."

He helps himself. He eats. He finds the croissant's taste marvelous. At last he has an agreeable contact with Paris. He asks
permission to take a second croissant and the blue-aproned proprietor shrugs his shoulders. Workmen in white smocks turn
around and look him over.

Two croissants . . . Three croissants . . . He is ravenous . . . It
seems to him that he has never been so hungry in his life. He
has already ordered more coffee twice, because the cups are
small here.

Finally sated, he temps his pipe and asks:

"What do I owe you"

"How many croissants?"

"Twelve."

The proprietor doesn't appear happy.

"Quit joking. I asked how many croissants you ate."

"Twelve."

Simenon seems to have been born with the imperious need to
devour life and its pleasures (when I posed the question to him
point-blank, he politely declined to deny the famous press report
that he had awakened with at least 10,000 women in his long and

hyperactive career) in the same maniacal manner as he attacked the typewriter when there was another novel within him, ready for birth. So, everything considered, it probably would be normal for him to wolf down a dozen croissants the very first time he encountered that delicate amber beauty which had seduced me aboard the Flounder, felt the indescribably desirable texture of its flaky, crisp and yet yielding crust over a gossamer white interior, tasted the magic metamorphosis of butter, flour and leavening into the archetype of the civilized urban breakfast. Moments of inspired gourmandise such as this happen only rarely in life, and when they do, the only proper course is to give in to the temptation. Simenon has known that all along.

If you come to Europe and you live in a city, sooner or later you will abandon your native breakfast habits in favor of the croissant. This is one of the few absolute rules of human behavior. In my own callow American youth, I gobbled stacks of leaden pancakes, with and without grits, slathered with industrial syrups and guaranteed indigestible; I have watched Japanese pushing down bowls of rice with spidery movements of their chopsticks, even though that gracious folklore has pretty much disappeared now, in favor of orange juice, scrambled eggs and toast; I have always wondered how people as fine and intelligent about food as the Italians could invent such awful and pallidly tasteless breakfast rolls (although they redeem themselves by serving The World's Best Coffee); I have contemplated Russians in Orwellian *stolovayas*, standing stolidly in half an inch of slush and mud, eating peas off their knives, accompanied by hideous Marxist-Leninist sausage and great draughts of bitter Czech beer; gazed in wonderment at Englishmen smiling and hawing and saying lovely weather as the rain drenched the streets without, then tucking into unspeakably loathesome dead fish; and participated with considerably more pleasure in the matutinal table rites of Teutons and Scandinavians, who have the curious habit of indulging in cold-cut sandwiches for breakfast, with side orders of herring a million times more desirable than the Englishman's kippered horror. Everyone has the breakfast he deserves, I suppose.

All this and much more have I done in my many years of buying and selling adjectives and subsidiary clauses throughout Europe, but it is in France that I live and so I cannot conceive of a breakfast whose focus is not a croissant or two, at room temperature if it must be so, but even better just slightly warmed. Countless are the breakfasts I have eaten exactly in the manner of Simenon—although, with less artistry resulting, *hélas*—in hundreds of French bars from Menton to Dunkerque, and the décor is almost always the same: the counter itself, zinc or stainless steel, the huge Italian coffee machine which can spit you out a tiny cupful of potent black nectar, steaming hot, in a matter of seconds (they don't call it expresso for nothing), the scruffy and psychopathic German shepherd lurking around the ankles of the *patron*, the distant tintinabulation of pinball machines, the three beer taps, the bowl of hard-boiled eggs and the attendant salt and pepper shakers, the workmen (their smocks are blue now) nipping back eye-openers of Calvados, wine or beer—and the baskets of croissants, placed along the counter so as to be within easy reach of the *consommateur*. Out in the countryside, peasants may tuck into *jambon* and eggs, or even soup, but the croissant is just the thing for the rapid, nervous pace of city life. You can consume one in the seated position if you really insist—the taste will not be dramatically altered—but it almost seems as if The Supreme Being created the croissant for the specific purpose of being eaten at a bar: LET THERE BE A DECENT STAND-UP BREAKFAST. It is the original fast food, both urban and urbane.

Mind you, it is not an absolute rule that it must be eaten for breakfast only. There are exceptions. My kids, like all others in France, are transfigured into terrifying savages at precisely 10:30 A.M. and 4:30 P.M., strategic moments of the day between meals when they blackmail their parents into expeditions to the *boulangerie*, where they choose their *goûter* (literally, a tasting), which is the way juveniles refer to a snack here. Inside the shop, on counters just at a child's nose-level, reside fresh, warm examples of the art of *viennoiserie*, the generic term by which French bakers render hommage to the city where the croissant was most probably born. *Viennoiseries* consist of the more rustic, everyday pastries, in contrast to the *pâtisseries*, the larger cakes and tarts and the elaborate creations such as charlottes, profiteroles, meringues and the like. Brioches are *viennoiseries*, as are *pains au chocolat*, the little flaky pastry buns with a bar of chocolate inside, and raisin buns and *chaussons*, "slippers" of pastry filled with applesauce, just right for squishing out the sides to sully clean dresses, books and the back seat of the car. But even with all this garden of juvenile delights facing them, one of the *goûters* children like best is simply a newly made croissant, ingested with all the finesse and tender attention of lion cubs, in the short intervals between fights.

For an adult in France, though, a croissant calls for coffee, and coffee means breakfast. I say this in spite of the fact that a whole army of criminals is presently engaged in stuffing "croissants" with pizza sauce, chicken soup, corned beef hash and God knows what other aberrations, and selling them to unwary pedestrians in the guise of nourishment (if they go for a fishburger, why not?), but I refuse to admit this nonsense into the category of the subject under consideration. I am a croissant purist, to be sure. Am I a croissant snob? It is possible. I will grudgingly admit some of the current variations, provided they are produced in good faith, as the chili con carne and egg foo yong croissants clearly are not. The Germans, for example, make curious little mutants out of bread dough, instead of a true *pâte levée*, encrusted with poppy seeds. Well, okay. In Switzerland they glaze them and add almond paste. That's unnecessary lily-gilding, but that's the Swiss for you. In Italy, croissants are as tasteless as those rolls. That's just one of the mysteries we have to accept, like the Holy Ghost.

If I must be brutally frank, though (brace yourselves), there are only two real croissants: plain and *au beurre*. The second category means that they are made with butter, and their shape is roughly rectangular, higher in the middle and pinched in at the ends. The plain one, which in France is made with margarine and hence is cheaper, has the incurvate, crablike form of the quarter moon, the original model for the pastry, and the one that gave it its name: *croissant* is the French word for crescent. Anything else is unorthodox. The American donut is what degenerate industry does to pastry. The Danish is a vulgar interloper. The bagel is only a primitive, unrefined ancestor, a Cro-Magnon of the *viennoiserie* League. Viennawise, the bagel ain't kosher.

Like Eliza Doolittle, croissants make the day begin. I was poignantly reminded of this essential verity quite recently, when I had to catch an early-morning flight for a semicolon and hyphen symposium in the Festspielhaus in Bayreuth, where Wagner's little-known masterpiece *Isolde und der Staubsauger* was first played in 1823. With plane changes at Dinkelsbuhl and Oberpfals, I had a long and trying day ahead of me, and I arrived at Charles de Gaulle, Paris's main airport, shortly before 6 A.M. Desiring breakfast—I had an hour before my flight was to be called—I descended into the catacombs of the monstrous Camembert-shaped concrete structure, where I knew the architects had hidden a twenty-four hour cafeteria. I found it all right, but apart from some bored Lebanese businessmen and a group of diplomats returning to Upper Volta, I discovered no solace beyond bottles of beer and Coke, hard-boiled eggs and an ineffable triumph of the Industrial Revolution which the French call *le cake*. (It isn't a cake at all, but a weird kind of egg bread, pre-sliced, peppered with candied raisins, candied cherries and orange rind, individually wrapped in cellophane and immutably "fresh" for at least six years. It is ineffably awful.) When I was told that I would have to wait half an hour—the bakery didn't deliver until six-thirty—for my croissant, I was torn between admiration for the French insistence on serving pastry right out of the oven and the nervous twitches I used to feel as a cigarette smoker when I knew I was running out of Gauloises and all the stores were closed.

Half an hour can be long when you're waiting for the day to begin. I felt myself floating free of the real world, in a state of edacious anxiety that focused my entire attention, my entire being, on two things: the minutes that crept past and the back doorway, where the croissant man would be entering before, I nervously hoped, I committed homicide on the person of the cafeteria attendant or an innocent sub-Saharan second secretary unlucky enough to pronouce the word "croissant" before my fix actually arrived. I passed the time and my spiritual crisis by endlessly repeating my mantra (another day, another dollar) and leafing through the dirty magazines in the newsstand next door. Finally they were there, soft and flaky and beautiful, awaiting my good pleasure, scattering a trail of honey-colored flakes down the front of my bespoke business suit as I savored their warm perfection. Even the coffee, which the French tend to spoil with massive injections of chicory, tasted delicious. I arose from my pale imitation of Simenon's orgy fully awakened, brimming with optimism and intelligence. The day had begun. I was ready. That afternoon, I gave a speech on the pluperfect subjunctive which the *Frankfurter Rundschau* hailed as a "seminal." (*Langweilig und stumpfsinnig.*)

After its invention by some unknown but talented baker (probably in Vienna and probably in the seventeenth century, if we are to believe most historians of the table), the croissant took root in France as nowhere else. Certainly the French consume brioches for breakfast from time to time, and those bar flies who are low on pocket money will occasionally substitute a *tartine beurrée* (a buttered slice of *baguette*) for the more expensive croissant, but everyone knows what the cornerstone of a real breakfast is. It is as much a symbol food in France as the hot dog is in the United States, and politicians use it here in exactly the same cynical manner as their *compères* Stateside. It was the French version of Nelson Rockefeller's celebrated chomp into a Nathan's red-hot when Valéry Giscard d'Estaing, French president from 1974 to 1981, enlisted croissants as an agitprop weapon early in his term as head of state by inviting a team from national television to come to the Elysée Palace and film him having breakfast at daybreak, as he briefly lay down the controls of the ship of state to nourish his meager body. *Monsieur le président* took his bowl of *café au lait* and then—and this was the point of the entire exercise—deliberately splashed his croissant into the coffee, thereby symbolically placing himself among the jest-plain-folks donut-dunkin' crowd and and confuting the pinkie-finger-in-the-air image that had been attached to him, like tin cans to a mongrel's tail. Some learned European political observers now attribute Giscard's loss of the 1981 presidential election to his unfortunate propensity for making speeches when he ought to have been dunking more croissants, or perhaps inviting more chefs to his table. François Mitterrand, the man who beat him, side-stepped the dilemma by never inviting television teams to breakfast, under any pretext.

In all but the poorest of households (it costs more than bread) the croissant reigns as supremely on French breakfast tables as corn flakes and fried eggs in the States. Nothing else comes even close. Almost all of them, I must add, are store-bought, but this is not because of laziness or incapacity on the part of French housewives. It is simply that France is still blessed with real bakers, neighborhood artisans who turn out fresh bread at least twice a day, and who offer their own croissants, brioches, cakes and tarts as well. If you have the energy, which most people can manage to summon up in the morning, to go downstairs and walk 100 yards or so, you can bring back your own batch of delights, wrapped in tissue paper, deliciously warm and exuding their irresistible aroma of festivity.

It was just in this manner that Gaston Lenôtre began the career that has now brought him to a summit of influence and affluence such as no other baker has ever attained, probably not even the God Carême himself, considering the modern communications and wealth-multipliers that our blue-eyed boy from Normandy has at his command. And the chances are good that it will not end with his demise 100 years from now, either, because with twelve members of the Lenôtre clan, and most especially his terrifyingly competent daughter, Sylvie, in key positions of authority, Gaston's operation looks with every passing year more and more like a dynasty.

In a way, the dynasty had been there all along, even before Gaston. His distant ancestor, André Lenôtre, who died in 1700, was France's most important landscape artist, having created with the Versailles gardens the biggest *pièce montée* in history. Gaston's own father had begun as a *pâtissier* and then chef at the Grand Hôtel in Paris, while *maman* had been cook for the family of Baron Pereire, a rail and industry tycoon typical of the sort that had replaced the aristocracy atop mountainous heaps of money, power and—of course—rich food. Little Gaston was born on a family farm in Normandy, but he had the bad judgment to come to adolescence during the Depression, so he was summarily apprenticed out to a *pâtissier-chocolatier* at age thirteen, taking the same route to Kicksin-the-Ass U. as the Bocuses, Chapels and Troisgros who are now his friends. (Like the best of them, he was a brilliant student, receiving an unheard-of grade of 99 percent from the professional jury at the end of his apprenticeship. It is no accident that people of this sort succeed.) Gaston's first move toward independence and self-expression was a ridiculously modest baker's shop in the farm town of Bernay, from which he tried to make a go of it during the German occupation, when nothing was available. When he married his wife, Colette, he sold the Bernay shop, borrowed what he could and bought another commerce in Pont-Audemer, on the River Risle halfway between Rouen and Le Havre. And there, twenty-five years old at the end of the war, already a professional with twelve years of experience, ready for anything, he fell into the same ancient routine that every artisanal baker in France still follows: cooking the daily fare of bread, croissants and brioches in pre-dawn batches that were ready for sale when the city awakened, then moving-on to the cakes, pastries, tarts and chocolates with which the artist *pâtissier* sets himself apart from the journeyman mass of *boulangers*.

What Gaston whipped up day after day in Pont-Audemer was so astonishingly sumptuous—the war and its rationing being finished, the French threw themselves upon cream, butter and eggs with a voluptuous greediness that had been honed by nearly a decade of deprivation—that his reputation spread far beyond the pleasant confines of his province. In 1957 he and Colette made the big move to Paris, setting up shop at number 42, rue d'Auteuil in the 16th *arrondissement,* an address that is now close to being a *monument historique* for the gourmet crowd. ("I used to buy in the shop when Lenôtre was doing the *pâtisserie* himself," is one of the most commonly heard bits of Parisian one-upmanship, roughly equivalent to having dined at Bocuse's when he possessed only one Michelin star and hadn't gotten the *grosse tête* yet.) From Pont-Audemer to Paris his route took him to the *centre de production* at Plaisir, and only the world remained after that.

Now, as we sat in his office while secretaries rattled telexes from Tokyo and Houston under his nose and vice presidents mumbled arcana about cash flow and amortization, he recognized with pleasure my passion for his croissants (he could tell by the tears streaming down my cheeks), and briefly took leave of his responsibilities to escort me to the section of the shop where the sorcery occurred. It was a large, well-lit room, as white as a hospital, filled with strange-looking machines, great tubs of butter, men in white and a fine, powdery film of flour over everything. Jean-Claude Sébin, *chef de section*, demonstrated for me how a *centre de production* such as this—shame on me for having thought of it as a factory—was able to produce *viennoiseries* as good as or better than those of any individual baker I had ever encountered. Sébin and his colleagues had machines for building their *pâte feuilletée* and *pâte levée*, of course—they are called *laminoires*, and they zip the raw dough back and forth through rollers, slowly kneading the butter into intimate companionship with the flour as the dough is folded over and over again upon itself—but so does every other professional baker in France, even the small, neighborhood ones. (The rolling pin is reserved for home use these days, or for domestic discipline in cartoons.) If the equipment is the same, then, the ingredients and the quality control are not, and no one else at his level of production has the Lenôtre touch, that indefinable knack that sets the good apart from the ordinary, and the virtuosi of the profession apart from the good. And this, of course, was what explained the perfection of the croissants which I had just enjoyed. A *pâtissier* may look upon a croissant the way a chef does on an omelet or a tomato salad but, like the Michelin man, I was able to see it as a small expression of the greater whole of Gaston's *nouvelle pâtisserie*.

Nowhere else—not even in dear old Vienna, alas—is the large-scale confection of pastry and its professional relatives (ice creams and sherbets, chocolates and candies, jams, creams, fruit preserves, *pâtés en croûte* and *galantines*) even close to the level of intelligence and sophistication to which Lenôtre has brought it, first in France and then beyond her borders as well, with an international expansion of his operations that has gone far beyond what anyone could have dreamed of just a few years ago. The last time I saw him—these things change from month to month, and trying to keep track of Gaston is like trying to catch a butterfly with your bare hands—his company, still private and mostly family owned, counted 800 employees, who were running 26 boutiques and 6 *centres de production*, in France, Germany, Japan, Singapore, Switzerland and England, in addition to the vast Lenôtre catering service, a school for professionals and the huge, elegant Pré Catelan restaurant (two Michelin stars and aiming for the third) in the Bois de Boulogne in Paris, all of this accounting for total group sales of 250 million francs, or about $22 million. This figure, by the way, does not include any of his revenues from the Chefs de France restaurant in Epcot which he shares with Paul Bocuse and Roger Vergé. If it did, we would have occasion to add another dollar or two.

Pré Catelan was an exemplary Lenôtre stunt. Until the mid-seventies he had contented himself with making food in his production centers and selling it in his shops and through the catering service, but when Pré Catelan came up for sale a few years ago he saw it as a fresh challenge for his demoniacal energies. It was a beached whale when he bought it, a relic of the Belle Époque, too big, with room for more than 1,200 customers, too expensive to run, too far from the center of town and impossibly out of fashion. Lenôtre imperturbably spent a million and a half dollars fixing it up, threw in his own staff (75 in all by now), designed the menu, invented the recipes and installed Colette as manager and his 27-year-old nephew Patrick Lenôtre as chef. Within a year he had made it over into one of the best and most beautiful eating places in Paris—and a money-maker, too, in spite of the monumental costs of running it. Nothing stops Gaston Lenôtre.

Well, almost nothing. There is the matter of America. Sooner or later, it was inevitable that Gaston would turn his arctic gaze toward Eldorado where, as any fool knows, the streets are paved in platinum in order to match the blondes, and the cigars inside the Cadillacs are lit exclusively with $100 bills. How could Lenôtre not give that a go? The Big Apple—*La Grosse Pomme!* Early in the seventies he made the plunge, accompanied by a Greek chorus of advisors, money-lenders and business brains who figured out for him exactly the wrong location and the wrong managers. Naturally, everything went wrong, and even if what he turned out in the Lenôtre shop was gastronomic, the prices were astronomic, and New Yorkers stayed away in droves. Gaston retreated from Man-

hattan in 1974, licking his wounds and vowing to return later, to a
better address. He looked around in other climes, sniffed the air and
expanded into Germany the very next year (there are Lenôtre operations in Munich, Hamburg and Berlin now), leaped across the Pa-
cific to Tokyo where the Japanese instantly began standing in line
to sacrifice themselves to the devilish Occidental joys of hot croissants, the Parisian-style *baguettes, petits pains au chocolat* or any of
the dozens of cakes, tarts and creams that have become status symbols as coveted as perfume by Lanvin, cognac by Rémy Martin and
silk scarves by Hermès. Beset with hungry investors on all sides, he
opened another shop and a production center in Tokyo and seven
more boutiques outside the capital. Singapore followed, and London and Montreal and Geneva. The Trois Chefs restaurant in Epcot
was almost an afterthought, but the 2,500 meals served daily were a
solid enough argument to persuade him that America was worth
another try on the *pâtisserie* and catering side. In 1983 he went
at it, and the address he found this time seemed to be a cinch:
Texas. Since Texans were even richer than New Yorkers, and presumably also hungrier, they ought to have had the good taste to
welcome a full-scale Lenôtre *centre de production* with open wal-
lets. As matters turned out they didn't, and the complications
of setting up a full-scale operation serving both Dallas and
Houston (airborne *petits fours!*) finally became too much for anyone to cope with. Writing off some impressive losses, he settled
for a couple of small shops in Houston, no *centre de production*
at all, and hopes of some hypothetical future breakthrough. The
American market is a tough nut to divine. Being French and being
good ain't enough.

Apart from his talents at the oven, his drive for work and his
winning personality, the stroke of genius that turned a successful
Parisian baker into a mini multinational conglomerate was the
brainstorm that came to Gaston in the late seventies, when, with six
boutiques scattered around the city, he realized that a lot of work
was being unnecessarily duplicated within his little empire. He decided to invent a factory that wasn't a factory.

The reasoning was simple enough: in each one of his boutiques
around the city, his staff performed the same gestures with the same

equipment to turn out the same *pâtisseries*. Why not centralize the basic preparations in a single *atelier*, deliver the half-finished goods into town by truck, and finish off the cooking in the ovens of each shop? Gaston bought a 5-acre plot at suburban Plaisir, built a 3,000-square yard plant, filled it with all the clever equipment with which the trade kneads, rolls, whips and shapes its wares, staffed it with 300 employees and set it asail on the seas of commerce.

It worked, so well that he has expanded the *atelier* twice since then, and has run out of space on his plot of land. It is a strange phenomenon, this *atelier*, the sort of thing that only the French seem capable of carrying off. Unquestionably its outward aspect is that of a factory, but it is astonishingly labor-intensive for its size, and the employees are all artisans rather than mere servants of machines. Ninety percent of the work at Plaisir is done by hand, the same way Gaston did it back at Pont-Audemer. From five in the morning to eleven at night, seven days a week and 365 days a year, two shifts of *pâtissiers, glaciers, charcutiers, cuisiniers* and *confiseurs-chocolatiers* cook up the 800 different items of the basic Lenôtre menu (as well as the 1,500-plus specialty items that change with the seasons) and send them off in white refrigerated trucks for the thrice-daily battle with traffic along the delivery route to the stores. The absurdly heavy emphasis on hand work would strike efficiency experts as folly, but the quality that results is so consistent that Gaston's army of customers seems happy to pay the higher prices that all those wages and social security contributions inevitably entail. Tens of thousands of croissants, the little darlings, are rolled by hand, pâtés cooked and molded, chocolates dipped and strung up to dry, cold sea bass glazed, turkeys carved, fat Provençal pears blanched and peeled, cakes iced and macaroons, so fragile that anything but a velvet hand would crush them, nested away in their little cardboard boxes, ephemeral pleasures awaiting some anonymous banquet, tea party or marriage. And, shades of Carême, Lenôtre swims against the current of contemporary fashion by employing six specialists to do nothing but construct *pièces montées* out of nougat and spun sugar. Usually they are small barques, swans or baskets for the presentation of ice creams and chocolates, but for banquets they can be up to five or six yards high, big enough to serve three or four thousand.

Gaston arrives at Plaisir by 8 A.M. on the mornings when he is not in Tokyo or Singapore or Berlin or Houston, dives into his white blouse, ties on the big chef's apron, dons his *toque* and barrels out of his office for a double-time inspection.

"Bonjour, les enfants!" cries the master as he bursts into a sweet-smelling room where he spots a boy meticulously wielding a paring knife to shave leaves from a loaf of fresh chocolate, the final decorative touch of a *vacherin Pré Catelan.* "We've got a special tool for that," he admonishes without breaking stride. "Use it." The boy nods and goes on shaving with the knife.

In the next room, mechanization has scored something of a triumph: a young man turns lemons on a tiny hand lathe, neatly excising the peel in a glistening yellow spiral that curls obediently up into a neat pile. Only a few feet away, two girls in blue blouses are peeling oranges by hand—so why not an orange lathe, too? "Too bitter," Lenôtre explains. "The machines take off too much of the white stuff under the peel. It's too bitter." Oh.

Over in a corner, a specialist with a sharp, pointy little knife is playing brain surgeon to fresh eggs, lopping off their crowns with an incision about the size of his thumbnail. Delicately, he passes the prepared egg to a lady who inserts the needle of an air gun into the other extremity and blows the quivering meat out into a basin, for use in some other preparation. The purpose of the emptied eggshells, which another worker stacks with infinite care, is to make chocolate Easter eggs, but ones whose shells are real chicken calcium, not just tinfoil. It is one of the best surprises possible for kids at Easter: crack open a hard-boiled egg and find it all yummy chocolate inside, and not just boring old egg.

The cakes and breads and chocolates and most of the meat and fish are cooked at Plaisir, but the pastry and tarts leave the *atelier* raw, either chilled or frozen, to be finished off in the ovens of the individual shops or in the kitchens of the private homes, offices, embassies or whatnot that have ordered them up for their receptions. In the first year that Plaisir was in operation, Lenôtre tried the experiment of cooking everything entirely and delivering only finished products to the boutiques. His business immediately fell by 10 percent, and he concluded that he had been stupid: Customers like a bakery shop to be filled with the aromas of cooking. How obvious. He changed back to the old system, and his sales shot up again.

Over in the catering section, a service which Gaston began from scratch and built into the biggest in France, three assistant cooks are removing the meat from fan-shaped scallop shells as another one bends over a cutting board to slice pink duck breasts into bite-size portions. Behind him, a young chef bangs a heavy casserole of vegetables over the flames leaping up from the stove. The *plat du jour* that day was *blanquette de veau*, but clients for banquets can order whatever they like, provided they have the budget for it, and in whatever quantity. The theoretical capacity of the Lenôtre catering service is almost unlimited (he has served receptions of up to 30,000 heads) and he regularly zips off three- and four-course hot gourmet meals for 4,000 guests as casually as a fast food machine spitting out triple burgers. The other extreme is there, too: on the day of my visit, an old lady in the 16th *arrondissement* had ordered one slice of foie gras.

Lenôtre swings over to the fish section, grabs a spoon and dips it into a bubbling cauldron of *sauce Nantua*. "Taste it," he insists. "All fresh. I never use anything but fresh. That's half the secret of my success. Only fresh ingredients. And the best ones, too. We never use anything but butter in our pastries—100 tons last year. Same thing with my colorings—they're all made from plants and fruits and leaves. Nothing artificial."

Charging into a refrigerated room the size of a movie house lobby, he displays a few of the items ready for transportation. There is a fat flank of fresh marinated salmon, three different kinds of ham, a baron of lamb, a *galantine* of duck, a roasted and glazed suckling pig, half a dozen platters of *paella* for someone's Spanish party, a *navarin* of lobster, a bass in seaweed, a vegetable *terrine*, chicken breasts stuffed with foie gras and six or seven different kinds of pâté. From the 250-acre family farm in Normandy where he was born, Lenôtre draws all the fresh, unpasteurized milk for his chocolates, ice creams, puddings and flans, the innocent creatures who finish their days reposing on bourgeois tables as roast suckling pig, many of his vegetables and the entirety of the 60,000 eggs he requires each week.

"Messieurs les glaciers, s'il vous plait," urges a disincarnate voice over the PA system, after the bong-bong-bong of chimes apparently borrowed from Orly Airport. "Prepare the order for the Grand Véfour."

Aha. Was that a little trade secret I wasn't supposed to know? Not at all, says Gaston. Maxim's comes to us for help with their desserts, and a lot of the other well-known Paris restaurants, too. "This place is like a rocket. We have to scramble to keep up with demand."

A new wing of the plant is filled with the workshops and classrooms of the École Lenôtre, the professional school, where bakers, *pâtissiers, confiseurs-glaciers, chocolatiers* and anyone else involved with catering and baking can follow graduate courses like decorating, modeling and painting cakes, traditional breads, spun sugar, ice creams and sherbets, chocolates, *petits fours, pièces montées* and the like. Fifteen hundred students pass through the school each year.

"Pâtisserie had remained pretty much stagnant until our days," he said. "It had hardly evolved since Carême. There was some wonderful traditional French pastry, of course, but too much of it was heavy and fattening. The new *pâtisserie* has become much, much lighter and more healthy. Now we have suppressed most of the heavy mixes of butter and flour and replaced them with fruits and eggs. We lean heavily on the eggs and light creams, and whip up mousses to make our pastry more airy. It's more digestible and it tastes better. No one wants to get fat anymore, and there's no reason why they should. *Pâtisserie* has evolved in the same way that new French cooking has. For instance, by using eggs and cream and fresh fruits and the mousse technique, we manage to use about one-fifth of the quantity of flour as in the old recipes. Our pastry isn't fattening!"

Fattening. The word arises with absolute inevitability whenever one of the ranking members of the French gastonomic establishment returns from America. Every professional who crosses the Atlantic for the first time has the agreeable surprise of discovering excellent elements like the meat, the fruits and vegetables and the California wines, but the reverse of the medal is the large quantity of mass-produced nutritional horrors and the endemic problem of obesity. For Paul Bocuse, the swollen waistlines he sees so frequently *outre-Atlantique* will always be imputable to dry martinis and pancakes (those *crêpes*, he says with a grimace), but for Lenôtre the villain is America's industrialized food industry in general and one of the most sacred of its institutions in particular: the donut.

"They are *dégueulasses*," he says with a sigh, meaning, in rough translation, bad enough to make him want to vomit. "The pastry they are made from is like blotting paper, so it absorbs all that cooking oil—and the combination of oil and flour is terribly fattening. Americans eat all those starchy things and all those horrible industrial candies and then drink huge quantities of beer and whiskey and soft drinks. No wonder they're always going on diets. Me, I'm against diets. What I'm in favor of is intelligent eating."

Hard to disagree with that. The problem is, Middle America is hopelessly impaled on its habit of industrial eating, because it saves time and gives the illusion of being cheaper. Deluxe handwork of the Lenôtre sort doesn't appear to go over on a large scale, if we are to judge from his two false starts. Much of this must be the fault of the geniuses who surrounded, financed and advised him in his American forays, but the fact remains that there is so much gastronomic invention, intelligence and practical experience lying behind Gaston's baby blue peepers that it is a pity his wonderful talents can't be exploited somehow for the greater benefit of the factory-fed American masses.

And if this strikes you as a call to action to United States industrialists, you're wrong. It's not a call, it's an entreaty: stop mucking about with chocolate chip cookies, hamburger mutants, TV dinners and all that and pay Gaston Lenôtre lots of money to come over and shape up your products.

Well, I can dream, can't I?

IX.
ON BECOMING SOCIAL, INTELLECTUAL, EDUCATED, RECREATIVE, SPORTING AND CULTURAL:

The Many Benefits to Be Derived from Drinking Great Quantities of Beaujolais

Although I do not presume to match myself with my intellectual and oenological superiors—why, Frank Prial alone has surely guzzled, with that infinite *délicatesse* which characterizes him, a hundred times more *grands crus* than have ever passed my lips, and *gospodin* Alexis Lichine ten thousand times more—I venture to say that the wine scene in France has changed over the past couple of decades in much the same manner as cooking and pastry. Tradition, consecrated by centuries of habit and rule of thumb, has given way to surer, more scientific treatment of the vines and vinification of their juice, with the result that the "lost" years, the vintages ruined by insects, foul weather or disease, have been virtually abolished. (Critics say that this bridging of the chasms has also lopped off the peaks, sacrificing the exceptional in favor of regularity, but I have not yet drunk enough to make such a sweeping claim.) What is beyond dispute is that as the demand for French wine has grown, a certain class of entrepreneurs has responded by sacrificing quality for quantity. In the south, for example, vast fields of recently planted grapes lie under the hot sun of the *midi* to carry out the ancient injunction of profitability: *faire pisser la vigne*, which, translated politely, means getting the maximum yield per acre. There are probably more discriminating wine-drinkers now—young people take it seriously—but they tend to drink less at each sitting, and restaurants lay in greater stocks of half-bottles in consequence. Partly because of taste, but also to a great extent due to the profit motive, the trend is to drink wines younger and younger. Keeping the better vintages and growths tucked away in cellars for aging usually makes better wine, but stocking means money tied up, so wine professionals have thrown up their hands and said what the hell: let them drink a 1978 Musigny in 1979, if that's all they know about it and all they care. Like food and pastry, then, today's wines are coming out seductively light and supple, and if they are somewhat lacking in body, it doesn't matter, because no one likes the "heavy" tastes anymore. The quest for lightness is further reflected by the habit of drinking wines cooler than ever, and chucking a lot of the traditional gastronomic *diktats* out the window: reds with fish and whites with cheese, sherry with artichokes, and watch me strut my stuff. As with *la nouvelle kiwisine*, there is the inevitable measure of silliness and exhibitionism—most often attributable to the PR and sales crowd rather than the vintners—involved with the modern wine scene, but on the whole the bottles we are uncorking today are a faithful reflection of our age: we are drinking the wine we want, and maybe even the wine we deserve.

When we can pay for it, that is. Fine wine has become a fashionable fad, alas, and when fashion sends its darts of love into the heart of a Tokyo micro-chip baron or a Fort Worth depletion-allowance cowboy, the result can be like a 1965 Gottlieb with all flags down and all the bonus holes lit: gling gling gling, and get me some more of that, I don't care what it costs. In the autumn of 1984, for example, American buyers more than doubled the price of Pouilly-Fuissé over the previous year by throwing around their inflated dollars with profligate abandon. Well, why not, after all? It is nice to see some of the world's wealth going into the pockets of the *vig-*

nerons, those most estimable of people. But these foreign dredging operations tend to play havoc with the prices of wines in France, turning the prestige growths of Bordeaux and Burgundy into objects of outright financial speculation that are purchased with all the affection and delicate attention which the market reserves for currency transactions. The result is that few, indeed, can afford a *grand cru* today, and so the French ferret cleverly through the two billion gallons of wine produced each year by a million or so growers to locate that most coveted of all beasts, *le bon petit vin pas cher.* This, the good little wine, not too expensive, may be a *cru bourgeois* from Bordeaux, a Corbières, a little Côtes du Rhône or a Loire Valley generic. The palate will discern great differences between them, but they all satisfy the basic requirement of the gourmet who does not happen to possess a string of factories or an oil well: good taste against a reasonable price.

Of all the *bons petits vins* there is one that deserves special mention, because its exemplary success story is the one that all the others envy and hope to emulate, and because, more than any of the other wines of this category, its character is the one most fittingly associated with the contemporary style of gastronomy. There is another reason: I like the wine, but even more than that I like the people who make it, for their hospitality, their simplicity, their generosity and their *joie de vivre.* As warm as is my relationship with them, though, it is also fraught with peril, as I learn nearly every damn time I go down there. The drink in question is called Beaujolais.

The first time I encountered the Beaujolais—I am speaking not about a bottle of wine but the whole region—I considered myself lucky to have escaped with my life, what was left of my rapidly waning senses and a hangover which even today, many years later, remains near the summit of my list of personal achievements. This was my baptism into the dangers of setting foot within that picture-book collection of hills, yellow-stoned villages and seas of vines lying between Mâcon and Lyon, which qualifies as well as any other place I can think of for the title of God's Own Country, specifically created for the growing of the Gamay grape.

I had entered the Beaujolais more or less by accident on that occasion, and I had paid dearly for my ignorance of the ways of the natives, who share the Lyonnais taste for practical jokes, and who like to test strangers with mirth and wine the way Russians do with vodka, production statistics and chicken *tabaka*. Returning from the south, my wife and I and the French friend we were traveling with had stopped for the night at a banal motel near Mâcon. Appalled by the plastic and concrete of the environment, we had decided to strike off into the wine country called *les Monts du Beaujolais* for a decent dinner in surroundings somewhat less reminiscent of Kansas City. The only place we found open at that time of night in late autumn was an odd little bistrot called Chez La Rose, but the menu was miraculously cheap and the setting was like the realization of an apprentice *bon vivant*'s cherished fantasy: Saint-Amour and Saint-Vérand were a couple of kilometers to the north, Moulin-à-Vent, Chénas and Fleurie to the south, the steeple of the village church of Juliénas a few meters above our heads, just across the town square, and *andouillettes grillées* crackling in a reduction of white wine and shallots on the plates before us.

There were a few bottles of wine—we were drinking Juliénas, what else?—and there would be a few more later, because the table next to us was occupied by a funny, agitated little man and a huge chappie in blue workmen's overalls, who looked like he could break any one of us in two with a casual twist of his calloused hands. The smaller of the two, it turned out, was a certain Pierre Martray, manager of Château de la Chaize, one of the biggest and most prestigious vineyards of the Brouilly growth. Not having failed to discern my charming little American accent or the presumptuous opinions of my Parisian *confrère*, Martray invited us to take a post-prandial look at his *cave* (famous as one of the longest and most striking in the Burgundy country), and maybe a little drink, just to maintain a salubrious rate of humidity in our gullets. It was nearly midnight when we left Chez La Rose, and in spite of the already respectable foundation of ebriety which we had built by then—or perhaps because of it—we felt no trepidation as we walked to our cars. But I couldn't help noticing that the big guy, Martray's chief *caviste*, bore a more than fleeting resemblance to Dr. Frankenstein's monster, and wondered if it might be a premonition of trouble.

Yup. Martray, who knew the cart tracks which twist through and around the vineyards like the inside of his pocket, opened hostilities by leading us to his place Beaujolais-style, in a hair-raising, 75-mph stock car chase up hill and down dale, just for the pleasure of seeing if we were good enough to keep up with him. Test No. 1. We passed it mostly because our car was a lot newer than his battered Renault, and we arrived at the château like horsemen of the Apocalypse. Minutes later we were treading over the dank clay of Martray's *cave*, glasses in hand, flanked by twin rows of enormous oaken barrels which stretched away to the dim horizon somewhere down there and preceded by Frankenstein, *pipette* in hand, moving languourously but unerringly to the first stop of his boss's A-1, see-what-they're-worth *dégustation*. Frankenstein clambered up the framework supporting the barrel, removed the bung, inserted the long glass tube of his *pipette* and deftly drew forth a column of ruby-colored liquid. He nodded at us, and we held out our glasses. He lifted his thumb from the orifice at the top of the *pipette*, and suddenly our glasses were full. It was time to drink—and there would be no spitting-out in this *tastevin*. Martray and Frankenstein gazed at us with the same intensity that comes to cooks' eyes as they watch you consume their creations, and we finished every last drop.

I can't say how many barrels we tried that night, because I don't remember, but I do know that Martray had a perfectly plausible oenological reason for every one—a different year, a different vinification, a different *parcelle* of his vineyard and so forth—and that we ended the visit with a bottle of champagne in his office. On the road back to Mâcon, we encountered the first sharp left-hand turn at about 2:30 A.M. but our car mysteriously ignored it and continued straight thump bump into a cow pasture. How humiliating. We could almost hear Martray and Frankenstein laughing.

Like a rider who has fallen off his horse and who is sitting there in the dust with the animal peering solicitously down at him, I knew I would have to either get right back on or give up, so I remounted. Time and again I have taken myself down the *autoroute du sud* on the beautiful drive south from Paris, through the Brie, the Gatinais, the Nivernais and Morvan, past the vast, sloping pastures spotted with albescent-faced Charolais cattle, past brilliant yellow fields of mustard and colza and the Romanesque churches so sturdy that no war has been able to dent them in a thousand years, down into Beaujolais' lushly harmonious hills, blessed by nature with a climate that is ideal for growing the Gamay and a soil, rich in granite and manganese, that generously provides its juice with the mysteriously perfect mixture of natural chemical elements—try to synthesize *that*, Dow Chemical—that creates the richly floral bouquet of the product made and drunk by the tens of thousands of natives whose devotion to their craft is infallibly signalled by the round, mirthful countenances, the good humor and the stoplight noses that bespeak generations upon generations lived in intimate association with wine.

A thousand or so years ago the region was an independent seignory, complete with knights and castles, named after the seat, the valley-hugging town of Beaujeu, and until the day before yesterday it was as poverty stricken as it was lovely to look at. The wine of Beaujolais, light, simple and abundant, had never been much of an earner, because there was so much of it—its present 50,000 acres of vine are more than four times as big as the priceless and prestigious Côte d'Or vineyards of Burgundy a few miles to the north—and because it didn't travel well as it was vinified in the old days. Beaujolais was pretty much reserved for the workers and *petite bourgeoisie* of Lyon, Mâcon and Saint-Étienne, drawn directly from casks into thick glass *pots* of 46 centilitres, the measure of an honest man's thirst. Like Coke for an American or tea for a Brit, Beaujolais was truly a popular wine, in the sense that it was drunk by the masses, while the wealthy stuck their patrician noses into goblets of Burgundy and Bordeaux. If Beaujolais was cheap it wasn't worth drinking, was it *mon cher*? Beaujolais was known as a *vin canaille*, more or less reserved for the rabble. But the workers and peasants had a secret: it was *good*.

This local popularity booted the *vignerons* little, though. Too many of them were competing for a market that was too small, and they were all in thrall to the wholesalers, the big wine merchants who bought their wine in lots, mixed it up, shipped it (usually in *pièces* of 216 litres, riding on barges down the Saône) and took the best part of the profit. Until the end of the Second World War the wine growers of Beaujolais lived on the knife edge of poverty, and in bad years it was common for them to barter jugs of their wine for the essentials of life, the bread and cheese that were "the meat of the poor."

Little by little, a few inevitable things began happening, and the hand of destiny moved toward Beaujolais. Life became more expensive as postwar France grew wealthier. More people were drinking more wine of better quality, and vinification methods improved, suddenly giving passports to wines that used to spoil during travel. That happened at just the right time, because big new export markets opened up throughout the Common Market, Switzerland and Scandinavia and, soon after, in America and Canada and then Japan. Wine prices rose everywhere, but most dramatically for the "noble" Burgundies and Bordeaux. Beaujolais, on the other hand, remained what it always was: unpretentious, good, honest quality wine that could be had for a reasonable price.

The Parisians discovered it. Suddenly, in the middle sixties—just as the modern school of French gastronomy began coming into bloom—the bars and restaurants in the French capital that served Beaujolais were not humble curiosities anymore. Beaujolais became the fashionable wine of the dynamic young crowd that would be called yumpies (yuppies?) in America today, who enjoyed the good things in life but were too busy for three-hour lunches and too strapped to pay for heavyweight bottles of rare vintages. The traffic pattern of sales began curving more and more northward, away from Lyon and toward Paris, and then toward all points of the horizon.

Around that time, a second important phenomenon occurred: Georges Duboeuf arrived on the scene. The youngest offspring of a family that had been growing wine since the days of Joan of Arc, he was in his early twenties when he set up a small bottling operation in the town of Romanèche-Thorins, sandwiched between the Saône and the hills of Fleurie and Moulin-à-Vent. A pensive, soft-spoken organizer with an insane capacity for work (he is in his office every day by 4:30 or 5 in the morning, and some day they're going to lock him up if he doesn't watch out), Duboeuf had two revolutionary ideas which over the years have brought him to his present eminence as the undisputed champion of Beaujolais dealers, the biggest and the best: bottling wines individually, by growth, and bottling them young.

Until Duboeuf came along, Beaujolais *vignerons* were like mutually replaceable pawns in the commercial game of the *négociants*, anonymous farmers of the juice which they sold to the dealers, who in turn passed it on to the public in one of the four categories authorized by French law: Beaujolais, Beaujolais Supérieur, Beaujolais-Villages or the nine *crus* (growths) recognized for their exceptional quality and character and hence awarded separate appellations by the very official Institut National des Appellations d'Origine. Moulin-à-Vent is the most esteemed, a wine of finesse and elegance that in a year of heavy sun (like 1976) could be mistaken for a Burgundy, a quality that can also be shared by its neighbor, Chénas. Fleurie is probably the most complex, scented and subtle, a wine of great class, while Morgon, with its more violent character, has a peasantlike strength to it. Juliénas is fat and round and powerful, just the thing to cook an old rooster in, for the most succulent *coq au vin* this side of Chambertin, and the two not quite identical twins, Brouilly and Côtes de Brouilly, are supple and generous, the Beaujolais taste that Paul Bocuse has always preferred. The lightest and most typically Beaujolais of all is Chiroubles, which grows atop the highest hills, and hence tends to be lowest in sugar. In bad years it is thin, but in good ones you feel as if you are drinking pure grapes rather than something called wine. Saint-Amour, all class and understatement, is the northernmost of the growths, the closest to Burgundy and generally described as the most feminine, whatever that means.

Starting at age eighteen as a merchant-distributor (his elder brother had inherited the family vineyards), Duboeuf became a wholesaler when he designed portable bottling plants mounted on trucks and went out to the individual growers to bottle their wine as it was, unmixed with others, directly from their vats. Even more important than his attention to individual lots was Duboeuf's influence on vinification. A born genius for this procedure that remains half art and half science—he still pays close attention to the phases of the moon—he came to the conclusion over years of tasting that most Beaujolais growers were going about their business all wrong by trying to ape the richer, more powerful Burgundies. Beaujolais, he was convinced, tasted best when it was young, and that was the ideal he aimed for. Traditionalists around Villefranche and Belleville shouted that he was mad to bottle Chiroubles and Brouilly as early as December 15—the old way had been to wait until the wine had passed Easter—but soon the Duboeuf taste became apparent to even the skeptics: light, singing and fresh, with the young flower still held captive. Paul Bocuse heard about it, came up to taste it and thereafter sold only the Beaujolais that was by Duboeuf. The other top chefs followed, and today there is scarcely a great restaurant anywhere in the world that does not serve Beaujolais by Georges Duboeuf. Now everyone in the Beaujolais country vinifies young. Tastes change, and Duboeuf did for Beaujolais what Bocuse and his pals did for cooking. Beaujolais has been *Duboeufalisé*, and this, in turn, has contributed tremendously to the present popularity of new Beaujolais, or *primeur* as the professionals call it. In effect, Duboeuf invented *primeur* by insisting on vinifications that were young and light. The new Beaujolais, released for sale on November 14 every year, barely two months after the grapes are picked, is the youngest and lightest of all. Demand is so great that no less than 60 percent of the 1984 vintage was vinified as *primeur*, which constitutes an all-time record for any growth anywhere, and an unbeatable financial proposition for the *vignerons*, who have their own saying to express their good fortune:

"*Le Beaujolais est bu, payé et pissé en quelques semaines.*"

"For me, a Beaujolais should never try to become a *grand vin*," Duboeuf was saying. "Its vocation is to be a light, friendly wine that you can drink with anything and at any time. It has to remain simple and pleasant and easy to drink. It doesn't have the capacity to stand the vinification into a powerful wine. It should also be drunk cool: 50 or 55 degrees is fine, and an ice bucket to keep it at that temperature is indispensable."

The man sitting opposite me—we were enjoying a little *casse-croûte* of *mousse de grenouilles* and braised pigeon in the wonderful Auberge du Cep in Fleurie—looked about as much like a *marchand de vin* as, say, T.S. Eliot. Thin, black-haired, ascetic of mien and piercing of gaze, he was the type whom Central Casting would have set up in a walk-on part as a Calvinist preacher rather than that of a man who is immersed in alcohol most of his waking life, and who on a good day of tasting in the *caves, caveaux* and *salles de dégustation* will lift 250 or more glasses to his lips, sip—and then spit it out. This hideous crime against nature is, unfortunately, the key to survival in the trade. Without this spitting (he has sand-filled *crachoirs* scattered around his own wine-tasting salon in the same profusion as stand-up ashtrays in airport lounges), Duboeuf would be falling all over the furniture three out of four days of his life. His naturally reserved character is restrained even more tightly, then, by this voluntary control he exercises over himself, and the result is disconcerting: Georges Duboeuf is a wine merchant who does not have the least trace of red in his cheeks, who never raises his voice, who rarely smiles and who has never been drunk in his life. He is a very dedicated man. And very, very serious. We had been drinking a St. Véran white (for unknown reasons, the *vignerons* of St. Vérand drop the "d" when they label their wine) and a delicious Côtes de Brouilly red, but I nearly spoiled everything by committing the gross barbarism of asking the waiter for a glass of ice water, too. What's the matter, wondered George, the Brouilly doesn't please you? Yes yes, I stammered, it's just that I felt thirsty. Duboeuf made an impatient gesture and I got a cold bottle of Fleurie instead. How clumsy of me. Never since that day have I had the effrontery to ask for water in Beaujolais country.

As if on cue, my friend Bobosse clattered up outside in his venerable Peugeot diesel. He had a few deliveries to make, he said, and would I like to go along with him? Well, sure I would. But even as I said yes I felt the old familiar Beaujolais conspiracy looming up over me. I was going from the company of Prince Hal straight into the clutches of Falstaff.

Bobosse is a great man, and I love him dearly, but he would be the death of me if I spent too much time in his presence. René Besson is the name he was born with fifty or so years ago, but everywhere within a couple of hundred kilometers around Lyon, wherever there are great restaurants, wherever a glass is lifted, wherever there are handsome women to be admired, hell to be raised or victims to be set up for practical jokes, Bobosse has passed, like Attila the Hun. Say the magic word "Bobosse" in Lyon, and people start laughing and shaking their heads, even before they hear what you say next, because they know it's probably going to be another *connerie*. A *charcutier* by trade, and probably the best one in France—which probably means the best in the world—Bobosse runs a tiny, three-man artisanal workshop behind his house in a hamlet near Belleville, and turns out such improbably succulent sausages, tripe, *pâtés, terrines, ballottines* and *galantines* that his customer list reads like a Who's Who of French restauration. His *galantine de canard* has been served aboard Concorde, and Paul Bocuse ritually offers his guests a warm slice of his *cervelas truffé en brioche* to fend off starvation while they peruse the menu. When he is not cooking, Bobosse's principal activity is enjoying life and laboring to spread his *joie de vivre* as widely and generously as possible. A born wassailer with the solid frame of the rugby player that he used to be, he is a big man, about half as wide as he is high, crew-cut and jovial and gifted with such titanic energy and capacity for alcohol that former drinking partners tremble and wives bolt the front doors when they hear the approaching rattle of his Peugeot. Bobossse is pure Rabelais, a truant from the Middle Ages, the friendliest, funniest and warmest lover of life I have ever had the pleasure to encounter. He is my hero.

"Let's see what Saint Joseph is up to," said Bobosse, pulling up in front of a dusty farmyard in the hamlet of Corcelles-en-Beaujolais. Saint Joseph, it turned out, was Joseph Boulon, producer of one of the finest Beaujolais-Villages in the region. His farmyard, full of animals and comfortably unkempt, looked like an *image d'Épinal* of a nineteenth-century bucolic scene, including the slothful cat and the enormous rooster strutting and fretting, the very picture of male imperialism. Boulon was out, but Madame was there with her wooden shoes and sarcastic smile, and she invited us into a dirt-floored shed across the yard from the house to *boire un petit coup*. This was a real peasant's *caveau*, musty and grimy and comfortable, about as big as the broom closet of Château de la Chaize, smelling of that same unmistakable dank acidity that Père Gelineau had loved so much as a child, but in this case further adorned with pages from girlie magazines, unstapled and stuck up on the walls. One *petit coup* led to another, and the conversation turned, as it always does sooner or later, to the harvest, the few hectic weeks in September and October when students from all over Europe flock to the French vineyards for healthy labor, extra money, good eating, even better drinking and as much play as they have energy left over for.

Madame Boulon wanted to pour another *coup*, but we demurred and regained the Peugeot feeling suffused with virtue. Hardly had we gone 100 yards down the road when whom should we run into but Boulon himself, returning from the fields on his high-legged *tracteur enjambeur*.

"*Vous boirez bien un petit coup,*" he said—it wasn't a question but an order—and we turned around and drove back to the farm.

"You people are going to kill me," said Bobosse in the pleasant coolness of the cave, watching Boulon dip into a barrel with his *pipette*. "When I'm in my coffin, my old lady is going to accuse you of being assassins. It's a good thing I'm going on the cure tomorrow."

It was true. The very next day, Bobosse was scheduled to leave for some gloomy thermal establishment in the French Alps, to drink—*pouah!*—mineral water for a week, give his liver some rest and lose a few kilos. The cure is part of his life now, and he looks forward to it the way a ten-year old boy looks forward to going back to school in the fall.

"Try this one," said Boulon. "Then we'll see what the '76 is like."

The '76 was just fine, although Bobosse pronounced it still too young. We left Saint Joseph and his wife in the company of a glassy-eyed neighbor who had wandered in for a free drink. A quick tour through the pretty little hilltop village of Saint-Lager, where they make an impeccable Côtes de Brouilly, reminded Bobosse of a bike trip he had made there a few weeks earlier, during one of his periodic seizures of remorse, when he feels he really ought to get more exercise.

"Climbing the hill got me pretty thirsty, but luckily I ran into a friend, so I offered to buy him a *pot*. When we finished my *pot*, he had to buy me one, of course, so we went on that way for a good little while. We drank nine *pots* before I got back on my bike. It was downhill back home, and I broke all the records. I could have won the Tour de France that day."

Turning a corner, we came upon a long driveway elegantly flanked by landscaped gardens, a layout which looked vaguely familiar. "Château de la Chaize," said Bobosse, and before I could say "Brouilly," I was following him down the brick stairs to that interminable tunnel of a *cave*. Far in the distance, barely discernible under the weak glow of a stingy light bulb, were three figures, one of them a good deal taller than the others. Could it be? As we walked closer the big fellow's features came into focus—Frankenstein! He was exactly the same as I remembered him from a decade earlier, even to the *pipette* in his hand.

"He's like a *coq au vin*," said Bobosse. "Being marinated preserves you."

"*Vous boirez bien un petit coup,*" said Frankenstein.

Half an hour later we stumbled back into daylight and made our way to Le Perréon, where Bobosse had some sausage to deliver to the Bar de la Cloche. Before he had put his package down, the *patron* was already filling three glasses from a chilled *pot*, glistening with pearly condensation. That afternoon, the talk around Le Perréon was of the funeral of a local notable who had died of cirrhosis of the liver without ever having known the taste of water. We continued onward, to Salles-en-Beaujolais, where we drove under the archway of a gorgeous Romanesque cloister, past the Benedictine church and to the gate leading to René Braillon's *cave*. We enjoyed two *coups*, one of a finished wine and another of one still infused with tiny needles of gas from its secondary fermentation.

"*J'adore ça!*" cried Bobosse. "*Ça c'est du Beaujolais. Et ça
. . .*"—he swept his arm out toward Braillon's courtyard, with the village square and the tenth-century ruins behind it—"*. . .ça c'est la France!*"

He was right. It was a wonderful, sunny afteroon, the architecture was authentic, the people friendly and the Beaujolais delicious. It was the best of all possible worlds. It was also time for another *coup*. We walked across the street to the shed where Bobosse's old pal Georges Texier was running a bottling machine, a Gauloise dangling precariously from his lower lip in the defiance of gravity of which the French are so especially capable. Texier preceded us down the stone steps to his *cave*.

"Ah, la la," said Bobosse tenderly. "The drinking I've done in this place." Just to prove it, he proudly pointed to an official-appearing certificate hung on a barrel: "Bresson, René, first-class drunk." It was dated Jan. 39, 1963, and signed by Georges Texier. As we were drinking our *coups*, two young locals in their early twenties came in for a refreshing drink. After all, why go to a bar and pay for it?

Bobosse and I drove on up the hill to Vaux-en-Beaujolais, a village so typical and picturesque that it could support an entire picture-postcard industry all by itself. Every French citizen who can read knows about Vaux-en-Beaujolais because of its alias, *Clochemerle*, the title of an immensely popular novel first published in 1934 and still going strong today. Set unmistakably in Vaux (the author, Gabriel Chevallier, simply took a map of the town, turned it around and used this mirror image in describing Clochemerle's street plan), the book's plot follows the ambitions, intrigues, boozing and sexual escapades of a caricatural population that is as maddening and endearing as the French are themselves. The mayor, Barthélémy Piechut, brings chaos to the town but succor to his political career by installing a *urinoir* next to the church, under the windows of an half-crazy old-maid bigot. Social climbers rise and fall, fortunes are lost and husbands famously cuckolded as the summer passes and the grapes ripen toward the apotheosis of what looks like a great harvest. Overseeing the town's spiritual health is the Abbé Augustin Ponosse, a holy man but a human one, too, who assuages the weakness of the flesh with the help of his housekeeper, Honorine, and his temporal thirst with at least two litres of Beaujolais a day, "any less than which would cause him to suffer."

"This system brought no soul back to God," Chevallier recognized, "but Ponosse acquired a real competence in matters of wines, and by that he gained the esteem of the wine growers of Clochemerle, who said he was not haughty, not a sermonizer and always disposed to empty his *pot* like an honest man. Over fifteen years, Ponosse's nose flowered magnificently, became a Beaujolais nose, enormous, with a color that hesitated between the violet of the canon and the purple of the cardinal. This nose inspired confidence in the region."

Now, with Bobosse, at the entrance to the *cave coopérative*, next to the municipal *pissoire* and just above the *boulodrome*, where fiendish old men schemed to destroy one another in cutthroat matches of *pétanque*, the tourist bar built many years ago to take advantage of *Clochemerle*'s popularity was full of locals, and there wasn't a tourist in sight—save for your humble servant. Fired to effrontery by the succession of *coups* already ingested, I made a rude allusion to the merits of Coca Cola as a replacement beverage.

"*Caca Calo?*" repeated a grizzled old-timer with unfeigned puzzlement. "*Connais pas.* I've never tasted that growth."

We drank a little *coup* with him nonetheless, and could hardly turn down Jonny Reynard's invitation to join him in his *caveau* for another. Reynard, I learned, was the village postman. Where else in the world, I vaguely wondered, would the village postman have a wine cellar full of his own vintages? But my head was too muddled to draw any pertinent sociological conclusions, so I resolved it all by obediently swallowing my glass and holding it out in fatalistic salute as Reynard approached yet again with his *pipette*. I was beginning to entertain serious fantasies about drowning in Beaujolais when Georges Duboeuf drove up in his Citroën—or, rather, rode up on his white horse, as it seemed to me in my perilous condition—to save me from further libations. For a few moments, at any rate. It was already suppertime. Did I catch the hint of a smile at the corner of his mouth?

Supper was just a few kilometers down the road, at the Hostellerie St. Vincent in Salles, the very town where I had been admiring, a century or two earlier, Bobosse's drunkard's certificate. Texier joined us, and within a few minutes we were all drinking something I had never come across before: a *rosé* Beaujolais from Texier's own vines. Bobosse drank it with relish, reminiscing about some of his best *conneries*, like the five tons of *gêne*. That had been a good one.

The *gêne* had been tit for tat, Bobosse's revenge against Jean-Paul Lacombe of Léon de Lyon. Jean-Paul had worked up a pretty good stunt several years earlier, when he and a confederate sneaked in and whitewashed the interior of his shop in Vaux. Bobosse took the joke in good humor and bided his time, knowing that sooner or later he would find the right response. It was nearly a year afterward that the inspiration came, when Georges Duboeuf phoned him with the information that Jean-Paul was looking for five kilos of *gêne*, the grape pulp which remains after the juice has been squeezed out of the wine presses. Apparently he intended to steam some sausages over the *gêne* the way Michel Guérard steamed sea bass over seaweed. Thanks for the tip, old buddy, said Bobosse, I'll take care of it for you. Bobosse dropped everything, borrowed a dump truck and drove it to a *cave coopérative*, where he loaded it to the gunwales with a fresh, dripping, odoriferous mass of *gêne*—five tons in all—and chugged on down the Nationale 6 with it, into Lyon. It was just past dinnertime when he got there, and Léon de Lyon was filled with customers. The rue Pleney, where the restaurant is located, is in the old section of Lyon and so narrow that Bobosse was barely able to squeeze through, but by dint of some skillful navigation he brought the stinking truck right up to the doorstep. And there he dumped it, Jean-Paul's delivery of five kilos of *gêne*, plus a little bit more. The mountain of vegetable matter entirely blocked the doorway, and the customers had to exit via the windows that evening. The next morning, Bobosse received a phone call from the Mayor of Lyon, who wasn't born yesterday.

"Bobosse, I know it's you," he shouted. "Bocuse is out of town, so you're the only one left who could do a *connerie* like that. Now come and clean it up!"

Bobosse sent a check and a couple of cases of Beaujolais to the Lyon sanitation department, and everyone lived happily ever after. It wasn't quite that easy with the police commissioner. That one had been Bobosse's *chef-d'oeuvre* of *connerie*, the one which had established his fame, for once and for all, throughout Lyon and its neighboring *départements*. The fatal machinery was put into motion a few years ago, on a sunny summer afternoon, when a *commissaire* of the Lyon police, a man who should have known better, came to Bobosse's house in Amorges for some trivial administrative matter and accepted his suggestion that they discuss it over a *pot* in a local bistrot. Naturally, the poor cop had to buy the next *pot*, and Bobosse reciprocated. So it went, well into the night and well into the depths of the many Lyon *bouchons* which they visited on their epic bar-hop. The cop may or may not have heard of Bobosse's reputation for *conneries*, but two things are certain: he presumed egregiously on his personal drinking prowess by matching himself head-to-head with the world champion of Beaujolais, and he was completely ignorant of the fact that Bobosse always carried two items in the trunk of his car, just in case, for use in improvised practical jokes. The first was a gendarme's uniform, presently unneeded, and the second was a *soutane*, the long, flowing cassock which country priests still wear in France. What had to happen happened: the *commissaire* passed out and Bobosse removed his uniform and dressed him in the *soutane* instead. (By happy coincidence, his black socks and black police brogans were of regulation ecclesiastical appearance.) He drove to Place des Terreaux, just in front of Lyon's city hall, and deposited the utterly schnockered cop like a sack of potatoes on a bench by the heroic equine fountain which dominates the square. And then he telephoned the *archevêché*, in the guise of a concerned bystander.

"Say, there's one of your priests drunk on a bench here. You'd better come get him."

The ecclesiastical authorities instantly sent a car around, thanked Bobosse effusively for his Samaritan spirit and whisked the offending father away. He awoke the next morning with a monumental hangover, loudly vociferating his indignation and wondering what in hell he was doing surrounded by a circle of concerned monks, clearly unconvinced by his ravings about being a policeman. Captive in his cassock, he gained his deliverance only after undergoing the humiliation of positive identification by one of his subalterns, dispatched *en catastrophe* from headquarters. He departed, fuming, in his underwear.

"He made me suffer a little bit for that one," admitted Bobosse. "*Ah, la la*, the miseries he made me afterward. But it was a terrific *connerie.*"

We left the restaurant at midnight and had gone no more than a kilometer when we were stopped at a crossroads by a police roadblock. This was too good to be true, I thought—but was it cosmic justice or the long arm of the *commissaire*'s vengeance? Neither, the matter turned out, but I still held my breath as the *gendarme* shined his flashlight into the car and leaned into the cauldron of alcohol vapors.

"*Bonjour*," said Bobosse imperturbably. "*Tu vas bien?*"

"*Ça va. Passez*," answered the cop, and waved us through.

There is a special god who watches over children, sots and René Besson, I was obliged to conclude, as we sped on through the night. Maybe they were looking for terrorists or something, and didn't care about mere drunkards. God knows that French cops are accustomed to dealing with them, and doubly so in Beaujolais, where the entire economy is based on alcohol that happens to taste good. If they started applying the letter of the law—and the law is liberal here—they would empty the roads of three-quarters of the vehicular traffic. How could they do that when every citizen in possession of his faculties, without exception, drinks wine the way he breathes, where wine-tasting shops and cellars positively cry out to passing tourists every few kilometers, the way fresh corn vendors do in New England in September, and where *dégustations* of one sort or another are a daily occurrence? No. The Gendarmerie Nationale is well equipped with breathalyzers and balloons and all the rest of the arcane paraphernalia of the profession, but they take it easy on the folks in the wine country. That may strike some of you as reprehensible, but that is the way it is in France. Otherwise, how could organizations like GOSIERSEC exist? I should like to know.

GOSIERSEC is the wine-tasting brotherhood of Beaujolais-Villages, and it has its headquarters and principal testing grounds in Vaux. Its full name is Groupement des Organisations Sociales, Intellectuelles, Éducatives, Récréationelles, Sportives et Culturelles, the initials of which translate, as you have already noticed, into DRYTHROAT. It was through the good offices of Bobosse that I gained the honor of being the first and, for all I know, the only American to be recognized by a bunch of drunks as social, intellectual, educated, recreative, sporting and cultural. You take your honors where you can get them.

Bobosse had convoked me to Belleville for the occasion. It was February, when the vines sleep, a blessed time of the year for partying, but the day dawned to an almost Mediterranean warmth, and I arrived at the great man's house in the hamlet of Amorges in my shirtsleeves. It was 8 A.M., breakfast time, but Bobosse, as pink and fresh as a virgin, had been up since five, packing his day's orders of *charcuterie* for shipment. Breakfast with a French *charcutier* is bound to be a serious enterprise, but with Bobosse it was even more special. There was the enormous loaf of country bread, of course, fresh from the baker and still warm, and *oeufs au plat*, a pair of eggs set astride a thick slice of his own ham, seared in the pan over a burner's open flame and then set to slowly firm up in the oven. None of this citified croissants and coffee nonsense for Bobosse. Jacqueline, his lovely wife, she of the quattrocento eyes, was removing our two cast-iron platters from the oven just as I walked into the kitchen, and she gently crowned the eggs' glistening summits with soft lumps of sweet butter, just the way Fernand Point would have done. How beautiful they were, these ham and eggs, a palette of orange and white and pink; only a monk could have resisted them. How in hell could anyone expect real cuisine, I wondered just then, to be even vaguely dietary? In the presence of Bobosse, one is given to wondering how anything can be anything but excessive.

"On dit toujours un bon gros et un petit con," he remarked,

settling once and for all the question of fattening foods, cholesterol and other matters unworthy of serious attention. "Burgundy, Bordeaux or Côtes du Rhône?"

I threw up my arms in despair. I generally prefer to have options like that a little later in the day. I love all Burgundies—who doesn't?—but not at 8:30 in the morning. Bordeaux is presumably lighter, to be sure, but its fine, tannic astringency was altogether too much to contemplate at that early hour, on an empty stomach.

"Côtes du Rhône," I said at length, without too much conviction. "But could I have, uh, a glass of milk first?"

Milk! Bobosse made a rude remark about American nutrition, but Jacqueline, who has a vast and forgiving heart, turned and opened the fridge. *Miséricorde.* After considerable rummaging she managed to find a bottle stuck off in a corner, for medicinal use, no doubt, as anomalous as a preacher in a whorehouse. I quickly drained half a litre, tucked into the steaming eggs and watched my glass fill with the deep, brownish-red of Hermitage-la-Chapelle '76.

Reinforced and ready for anything, I put my fate into Bobosse's hands and we clambered into his Peugeot wagon for the long drive up to Vaux-en-Beaujolais. Over the Mont Brouilly we rambled, through immaculate geometric patterns of vines trimmed back for winter, now coiffed with a bluish mist backlit by a low February sun, through Saint Lager, Saint-Étienne-la-Varenne and Le Perréon, where we hooked south for a little detour to Salles, because Bobosse wanted to say hello to Texier, he of the dangling Gauloise and the Beaujolais *rosé*. We found Texier the way we had left him the last time, at work in his *cave*.

"He's going to be a *gosier sec* today," Bobosse announced.

"Ah!" replied Texier, with a phlegmatic grunt that signified interest, irony and empathy, all at once. His gaze heavy with consequence, he raised his glass to me and smiled. Bobosse and I walked back to his car, U-turned and headed back uphill toward Vaux. He reached an arm into the back seat and placed a yellow straw boater on his head. The green and yellow trim which wound around the hat and tailed off the brim were the GOSIERSEC colors, and the heavy bronze medal hanging from a ribbon he hung around his neck was the badge of office. We parked on the main street, opposite the entrance to the church. Everywhere around us, similarly boatered men, and a few women, milled about, waiting for things to get going. From somewhere came a few desultory blats of a brass band warming up.

Bobosse made straightaway for the nearest bistrot, where most of the band, The Echo of the Vine by name, was wetting its collective whistle with a little *coup*, in the company of a not negligible percentage of Vaux's male population. Since there remained half an hour or so before the beginning of festivities, Bobosse led me and five or six other barflies downhill, past the *boulodrome*, where four matutinal athletes were rolling steel balls with infinite care and concentration, and into Jonny Reynard's *caveau*. Reynard was seventy by then, I learned, but he appeared as fresh as a stripling and didn't look a year over forty-five. Such are the wonders of marination. Standing in a shaft of sunlight by the open door, glass in hand, I heard a distant tintinabulation that grew steadily more distinct as the minutes passed, a sound very reminiscent of herds of Sancerrois goats being driven home for milking. It turned out to be a troop of *gosiers sec*, boatered and beribboned, walking up from the parking lot, their medals of office and their silver wine-tasting cups tinkling musically against each other.

We joined the rear guard of their group and sauntered up to the Place de l'Église, where The Echo of the Vine executed a lively fanfare for the obligatory ceremony at the monument to war dead, ending with taps and a minute of silence that was broken only by the musings of a solitary drunk. After a summary rendition of the Marseillaise, the band wheeled around and led the entire company back downhill to the Place des Caveaux (Wine Cellar Square) to preside over the inevitable speech by the mayor. The tune to which we marched was "The Yellow Rose of Texas." I have no idea why, but it seemed quite fitting at the time.

Bobosse was having none of the official business. He led a dissident group into a barnlike building at the edge of a steep hillside of Gamay vines, the combination *cave*-garage of Jean Balandras, an old friend somewhat more advanced in years than the vintner postman but no less florid and hale. Bobosse was full of admiration for Balandras, and for several reasons. Firstly he was a *vigneron*, which is always a good sign, and, secondly, he had preceded Bobosse by a couple of decades in the recondite art of the *connerie*. Nor was his appearance a negligible factor. A thoroughgoing heller when he was younger, Balandras had chosen, with the seventy-five or so summers that lay upon him, to remake his image into one of mysterious evanescence. He did a marvelously effective job of it, too, and with his gray fedora and gray overcoat framing a gray, sharply angular face entirely innocent of teeth and capable of only the briefest of sardonic smiles, managed to project an aura of sinister menace. Bobosse introduced him to me as The Godfather.

Twenty years earlier, he said, his voice heavy with respect, Balandras had driven all the way from Villefranche to Vaux in reverse, just for the hell of it, fueled by a surrealistic attitude toward life, a monomaniacal determination and uncounted litres of Beaujolais. After a *coup* or two with Balandras, it was time for lunch. We walked back uphill to the center of town and into the vast dining hall of the Auberge de Clochemerle, a restaurant whose terrace overlooked the vineyards on the back side while the front entrance was exactly opposite the church. This symbolic balance between body and soul has never fooled anyone, and least of all The Supreme Being, in the Beaujolais country: the church was as empty as an Irish parlor, and I have no doubt whatever that the *curé* was among us at the banquet that afternoon, drinking and eating and carrying on. From 1:30 P.M. until past four o'clock the lunch flowed on in its majestic pace, a hot Lyon sausage *en brioche* following the *terrine* of scallops, and the *gratin dauphinois* coming hard on the heels of the *civet de lapin*. The cheese tray reluctantly made way for sherbet and *digestif*, the explosive white lightning well known in every vineyard region as *marc*.

With it all, over it, around it and even within it (what else would the rabbit be stewed in?) flowed Beaujolais-Villages *à volonté*—torrents, maelstroms, Mississippis, Niagaras of Beaujolais-Villages, ineluctable, unavoidable *pots* reappearing before our eyes in a kind of oenological resurrection as soon as an earlier one had been drained. Before an hour had passed, the wine began demonstrating its subversive powers. At the table behind us, a group of Italian guests slowly foundered in the sea of Beaujolais. Doubtless accustomed to the softer embrace of their own tender wines—those admirable, light Italian wines which go down like lamb's milk—they got blind-sided by the Gamay grape and reacted accordingly, singing as if they were on stage at La Scala. As the afternoon drew on, their first few melodies developed into full-scale *opera buffa*, complete with choruses, *recitativo accompagnato*, and tenor renditions of all the greatest hits of Puccini, Rossini and Verdi, with occasional forays into Mozart, Wagner and The Volga Boatman, whoever wrote that. By the time we were into the cheeses, their strongest vocalist, seized by some inexplicable Neapolitan atavism, had stripped off jacket and shirt and was bellowing out "O Sole Mio" in his *maglia*, now richly stained down the front with Beaujolais-Villages. Around him, at the tables in closest propinquity, the French gaped in astonishment, exactly the way Anglo-Saxons do when they are faced with manifestations of Latin excitation.

When the last morsel of sherbet had been consumed and the last glass of *marc* emptied, it was back to Bobosse's subterranean *caveau*, underneath his shop. Quicker than a wink he broke out a jeroboam of champagne for the crowd. On the wall, framed in gilt, was the hand-printed advice of Molière:

> *Buvons, mes chers amis, buvons, le temps qui fuit nous y convie. Profitons de la vie autant que nous pouvons.*

Bobosse allowed me a dispensation from champagne and poured me a tot of Beaujolais. It was nearly five o'clock when the call went out for the enthronement ceremony. *La bande à Bobosse* rolled out of the *caveau* for a brief struggle with the force of gravity, marching even further uphill, past the entrance to the church (bolted tight), past the *monument aux morts*, up to the *salle des fêtes*, the all-purpose municipal meeting room where, for all I knew, they probably held catechism classes when nothing else was going on. The GOSIERSEC were lined up in great pomp, ordinary members with boaters and medals and senior members of the Board of

Directors with the long, black aprons worn by cellar masters the world over. The lead man bore the giant silver *tastevin* cup, capacity 75 centilitres, or exactly one bottle of Beaujolais.

Tinkling and clanking, our august assembly stumbled forward into the long, low-ceilinged room. Along with the other postulants, I took my place by the side of the stage, where a three-man orchestra stood next to a large keg of Beaujolais, and where a master of ceremonies was already making his announcements. One by one, the thirty or so pretenders to the title of Dry Throat were called to the stage, introduced to the crowd and then given to drink from the *tastevin* cup. As each one drank, the orchestra played a suitable accompaniment, the drummer rhythmically rang a cowbell and the chorus of seniors chanted *glouglou glouglou glouglou* until the cup was emptied, at which time the chorus announced that he had drunk his cup like an honest man. The apprehension which had been building within me concerning those 75 centilitres abated to foolhardy light-heartedness when I saw that the master of cermonies, whom I had been carefully scrutinizing, never filled the cup more than about one-third of the way to the top, and that for eminent notables like the deputy prefect of the Rhône *département* the measure was merely a symbolic splash of wine. This was going to be a cinch.

I should have known better. When it came my turn to climb to the stage, I was suffused not only with Beaujolais but also with a grossly misplaced self-confidence. As I was introduced to the assembly, I was positively looking forward to having a drink. Did I really think Bobosse would let me off that easily? I suppose I did, in my criminal naiveté. Now, suddenly, my sponsor himself was up on the stage, and it was *he* who was at the keg with the cup. Naturally, he didn't stop until it was filled to the brim, clinging there by the miracle of surface tension. In a few seconds I was presented with the contents of a full bottle of wine, shimmering ruddily and dancing with silver highlights. The size of a large soup bowl, the cup was surprisingly heavy in my hands. I began to drink.

"*Glouglou glouglou,*" chanted the chorus behind me, accompanied by the pitilessly insistent cowbell, wonkydonk, wonkydonk, wonkydonk. The footlights blazed up at me, blinding me to the presence of the crowd and giving me stage fright at the same time. After thirty seconds or so I had the surrealistic experience of feeling I was suffocating on Beaujolais. I stanched the flow of wine for a moment, took a deep breath through my nose and continued, realizing to my chagrin that it was going to take much longer than I could have imagined. Above all, I must not lower the cup, I knew; that would be not only a breach of etiquette, but a devastating loss of face as well, for me and for Bobosse, my sponsor. I continued drinking. *Glouglou glouglou glouglou.*

It was a curious sensation, very interesting. Everyone who has done a little wine-tasting knows that there are three stages for civilized drinking, each one of which is subdivided into several steps, categories and procedures: the visual inspection, the olfaction and finally the actual tasting. All of that was thrown out the window now, in favor of the timeless challenge of the chugalug, which afforded me a nice object lesson in why wine should never be drunk that way—it is awful. My mouth overloaded and my taste buds drowned, there remained absolutely nothing of the fine, friendly subtleties of good Beaujolais, none of the old familiar floral-fruity bouquet of currants and violets reminiscent of English rock candies. Everything was absent now except for an overwhelming sensation of acidity, pinching at the back of my throat, on either side of my tongue, as the contents of the cup flowed past, *glouglou.*

A few more deep breaths through the nose, a last deep draught, and the wine was finally gone. I held the cup out to the crowd, bottom up, to prove that it really was empty, feeling like Perseus brandishing the Medusa head. Bobosse came forward, gave me the accolade traditionally reserved for heroes, handed me my new boater and slipped the ribbon of the heavy bronze *GOSIERSEC* medal over my neck. From some other hand came my own silver wine-tasting cup, of normal size this time, attached to a green and yellow cord which went around my neck to join the medal. The orchestra released a lively fanfare and I walked off the stage. I was pleased to note that I was able to walk.

I continued to walk, with Bobosse and his gang, from *cave* to *cave* for the rest of the evening and well into the night, the rhythm broken only by a return to the restaurant for a cold buffet supper and an improvised dance under the ministrations of the same orchestra and the same cowbell. One by one, various members of our group of drunks peeled away as the hours went by, some driving home, some disappearing into the night, and, for two of them at least, politely passing out. Bobosse's Peugeot, which apparently knew every Beaujolais road by heart, took me back to my hotel in Romanèche-Thorins without the least hint of a problem, but not before Bobosse had asked it to make one final detour, to Fleurie this time, for a brief but reverent pilgrimage to the important local monument: the Fleurie municipal water tower. We stood in the starlight, gazing upward through the gloom, barely able to perceive its ponderous concrete silhouette, remarkably ugly, stretched out against the sky.

The moment of silence we observed was dedicated to the glory of Marguerite Chabert, *grande dame* of Beaujolais, who, in a single profound flash of inspired wisdom, demonstrated the qualities that make true leaders and assured herself of her place in history. In 1960, Bobosse explained, the harvest had been particularly abundant, and the *vignerons* found to their dismay that every single barrel, vat and cistern was filled to overflowing while more grapes were still coming in. It was a time of crisis, calling for swift and decisive measures, and Madame Chabert proved to be the woman of the hour. Girt with the authority of her position as *présidente* of the Cave Coopérative de Fleurie, she cut the Gordian knot by commandeering the water tower and filling it with Beaujolais until the excess could be placed in more traditional receptacles. God knows what the local population did for water during the crucial period, but they never did drink much of it, anyway.

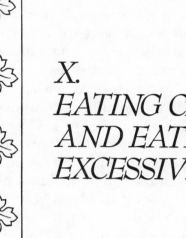

X.
EATING CHEAP
AND EATING
EXCESSIVELY DEAR

I was returning from an emergency consultation at the office of Dr. Troisgros in Roanne (the treatment he had administered consisted of a *pavé* of Normandy beef with shallots, fresh spinach with croutons and a salad of mixed lettuces and sautéed duck filets, *déglacés au vinaigre;* I had managed to choke his medicine down only because he had prescribed a Romanée-Conti '66 to accompany it, and the fact that there were some rather exceptional goat cheeses after didn't hurt), and the train returning us to Paris was making a beeline along the banks of the Loire, with the Nivernais on one side and the Sancerrois on the other: cattle and grain against goats and vineyards, what a matchoff. My attention was irretrievably captured by a fellow traveler who had been anonymous until then, but who assumed an entirely new dimension when he became engaged in one of the strangest and most humiliating struggles it has ever been my privilege to watch: trying to open his dinner. It was an edifying spectacle.

The poor man had obviously been so starving that he was unable to wait for his nourishment until our arrival in Paris. Consequently, he had walked up to the combination bar car and grill to buy what the Société Nationale des Chemins de Fer Français (SNCF) calls a *plâteau repas,* or a cold meal tray. The plastic strongbox with which he returned, glistening and rattling like something that E.T. would have stashed aboard his intergalactic vessel, had clearly been spat out by a factory somewhere, robot-loaded with rations which had emerged from high-pressure tubes, hefted aboard the train by forklift and probably sterilized, too, somewhere along the route, the whole monstrous operation untouched by human hands from the moment it had been designed by some criminal engineer. And now, at the end of the line, came the final desperate *mano a mano* for which it had been born. As the poor wretch who had made the mistake of acquiring it fought against the plastic cover's limpet-like grip to get at his victuals, knitting needles fell silent, newspapers dropped to laps and conversations trailed off in mid-substantive. Every head in the car turned his way, and before he had even reached the edible part he was the absolute center of attention, and not too comfortable about it, either.

CRAC! With a surge of energy he sprang the cover free from its base, but this was only the first step, the scaling of the walls as it were. The dungeon keep remained, and to vanquish his first course the fellow had to peel away and prise off some of French industry's finest efforts of hermetic sealing. The first course, pâté, was one of those little round kitty food cans with the grenade-like opening system on the cover: pull the ring and you've got seven seconds to eat it before your illusion of a decent meal explodes. The smoked ham that followed was sealed in clear plastic, and the packaging had to be, well . . . unzipped in order to free the content of its confinement *in vacuuo.* The fellow smiled sheepishly—it's not my fault—and some of the ladies averted their eyes. Once he had it out, he vainly tried to cut it with the little-bitty white plastic knife and fork provided with the *plateau,* but gave up after a brief struggle and picked it up and placed it on his *petit pain,* regulation caliber, with some mustard squeezed out of a silvery sliver of foil. The bread's dry crust cracked and he gnawed into the ham, simultaneously clawing free the aluminum cover from his chemical orange drink, from which he swigged from time to time to ease the passage of his dessicated collation. And so the cruel charade continued, through the metal-girt cheese and the die-stamped portion of *cake*, until the poor man had drunk his horror to the dregs and was shaking his head in wonder at the folly he had committed by buying it at all.

It was a pity that Jacques Tati had died before seeing his most outrageous fantasies come true, bigger than life, even worse than he had imagined. The French, he knew, are a very odd people: geniuses, but unstable. Their country is so beautiful and they do things so well that everyone envies them, but every now and then they are seized with an inexplicable passion for what they call *le progrès* and proceed to wreak the most appalling destructions in its name. It must be the legacy of Descartes: trust your reason too much and you become so rational that you can calculate everything about the world except the fact that it is inhabited by human beings. One of the results of this hubris, undoubtedly perpetrated in some Parisian *bureau d'études*, was the gastronomic alienation which I witnessed that evening aboard the train. Alas, that plastic *plateau repas* was perfectly indicative of the larger picture, and the message it delivered was simple and depressing: food has gone to hell aboard French trains.

In giving this report on the French at table today, I would be remiss if I did not include in my inventory the *chemin de fer*, that most romantic old symbol of elegance and adventure in nourishment, and this is why I am obliged to sully the otherwise cheery picture with the vignette of the *plateau repas*. The great ocean liners (called *paquebots*, a happy derivation from the English packet boats) are gone forever now, and their grand Escoffier style with them. In the commercial skies, Air France occasionally makes an effort toward microwave gastronomy (as when they spend the money to hire Bocuse and friends as consultants), but the results rarely seem any better than Pan Am, Air Afrique or Orkney Airlines unless you judge them after several splits of champagne. The trains remained, and the SNCF held the line for a number of years, but gradually the dread hand of *le progrès* began to make its influence felt, and the service and quality dwindled. There are still some lines where you can be served a passable meal at real tables with real tablecloths, but the food is reheated, the style desultory and the prices inflated. The old trains with dining cars, compartments and the long corridors down one side are being replaced as fast as the budget permits with awful modern cars of plastic and steel called *le train corail*, for the red color they are painted on the outside, and for the vague play on words with "rail." The *corail* train is ugly and uncomfortable, but the French have accepted it with enthusiasm because of a vast SNCF propaganda campaign which has persuaded them that leg-cramping airline-style seats with fold-down plastic trays represent *le progrès*. It was aboard a *corail*, naturally, that the drama of the chastity-belted dinner unfolded.

The *corail* in turn is being one-upped by the TGV, the *train à grande vitesse*, the high-speed bullet train which zips along at nearly 200 mph, and aboard which food has become virtually irrelevant, since the time between cities is so short. Still, to throw a bone to the diehards who insist on eating, the SNCF offhandedly contracted the TGV nourishment out to a Belgian company which caters to airlines and which manufactures a *plateau repas* whose industrial packaging is second to none, and a hot meal which the lucky passengers may consume leaning forward into the fold-down trays in front of them. The last time I encountered one of these was in the TGV bar car, where I watched a wagon load of fodder being wheeled up to the front lines. I was on my way to Pic in Valence, so I didn't feel an overwhelming need to buy one for lunch, but out of curiosity I asked the hostess who was directing operations what they were like.

"It's the same food as on the planes," she said. "You have your choice of grilled lamb or a *plat du jour* like *canard mandarine, saumon à l'oseille* or *daube de boeuf*."

"And how are they?" I wondered.

"Oh, horrible," she said matter-of-factly, and I was relieved of any *Angst* I might conceivably have felt about missing a 300 kph Belgian delight. This enabled me to turn my entire attention over to anticipating the glory of my lunch at Pic. I was not disappointed, I might add, but then again, no one sensible ever is, *chez* Pic.

Even if the trains are out of the gastronomic picture, all is not entirely lost for rail travelers over here. French honor and your finely tuned appetites are saved by the century-and-a-half-old institution of the *buffets de gare*, the railroad station restaurants. These hybrids, operating in premises that are the property of the SNCF, but run by private entrepreneurs who pay their rent by diverting a percentage of turnover back to the owner, served in the nineteenth and early twentieth centuries exactly the same function that the more plausible airport restaurants do today. Catering to a city's inhabitants as well as train passengers, they were all built with one set of windows overlooking the town and the other giving out onto the glistening ribbons of steel which signified the adventure and exoticism of travel. The excitement of faraway places was an integral part of the aura, and the *buffetiers* did not fail to take advantage of this special *cachet*, often decorating their dining rooms with paintings and frescoes designed to induce reveries about getting away from it all. There were several minor masterpieces in this genre, like the five-story Chinese pagoda at Arcachon and the Wagnerian medieval fortress in Metz, but the uncontested winner of the *dépaysment* sweepstakes, today as yesterday, is the *buffet* of the Gare de Lyon in Paris, which André Malraux, culture minister under De Gaulle, personally classified as a *monument historique*.

Like the Grand Palais, the Petit Palais and the gracefully curving Pont Alexandre III which dives with its ornate *lampadaires* over the Seine from the Esplanade des Invalides, the *buffet* of the Gare de Lyon was built especially for the World Exposition of 1900. A masterpiece—for all I know *the* masterpiece—of the florid academic style that was breathing its last (by then, even Impressionism was considered *dépassé* by the in-crowd), it is utterly unique. I'm not certain that I am qualified to speculate what Paradise looks like, but I have a strong suspicion that at least a corner of it bears a sneaking resemblance to the *buffet de la Gare de Lyon*.

Uninitiated first-timers have been known to stumble headlong into tables or knock over hat racks. The décor that envelopes the arriving customer is so insanely, so astonishingly sumptuous, the architecture so overwhelming, that life seems to take on a new dimension, complete with free-floating celestial music. To the right and left soar walls decorated to the last square inch with creamy, sculpted paneling and gilded wood, plaster and ironmongery. The windows—ranks of proscenium arches—are framed by heavy red velvet curtains and then even further embellished by spiderweb filagrees of macramé. The gold-and-pearl chandeliers throw soft light over a series of brilliantly colored frescoes, allegorical representations of the French provinces, which included Algeria, Morocco, Indochina and the Congo, among others, in those days. The paintings are so gloriously pretentious that they become beautiful in spite of themselves. Everything fits: President Émile Loubet and Sarah Bernhardt painted into the pictures, the brilliant brasswork reflecting the amber tones of old wood and leather, the ample female creatures gracing the arch of the ceiling twenty-five feet above— positively luscious; pseudo-human constructions of *crème fraîche*, raspberries and *fromage blanc*. There is no other restaurant, anywhere, like this one. It is the only one I can think of in France where eating truly does become of secondary importance—though the food there can be excellent on the days when things are going right and the chef is in form. But as a general rule, you go to the *buffet de la Gare de Lyon* to look up, not down into your plate.

France has just under 3,000 railroad stations, and scattered among them are more than 300 *buffets*, full-time, professional restaurants, which constitute the largest single grouping of eating places in the country, the fast-food joints excepted, but please don't ask me to include these in the same category. In the provinces, the *buffet* is sometimes the best restaurant in town, and places the size of Booneville, Arkansas and Yuma, Arizona offer railroad-station restaurants that can legitimately be classified within the aristocracy of French gastronomy. There are admirable *buffets* in tourist towns like Strasbourg and Bordeaux, but also in lesser-frequented places like Mulhouse, Longuyon and Nantes. In the *buffet* of the monumental, neo-Byzantine railroad station in Limoges you can drink a very curious *rosé de Verneuil*, and taste lamb's tongue *limousin* or sweetbreads *bénédictin*, while in the *buffet* of the Gare d'Austerlitz in Paris, René Rouillon offers *foie gras des Landes, turbot grillé sauce béarnaise, lotte aux petits légumes* and other such trifles (and truffles) that do not suffer too cruelly from comparison with the hot dogs and Pepsis available in the few remaining railroad stations in the United States.

The *buffets* in the lovely Flemish-fronted town of Arras and the less lovely city of Valenciennes (twice flattened by passing world wars) earned stars for themselves in the *Guide Michelin,* and the one in the southern city of Millau, stuck off on an arid plateau halfway between Toulouse and Avignon, entirely deserves one. Its refusal of a star by the Red Bible is quite inexplicable, and only goes to show that nobody is perfect, not even Michelin. In Arras, Robert Chavroche's dining room is decorated in Louis XVI style, about as far from a railroad station as you can imagine, and his menu includes duckling with raisins, turbot poached in champagne, Flemish pork chops and trout stuffed with seafood mousse. François Benoist, the whirling dervish restaurateur who presides over the destinies of the Valenciennes *buffet* at the same time as the admirable one-star Chez les Anges in Paris (one of Julia Child's favorite restaurants, by the way), makes travel in the north more bearable by serving up calf's tongue stuffed with foie gras, kidneys cooked with juniper berries, pigeon with crayfish and a *terrine* of veal sweetbreads with hazelnuts. And in Millau, hard by the Gorges du Tarne, France's answer to the Grand Canyon, the gentle Albert Négron will tell you about the old days of trapping thrush up on the Plateau du Larzac and congratulate you if you can get through his stupendous six-course *menu gastronomique,* which includes foie gras, scallops, trout or crayfish, veal sweetbreads, sautéed wild mushrooms, *entrecôte au roquefort* or *tournedos sauce Périgeux,* endless cheeses and a selection of desserts that can make any weight-watcher abandon caloric virginity.

How long the *buffets* will be able to continue the French traditions of excellence is a matter of some concern, over which I have lost several nights of sleep. Passenger trains continue to be popular in France, and of first-rate convenience, mostly because the rail system is nationalized, and, as a public service, is not expected to turn a profit, but even so, the *buffet* is no longer as attractive an investment for a young cook's time, money and devotion as it was in the days when the rail held a virtual monopoly on travel. More and more, the *Zeitgeist* is toward the hurry-up style of travel when it is not by private car. Gone are the days when the trains used to actually *stop* for the passengers to take their meals at the railroad-station restaurants—*"arret buffet, dix minutes!"*—had been the conductor's cry, and rare, indeed, are the travelers who plan their trips to include a leisurely predeparture repast at the *buffet*. The result is that there are fewer *buffets* and the approach is more cafeteria-style, what the French call *le snack*. Still, the quality is honorable enough, even in the simplest of them, and if you are ever stuck in a strange town while suffering from flattened finances, it is always reassuring to know that you have only to follow your nose to the *gare* to get a decent *choucroute garnie*, a *poulet rôti* or a *saucisse-frites* at the *buffet*, and that you will probably have enough change left over to buy a copy of *Le Monde* or to play a game or two on your favorite Gottlieb. It is nice to have fallback positions in life.

If the private car, in France as elsewhere, has ended the railroad's monopoly for travel, so has the truck for freight, and this phenomenon, too, has its reflection on the nourishment scene. The professionals of the open road, *les routiers*, deserve a mention here for their species' feeding habits. It may not be *la gastronomie*, but it is interesting and worthy of esteem. Truckers tend to be pretty much of the same breed everywhere: independent-minded, tough, rough-mannered and slightly narcissistic dwellers on the periphery of society, they are an international club whose members understand one another the same way nuclear physicists or philatelists do. Still, there are bound to be differences of national character, and in the case of the French, the main item that sets them apart from their *confrères* around the world is the matter of food. *Vive le différence:* the French truck drivers like to eat well, and if they manage to do so, it is because of the truck-stop restaurants known as *les relais routiers*.

When I was an innocent child in the States I had often heard that platitude about stopping where the truckers stop, because the food is bound to be good there, but many trips from one end of the country to the other thoroughly dispelled this illusion as one of the cruelest canards ever visited on the American people. The men who heave their bulk atop those foolish little round chrome stools, I discovered, own stomachs like rock crushing plants, capable of digesting king pins and tie rods and ball bearings and sticks and stones and the puppy dogs they run over on Oklahoma highways. Which, come to think of it, could hardly be worse than the oppressive procession of burgers, chili, canned soups and industrial pastries which they ingest, washing it all down with that stuff that roadside diners have the effrontery to call coffee. There must be other attractions to the job. The pay must be terrific.

In France, the truck stop legend is closer to the truth. The *relais routiers* are the French equivalent of the American roadside diners, a loosely linked association of some 4,000 family-owned restaurants catering to professionals of the road and identified by a characteristic red-white-and-blue disc prominently displayed outside or on the front window. The last authentic bistrots, they have been called—not a complete exaggeration. The *routiers* are simple, cheap and unpretentious, both in the décor and the food they serve. If the biggest ones, along some of the main truck routes, resemble professional canteens, the more humble operations inside or on the edges of cities do manage to conserve much of the mom and pop charm of the vanishing bistrots. The *routiers* are not a chain, and even less a franchise. Each restaurant is completely independent of the others, and the only semblance of an organization binding them together is the guidebook from which the idea sprang in the first place, and which awards the tricolor plastic disc. *Le Guide des Relais Routiers*, it is called, and it is the *Guide Michelin* of the truck stops.

What does the French truck driver typically eat to ease his hunger and break the tedium of a long run between Lorient and Belfort? Why, oysters, *mon cher*, and frogs' legs Provençal, and *coq au vin*, and veal Marengo, and trout *meunière*, and *steak au poivre* and, if he feels like spending a few francs more, lobster *à l'armoricaine*. French food is French food, and the French are the French, even if they make a living jockeying semis. I have encountered, and tasted, all of these above-named specialties in different truck stops around the country. Yes, and quiche, too. (Don't try to tell a French truck driver that quiche is for sissies. You're likely to regret it.) I have also watched, with a combination of admiration and apprehension, as they attack their meals with pitchers of *vin du pays* and tamp them down with cognac, *mirabelle* or other such explosive accompaniments to their black coffee.

"It's strictly family style," says Bertrand de Saulieu, the Parisian editor of the guide which his father founded in 1934. "That's what make the *relais* different from other places. Everyone knows everyone else and there's lots of noise and joking going on. Often it's the father who does the cooking and the mother and kids who wait on the tables. I know some places that barely make any money because the owners are so reluctant to raise the prices on 'their boys,' the truckers. The *relais routiers* are, I think, the last bastion of truly popular cooking in France."

This combination of cheap food and relaxed atmosphere makes the *routiers* tremendously popular with young people and budget-conscious foreign tourists. (Seventy percent of the guides are bought by tourists, and only thirty percent by the truckers themselves.) So taken are the English with the *routiers*, for example, that De Saulieu has branched out across the Channel and now lists more than five hundred *routiers* in Britain, although I suspect that this has as much to do with the English passion for collecting French memorabilia as with any service for truck drivers. That *routiers* disc may look wonderfully authentic outside the door of Pissaro's Wine Bar in Kew, but I doubt that there are many thirty-five-ton rigs parked outside.

The restaurants aren't always good. In fact, I have known some to be pretty awful. But the food is always plentiful and cheap, even more so than in the *buffets*, and that's what a lot of travelers in France are looking for. Every *routier* has a daily menu offering *hors d'oeuvre*, meat and vegetable, cheese, dessert or fruit and coffee for a price that scarcely seems more than what it would cost to buy the raw materials in the market. It is hard to find cheaper eating than this in France, but that doesn't prevent some clients from trying to push the miracle too far. "*Attention,*" De Saulieu implores his readers in a preface to the guide. "In France it is considered extremely bad manners if you take advantage of the owners' confidence in you by filling your pockets or bag with fruit or cheese." Bad manners, hell—that's called stealing, but the fruit basket and cheese tray are about the only aspects of a *routier* where any etiquette is involved. For the rest, the atmosphere is strictly barracks room. De Saulieu, who never tires of giving advice to unwary tourists, made that clear several years ago, when he wrote a brochure introducing the *routiers* to foreigners.

> If a *relais* seems to you to be less clean than others, and it is jammed with truckers, you're not obliged to stop. The *relais* are first of all for these working men. But if you persist, take it as it is. If you are accompanied by a pretty woman don't be angry if you are greeted by whistles or songs—it is a homage to your companion.

All of which goes to prove that De Saulieu is an abominable male chauvinist for having directed his brochure exclusively toward men in the first place, that the truck drivers are no better than he is, and that they have bad manners to boot. It is beyond my powers to do anything about this lamentable situation, but the single paramount fact of life concerning the *relais routiers* remains: they are ubiquitous, they are cheap and some of them are very good. If you have the good luck to motor through France, then (and I fervently wish you that pleasure), sooner or later you will have to choose between ideological purity and the alliance of your stomach and your pocketbook. The world is a cruel place.

If you are untrammeled by vulgar matters like money, you have only to follow the advice of the Michelin or the *Bottin Gourmand,* and I can give you a flat guarantee that you won't suffer. Or if you do, if the finest France has to offer deranges you dyspeptically, why, then, it is only proof that you are not a trooper, and don't expect any sympathy from me. I have reached this heartless disposition not only as a result of my epic *tournée* with Jean Didier, but also because of Craig Claiborne and "The Dinner of the Century." It was an illuminating experience and about as far removed from a *buffet de gare* or a *relais routier* as it is possible to imagine. I know, because I was there.

Senior food writer of *The New York Times,* gastronomic guru to untold millions of American *fines gueules*, Claiborne is a man estimable in all ways: cultivated, friendly, scholarly, competent—and a gentleman, too, which sets him apart from a lot of his professional peers. I hear he is also a terrific cook, although I have never had the honor of his table. All of these qualities add up to a personage who is a giant in his field, then, and I am happy to lend my voice to the chorus of homage that is clearly due to him. Still, I am compelled to reveal a dark secret about him: he is a liar. Or, let us say, he does not tell the entire truth. The entire truth is that the Dinner of the Century was not thirty-one courses, as he claimed, but *thirty-two*. What was that mysterious thirty-second course, and why has Claiborne remained mute about it all these years? What does he have to hide? I should like to know. Perhaps it is those 85 cents. Allow me to explain.

Those of you who follow culture and current events carefully will recall that in the autumn of 1975, between more Watergate sentencings, the death of Haile Selassie, the evacuation of Saigon and yet another OPEC price rise, a truly significant story finally hit the pages of your favorite journals: the $4,000 dinner. Remember? As part of a fund-raising campaign being carried out on Channel 13, American Express had been foolhardy enough to sponsor one of the prizes being put up for auction: dinner for two at any restaurant, anywhere in the world, at whatever price it might cost. "The sky's the limit," their PR people somewhat temerariously put it. Never one to turn down the chance for a good meal, Claiborne phoned in a desultory bid of $300, not really believing it.

"I was ready to go up to $500," he said later, "but I was pretty sure that someone else would take it away with a bid in the thousands. I was really surprised when my bid won it. That was a good deal."

A good deal? It was probably the best bargain he had ever made in his life. After a lot of mouth-watering fantasizing—shall we try it in Tokyo? Hong Kong? Stockholm? Rome?—and some scouting *in situ*, Claiborne and his friend and colleague Pierre Franey settled on a small, fashionable and ridiculously expensive restaurant on the Right Bank in Paris called Chez Denis. They made the choice not because they thought it was the best restaurant in the world, but because it was the best they could think of at the time which also accepted American Express cards in payment, which was the only precondition for the free meal. American Express may be dumb, but they're not *that* dumb. It was Carl Sontheimer, gourmet, scholar and inveterate inventor of a thousand esoteric devices—best of them all, the Cuisinart food processor—who steered them in that direction with the Sibylline advice that "Denis is one of my favorite restaurants, if not one of my favorite people." A quick visit for a test dinner confirmed for them that Sontheimer was right, as he usually is. On both counts.

"We visited Chez Denis in a party of three to reconnoiter," Claiborne explained later. "It was not hard to go incognito, for we suspect the proprietor, Denis Lahana, does not credit any American with even the most elementary knowledge of French wine and food."

We are planning a special birthday celebration, they told Denis over coffee. For this occasion, could you arrange the finest dinner you could think of? Price is no object.

"I will think over," said Denis, a man who enjoyed speaking English, but who was impatient with mere grammatical rules. Not long afterward, he sent Claiborne a letter outlining his intention to create a *dîner à la française*, in the manner of the meals at Versailles, before the *service à la russe* became the rule in France. There would be thirty-one courses, served with a selection of wines so rare as to be priceless, and the bill would come to 17,600 francs, or exactly $4,000 at the paltry 1975 exchange rate for the dollar. Okay, responded Claiborne with all the assurance of a man with a blank check from a giant multinational, that sounds fine. We'll be right over.

It was around this time that I received a rush phone call from Dick Stolley, then editor at *People* magazine (presently in charge of the mailroom and a few other antic activities at *Life*), at my garret in Paris. Although he knew that I had little experience in writing, Stolley asked me if I could cover the $4,000 meal, because he knew that I was cheap to hire and that writing didn't count much for *People*, anyway. Sure, Dick, I said, anything to help you out, and I quickly dialed Chez Denis.

"*Monsieur,*" Denis said, "At first I thought this was a joke, but now I promise it will be the dinner of the century."

Things were starting well. I had hardly been into the story for ten seconds and I already had a lead. Denis never did suffer from excessive modesty, as Claiborne had already noticed. Sixty-five years old at the time, huge and aloof, as arrogant and prideful as an overgrown bantam rooster, he was as famous for his execrable character as he was for the extravagance of his creations. (He did not do the cooking himself, but rather supervised it in the manner of Fernand Point—with considerably less genius, though.) The excellence of his opinion about himself was matched by a symmetrical disdain for just about everything else and by his skill at name-dropping, and he was fond of tossing off references to "my friend Mrs. Onassis" or "my friend Orson Welles," for whom he had created a new dish, *filet de boeuf Oga Palinkas.* Denis was so impossibly irascible and self-assured that the *Guide Michelin* refused purely and simply to list his place in its pages. (He was rumored to have thrown an inspector out.) Withal, he was something of a genius about food, even if he lacked a sense of measure. Gault and Millau, the rover boys of gastronomic journalism, were so impressed with Chez Denis that they classed it among the world's greatest restaurants. Denis has left us by now, but he is surely enjoying himself in Paradise, ordering God about.

Denis's *dîner à la française* was a direct return to the days of Carême, and the table that he laid out that November evening was like a miniature replica of the kind of feasts with which Tallyrand and Cambacérès enjoyed dazzling their foreign guests. In order to prepare the dishes properly, he had been obliged to make portions that in normal circumstances would have been enough for eight or ten, but that didn't change the price—Claiborne and Franey could have brought several guests along for their little party if it had not been for American Express's stipulation of dinner *for two.* Never mind, said Denis, the boys wouldn't be expected to eat up everything.

The dinner as Denis had planned it was broken down into three services, beginning with grilled almonds and tiny cheese-

pastry *amuse-gueules*, then getting more serious with Beluga caviar
and moving on to three soups (wild duck consommé, *germiny* and
velouté andalou), to three "soft" meat entrées (foie gras and truffle
tartlets, sweetbreads and tartlets of wild quail mousse), to three
seafood entrées (baked oysters in *beurre blanc*, lobster *au gratin*
and red mullet *en croûte*) and finally to three meat dishes from
three different beasts: chicken filets and excised chicken oysters in
wild mushroom sauce, a *chartreuse* of partridge and a beef dish. A
beef dish, indeed—this one was nothing less than the famous *filet de
boeuf Oga Palinkas*, in person.

That took care of the first service.

An intermezzo of sherbets—orange, lemon and black current—was designed to cool the stomach and give it the courage to
mount to the attack of the second service, which would open with
the tiny grilled birds called *ortolans* (cousins of the American bob-
olink), move on smartly to the wild duck filets, *rognonnade* of veal
served with whole fresh truffles, purée of artichoke hearts and that
eternal champion of potato dishes, *pommes Anna*. The meats of the
deuxième service would end cold, with the presentation of fresh
goose foie gras, cold woodcock filets cooked in Chambertin and a
salmis of wild pheasant with nuts, mushrooms and truffles. The
service itself would wind up with iced charlotte, floating island and
pears Alma, poached in *porto* and served with grilled almonds and a
Cointreau-based sauce.

The third and last service would be an interminable array of
baked fantasies and pastries, candies, preserves and nuts. Depending on how one counted, the meal could be described as anywhere
from twenty-seven to thirty-three courses. Claiborne called it
thirty-one, Denis twenty-seven, but it really didn't matter. Dis-
dainful, Denis feigned to toss it all off as the merest of bagatelles.

"Bah!" he told me over the phone. "The food's nothing. It's
only something to go with the wines."

He had a point, but, Denis being Denis, he exaggerated it.
Most of the wines planned for the Dinner of the Century were rare
enough to be true collectors' items. The only way to fix a value to
them, Denis suggested, would be to put them up for auction:

Champagne Comtesse Marie de France 1966, Château Latour 1918, Montrachet du Baron Cher 1969, Château Mouton Rothschild 1928, Château Lafite Rothschild 1947, Château Pétrus 1961, Romanée Conti 1929, Château d'Yquem 1928 and a Madeira dating from 1835. Afterward with the cigars, there would be an 1865 Calvados and a cognac from Denis' personal reserve, classified as "ageless."

On Sunday morning, D-Day, Claiborne and Franey took a light continental breakfast of *café noir* and croissants at the Deux Magots on Saint-Germain-des-Prés, then strolled through the open market on nearby rue de Buci to reaccustom themselves to French produce and, incidentally, build up their appetites. Claiborne was aglow with enthusiasm for the city he loves most of all.

"Anyone with any sensitivity who doesn't want to live in Paris is out of his mind," he declared, happily loping down the rue de l'Abbaye, the collar of his raincoat raised against a damp and frigid breeze. "Hey, Pierre, why don't we have some couscous for lunch?"

Franey grunted and looked impatient, but Claiborne was launched down the chute of his fantasies; "Maybe we could just have some oysters. Or how about a Vietnamese place?"

"Are you out of your mind?" asked Franey, cutting him off in mid-fantasy. Denis had warned them: breakfast was all right, but there should be no lunch. Claiborne gazed at Franey reproachfully, looking disapppointed. He was sure a little lunch would do no harm.

"The secret is to take small portions," he explained. "That way you can go on almost indefinitely. But Pierre, being a chef himself, feels he would be insulting the chef if he doesn't eat everything. Once when we made a tour of the three-star restaurants he felt obliged to finish his plate and what I had left on mine, too. That man has the most incredible appetite of anyone I have ever known."

Over on the rue de Seine, a poultry dealer had made the macabre joke of hanging a dead crow up among his pheasants, partridges and *volaille de Bresse*.

"The French will eat anything," someone remarked.

"So will I," Claiborne admitted.

"This evening I am amusing myself," Denis proclaimed, striding back and forth beneath the plastic vines and flowers that decorated the ceiling beams of his dimly lit dining room. "I like American Express."

The wines were already decanted and lined up at a sideboard when Claiborne and Franey arrived at seven on the dot, both dressed in navy blue pinstripe suits. I was there to record the occasion for history, and with me was photographer Loomis Dean, Florida's answer to Henri Cartier-Bresson.

"Dressed for a funeral," Claiborne said. "It's my only dark suit."

A photographer for *The New York Times* quickly ran off a series of snaps of Claiborne and Franey with Denis, then thanked all present and went off to other pursuits, like, probably, having dinner. That was a very sensible choice, indeed. I was getting hungry myself. One more photographer remained somewhat longer (Denis identified him as "the photographer of my friend Alain Delon") to record the scene as the two friends shyly took their seats at the corner table which had been reserved for them. With the photographers ordering them from one pose to another and Denis looming over them like a schoolmaster, Claiborne and Franey seemed more like well-behaved children than the two most powerful figures of American gastronomic journalism. The entire northeastern end of the room was occupied by their table, the two sideboards for the wines and the prepared cold dishes and *pièces montées*. In all, Claiborne and Franey were using up the space of fourteen potential clients. No matter: the rest of the restaurant remained half-empty for the rest of the night in any case.

"What are you going to do with the leftovers, Monsieur Denis?" Loomis asked, hungrily eying the enormous portions displayed on the sideboard. In the old days of Carême, it had been customary for the aristocracy's *maître d'hôtel* to inherit dishes which had been untouched, for resale to other high-born folks. The waiters got the slightly touched pieces, cleaned them up and sold them to the bourgeoisie. The rest of the help got what was left—the *reliefs*—for sale among the poor. The dishwashers—*les plongeurs*—

were allowed to scum the grease floating on their water and sell it to soap-makers. One is never too good with one's personnel.

"The staff and I will tranquilly eat the leftovers on Tuesday," Denis said.

"Are you hungry?" I asked Claiborne.

"Yes," he said emphatically. His eyes were glistening.

At precisely 7:42 P.M. the hot toasts—unbuttered, of course, as they must be—arrived from the kitchen and the *maître d'hôtel*, Jacques Manière (no relation to the famous restaurateur), began ladling out the pearly black Beluga caviar—Iranian, of course, much better than the Soviet—as the sommelier, Marc Fourmet, poured icy, crystalline bubbles of Comtesse Marie De France into the champagne flutes.

"Let the hostilities begin," Denis intoned, rubbing his hands.

The two friends spooned great devil-may-care portions of caviar into their mouths, as insouciant as if it were Cream of Wheat. Franey added a drop of lemon juice; Claiborne mainlined it straight.

"Do you ever serve white caviar?" Franey asked. Denis was at tableside, where he remained, hovering, through the rest of the evening.

"No," he said with finality. "That comes from an albino fish, a fish that is sick. It is less good."

"Mmm," said Franey, and continued eating. As the soup courses were dispatched, one after the other, Loomis Dean and I realized why the rest of the press had gone home: there is nothing that looks so much like a man taking a spoonful of soup as a man taking another spoonful of soup, even it it's a different kind.

"You suppose he's going to let us have any of it?" Loomis wondered.

Fat chance. Into the *tartelettes Montglas* they ploughed, through the *parfait de ris de veau Denis*, on toward the *tartelettes de mousse de caille*. Eight o'clock came and went, then nine o'clock, and nine-thirty. The vicarious sharing of the Dinner of the Century by nose and eyes only multiplied many times over our normal suppertime hungers, but Denis was far too involved with his pedantic pirouettes to think about the working stiffs. By now Loomis and I were feeling less politely disposed than before.

"The bastard's not going to give us a scrap," Loomis whispered urgently. "Not even a ham sandwich. Ahm hongry!"

I was forced to admit that he was right. This sort of thing would never have happened in Beaujolais country, but Paris is Paris. Loomis and I excused ourselves and went out to look for some dinner of our own, at the risk of missing a mouthful or two of history. Late on a Sunday night around the Place des Ternes, there were only two possible choices: the Brasserie Lorraine and Goldenberg's, one of Paris's exceedingly rare delis (who needs a deli in a city with the kind of restaurants they have here?), and it was this we chose, mostly because it was closer than the other place. Loomis and I fell upon our hot pastrami sandwiches and cold beer like famished savages, and between mouthfuls exchanged rude reflections on Denis's treatment of intellectuals and men of destiny like us. It was at this precise moment that the inspiration arrived. The light bulb still alight over my head, I summoned the waiter to our table.

"Bzzz, bzzz, bzzz," I instructed him confidentially, adding: "And make it gift-wrapped."

We returned to Chez Denis, where the hours were passing in majestic, deliberate delectation. By now the dozen or so other clients who happened to be there that night had abandoned their own pedestrian fare and were unabashedly staring at the two Americans. Just like the monarchs at Versailles, they ploughed on obliviously, passing effortlessly from one wine to the other, and helping Oga Palinkas along with *two* of them, first the Château Latour and then the Mouton-Rothschild 1928, fuller and more generous to the palate.

When the first service had finally been disposed of, they refreshed themselves with sherbets ("the thermal hole," as one French food critic describes this mid-meal pause) and were ready to confront the second. The high point was the arrival of the grilled ortolans. Denis could not restrain his emotion as he watched Claiborne pick fastidiously at his with knife and fork.

"Here. Let me show how we do it in the Landes," he said, snatching up one of the birds. Quick as a wink, he removed the beak and feet, then popped it into his mouth whole, head and all. It was about the size of a lemon. As he crunched and masticated his way through the luckless beast's fragile carcass he closed his eyes in sensuous ecstasy and made unctuous, caressing motions with his hands over his stomach. In a moment it was gone, and Denis was smiling beatifically.

"Have they been cleaned?" asked Claiborne suspiciously.

"No, of course not!" Denis shot back with more than a hint of indignation. "The ortolan is a clean bird. Only the feathers have been removed."

As courageous as they come, Franey opened wide and grimly ground his ortolan down to destruction. Claiborne refrained. The sissy.

"The ortolans are caught in nets during migration and then fattened up for a month," Denis explained, peering down over his glasses. "Then they are killed by being drowned in Armagnac. That is what gives them their special flavor."

At 11 P.M. the two friends were still rock-steady, going along powerfully. "*Ça va?*" someone asked Franey. "*Ça va!*" he said with a grin. "We're in great shape."

It was at the arrival of the *rognonnade* of veal, hidden under a beautiful, golden pastry shell, that Claiborne finally broke down and displayed his emotion. Reaching his fork into the steaming crater made when Denis lifted off a piece of the crust, he speared an entire truffle, nearly as big as a tennis ball.

"Oh, my God," he said. He looked like Little Jack Horner.

I asked Franey how he was holding up.

"Holding up?" he retorted. "Holding up? What do you mean? I'm *hungry*."

At 11:20 Franey arose—"*par nécessité*"—for a short turn around the room at the end of the *deuxième service*. There remained only the pastries, preserves, candies and fruits. He sat down with a huge smile as the polychrome parade of sweets headed their way.

"Right now," said Claiborne, "he could go to La Coupole and eat a couple dozen oysters."

"How about some onion soup?" Franey asked innocently.

By 11:45 it was all over, and there remained nothing but the

Calvados and the ageless cognac to help it all get digested. What was the verdict?

"*Formidable!*" cried Franey. "*Fantastique! Première classe!*"

This was the moment, it seemed to Loomis and me, to make a little presentation ceremony, our manner of picking up the French challenge and reaffirming the importance of the greatness of the American school of gastronomy. Prudently waiting until Denis had turned his back, I stepped forward and presented Claiborne with the gift-wrapped parcel. Denis bounded across the room at this intrusion, leaned over the table and peered suspiciously at the package as Claiborne unwrapped it.

"A hot pastrami sandwich!" exclaimed Franey joyously.

Prompted by Loomis (photographers will do anything for a picture), he seized it in two hands, took a large bite for the camera, and then softly disposed it on his Limoges plate. Now, finally, he had had enough. Denis snapped his fingers for the waiter and had the unannounced thirty-second course—it was the first time in his life he had seen such an object—carried back to the kitchen for analysis.

Denis never spoke to me after that, of course, but that was all right: I couldn't afford dinner there, anyway. But I am a little bit disappointed with American Express. They still owe me 85 cents for the part of the banquet I paid for.

XI.
THE WOMEN

She alone is the joy of my eyes,
And my love for her is undying.
When I see an object so divine
'Tis not for her bed I am sighing
But rather to drink of her wine.

Claude-Emmanuel Chapelle, a mid-seventeenth-century poet known as something of a libertine, wrote this rather better in French than I in the plodding translation I offer here, but you get the message. He was singing the praises of *la joyeuse Coiffier*, a famous *cabaretière* whose place of business, La Fosse-aux-Lions, or The Lion Pit, was located near the Palais Royal in Paris (which used to be the capital's swinging address) and who was famous for the quality of both her food and her drink, a combination that was excessively rare in those days.

Ever since cooks were cooking professionally in France, and especially since the invention of the restaurant, it has been the men who dominated the trade, while the women either stayed home wiping bottoms or, if they were involved with the professional side, were relegated to the more humble tasks of the culinary arts, like scullery duties, for instance. The men, in all their God-given magnificence, puffed out their chests and their heads and swaggered about giving each other orders, playing the most ancient masculine game of all: king of the mountain, cock of the walk. He who won was the *chef*, which doesn't mean cook at all, but chief, leader, honcho, boss man.

To lead a *brigade* of perhaps dozens of *chefs de partie, sous-chefs, commis* and apprentices required not only the knowledge to spot errors as soon as they were committed—no dawdling in this line of work—but also a dominating physical presence, a self-assurance and the authority to deliver remonstrations and the famous *coups de pied au cul* on which western civilization, gastronomic and other, has been built. Until now, few women cooks have ever possessed the sum of these disagreeable attributes, and I, for one, cheer mightily that this is so. In my feminine ideal, there is no place for gauleiters. And if you say this makes me macho, I'll cry.

As a general rule, then, the women stayed around the edges of the big, prestigious playing fields, but that didn't prevent them from developing their own gentle science at home, slowly developing through the centuries, by hit-and-miss pragmatism as much as anything else, the basic vocabulary of what is now known as classical French cuisine. While the men were serving flame-spitting peacocks to princes and *pièces montées* to bourgeois millionaires, the women at their hearths nourished the kids with the bread they baked, the vegetables they grew, the cheese they made and, when meat was available, their *plats mijotés*, the slow-cooking stews, ragouts and *daubes* that can go on for hours and hours on the back of a cast-iron stove or on the fender before an open hearth, in heavy pots as black as an editor's soul. Sometimes they'd even go to bed with their creations—who needs husbands?—wrapping the receptacle in blankets to permit it to simmer all night long. If that's not soul food, I don't know what is.

The most striking exception to this rule of sexual apartheid were the *cabaretières* like La Coiffier, a tough, strong-willed breed of women born with the talent and strength of character to take on the men at their own game, using whatever weapons they had at their disposal. Not so much cooks as hostesses, their clients conjure up images of Prince Hal and Falstaff, their establishments the Boar's Head Tavern in Eastcheap. My favorite among them is the one known as La du Ryer (no one seems to have used first names in their regard), who makes Mistress Quickly look like a modest beginner.

La du Ryer was a poor girl from the region of Mons (now in Belgium) who became the mistress of a French nobleman named Saint-Prieul and amassed a fortune as a camp follower to his army, selling not her person but the food she cooked for his hungry army as official *vivandière* (victualer). Married and set up with her own country inn after returning from the wars, she did not hesitate to round out her income with the occasional trick or two, but when her old benefactor Saint-Prieul galloped up for a gambol in the sack one fine evening, she made the mistake of asking to be paid, and he promptly beat her for her impertinence. I should have known better than to ask you for money, she observed with cruel lucidity, because you're always broke.

She had a good heart, though, La du Ryer, and when in 1641 poor old Saint-Prieul was implicated in a case of misappropriation of public funds and decapitated for his philandering, she caught his head in her apron and paid for a sumptuous funeral. With her second marriage (no one seems to know what became of du Ryer, her first, and for all I can tell you he might have ended up in a stew pot), she acquired a richly appointed cabaret in Saint-Cloud, close to Paris but also strategically astraddle the route to Versailles, the best possible location of all. Every nobleman on his way to pay homage to the king was bound to get hungry sooner or later, or thirsty or tired. Or, for that matter, concupiscent, and La du Ryer was happy to oblige by renting out one or several of her eighty rooms—an enormous number for the time—as *lieux de rendezvous* for various princely dalliances and orgies. Terrible-tempered but tender, mercenary but generous, light of virtue but irretrievably motherly, La du Ryer had a full fund of contradictions about her, but she probably had to possess every quality and its opposite to survive and prosper as she did in the man's world of the seventeenth century.

There were few such dominating figures like her and La Coiffier, though, and the overwhelming majority of their culinary congeners worked in domestic anonymity. Did they suspect, these millions of unknown wives, instinctive artists clomping around primitive kitchens in long dresses and wooden shoes, that they were building the single strongest tradition and social bond in their country? Ever so gradually, as these admirable women tried all manner of different combinations, marrying the ingredients that were available at any one time of the year, varying the methods of cooking them and building up their mini-cathedrals of savors and flavors, they evolved the gastronomic perfections which today, now that the work is done, may strike any beginning *cordon bleu* as obvious, but which in fact are highly sophisticated products of intelligence, imagination and love. The flawless *pot-au-feu*, as Dodin knew, is a lot harder to create than most of the worldly exercises of the male of the species: head-bashing, chemical synthesizing, expense-account chiseling or whatever other masculine triumph you care to cite. I am certainly grateful to Dr. Einstein for having invented the double overhead vacuum-dezincking planetary worm gear, and to Dr. Vicky Tooley for the combination bloffing and it-otting machine (pride of South Norwalk, Connecticut), but neither of these masterpieces can match the complex simplicity of a properly constructed *cassoulet, blanquette de veau à l'ancienne* or that absolute apotheosis of domestic cooking, the *poulet à la crème* of mother Blanc. True genius always looks simple, and the best of creations are "obvious." But you have to find the obvious, don't you? We blithely take the force of gravity for granted now, but where would we be today if Isaac Newton hadn't come along to invent it? Up in the air, I'll parry. So it is with the recipes for *navarin d'agneau printanier, potée auvergnate* and, yes, even good old *boeuf bourguignon*, which isn't as easy as all that to get right, and as a result is one of the most massacred dishes in the world, right after *coq au vin.*

"*La cuisine de l'amour,*" Paul Bocuse calls women's cooking, and I would be hard put to find a better description, in English or French. Neither Bocuse nor his master, Fernand Point, hesitated to base his departure from Carême's and Escoffier's *grand cuisine* (utterly masculine in its deliberate complication and showiness—

hey, lookit this one guys, now I'm gonna stick a truffle on top of the foie gras!) on the wisdom he had all around him in the menus and in the hearts of the famous women chefs of Lyon, the *mères lyonnaises*. Today still, probably half the items on Bocuse's menu are unabashed copies or derivatives of the country dishes that he grew up with. The great man may have won his medal of Meilleur Ouvrier de France with the typically masculine *loup en croûte farçi d'une mousse de homard, sauce choron* (sea bass stuffed with lobster mousse in a pastry shell served with Choron sauce, which is a béarnaise with tomato), but he takes just as much pride in recommending his *poulet en vessie* (chicken cooked with vegetables inside a pig's bladder), which grannies around Lyon had been serving up for centuries. Alain Chapel, over in Mionnay, is unquestionably one of the world's most dazzling magicians of the stove, but the dish with which most people identify him, the *gâteau de foies blonds* (a hot mousse of chicken livers), is an ancestral recipe that both his mother and Bocuse's mother used to make when they were kids, in the benighted days before anyone was able to reap the benefits of Big Burgers and Twinkies. Come to think of it, these industrial horrors are typically masculine expressions—as was, indeed, that excruciating *plateau repas* which I and my fellow passengers watched in terror aboard that train the other day, wondering in dread if we were looking at our future.

The future of nourishment *may* be bright for industry in France, because more and more women are working and fewer and fewer cooking. Michel Guérard, for one, has decided that French traditional home cooking is on its way out, and has thrown in his lot with the industrialists to develop Lego-style products which working women—or men or children or robots—can put together, click-clack (but at what price?) to build meals of somewhat higher quality than a can of corned beef hash. Note, though, that the capitalists who own and run the factories which turn out industrial food stay away from their own stuff when it comes to the most important question of all: feeding Number One. For their expense-account lunches they go out to proper restaurants for a proper nosh, and when they get home they have their cooks fire up proper dinners which bear no resemblance whatsoever to the canned abominations they sell to the drones. You may be sure that the dishes they prefer are the classics of *cuisine de femme* and not the plate-decorating exercises of *nouvelle kiwisine.*

"Just the other day we had the president of a big company in for lunch," said Marie-Claude Gracia, a red-headed, brown-eyed explosion of energy who owns, runs and does the cooking for a wonderful little restaurant in the middle of nowhere (Poudenas is the name of the town, and if you look very, very carefully, following the Michelin star in the east, you might find it on the map, roughly in the vicinity of Agen), "and when he left, I swear to you that he had tears in his eyes. He told me that my cooking reminded him of his mother."

The best cooking in Paris went on not in restaurants, Balzac said, but in the *loges* of the city's *concièrges*, ill-tempered old dames in slippers who had no space, no elegant kitchen gear and no budget for truffles or foie gras, but lots of time and patience and the canny intelligence that tells a cook just how long to leave vegetables in the pot to be perfect or how much *crème fraîche* is right to make a dish smooth and unctuous and how much renders it cloyingly rich. This is the same kind of intelligence that led Point and his disciples to make their departure from Escoffier, but to handle it in a measured and sensible way. When those who followed them pushed cooking into exaggeration and caricature, it fell into this "new cuisine" nonsense. That's men for you: always trying to show off.

Until today, the greatest burgeoning of female cooking talent came, as we have seen, in the (generally rounded) form of the mothers of Lyon who simmered their dishes in tiny *bouchons* located on obscure back streets, the geography of which every serious gourmet in France knew by heart. Like the Parisian *concièrges*, they were limited in funds and space, and the traditional mock-grumpiness of their characters hid a modesty which abhorred the pirouettes of *grande cuisine.* The result was a limited number of familial dishes, cooked to perfection and delivered to the tables by the *patron*, whenever he could take time off from playing *boules* or drinking Beaujolais. They were a hardy, truculent lot these women, independent, self-reliant and utterly unimpressed by titles, money or the reputations they had made for themselves. No staff, no décor, no apprentices, no pretension and, usually, not even any written menus: just the *pot-au-feu* bubbling on the back burner, next to the *boeuf aux carottes*, the *poule-au-pot* or the *blanquette*. Add a cold bottle of Brouilly, and who demands anything more of life?

These saviors of humanity had probably been around forever in Lyon, making life more civilized in cabarets and taverns whose names are now lost to history, but the ancestress who is usually held up as the prototype, the first of the species, was La Mère Guy, who opened shop in 1759 (six years before Michel Bocuse, the founder of the cooking dynasty presently presided by Paul), and whose restaurant, bearing the same name, continues today under the hand of the excellent Roger Roucou. Many, many more mothers followed, and *les mères* Bigot, Pompon, Coquit, Terrasse and Carton achieved their own manner of sainthood for serious eaters, as did Georges Blanc's illustrious forebears up in Vonnas. They are all gone now, and if La Mère Brazier and La Voute, two of the greatest of the temples of women's cooking, are still there now, the *mères* who made them famous have hung up their aprons. The one whose memory the Lyonnais cherish the most ardently is Françoise Fayolle, the *cordon bleu* cook who married a certain Louis Fillioux in 1890 and became the immortal Mère Fillioux, bringing honor to Lyon and succor to innumerable hungry souls until her death in 1925, a far more bitter loss to the French social structure than the passing of any *président de la République*.

"I've spent my whole life making four or five dishes," *la Mère Fillioux* grumbled in one of her definitive pronouncements, "so I know how to make them. And I'll never make anything else."

What were the dishes that could occupy a lifetime? *Potage velouté aux truffes, quenelles de brochet au gratin au beurre d'écrevisses, culs d'artichauts au foie gras* and *volaille demi-deuil*, the latter dressed in a subcutaneous mourning suit of truffles and served, falsely modest, with a down-home garnishing of pickles, rock salt and mustard. That's what. On special order, and if she felt you were worthy of it, she would consent to make you a lobster *à l'américaine.* When she finally took her retirement, some mathematical whiz estimated that she had cut up half a million chickens, and the knife she used—*the* knife, worn paper thin by decades of grindstone sharpening—was immediately confiscated and put on display in the Escoffier Museum of Gastronomy in Villeneuve-Loubet, above Nice. Such was her skill with the fabled shiv that the wings, thighs, and breasts of the birds used to fly off as if by magic at her feathery touch, separated at the joint as cleanly as petals from a rose. One day, the story goes, a famous surgeon dining in her place was so mesmerized watching her operate that he could not restrain himself from asking if he, too, could give it a try. Suspiciously, against her better judgment, she consented, and the doctor did his number so clumsily—malpractice!—that she was moved to professional indignation.

"Stop, unhappy man!" she cried. "You are making an assassination of it."

Paris, too, had its share of holy mothers, although not as many great ones. Of these, perhaps the most famous was Madame Gênot, who installed the tools of her trade, her perfectionism and her *mauvais caractère* in a little bistrot of most modest mien at number 20, rue de la Banque, near the Grecian-columned stock-exchange building. *La Mère Gênot* was at the height of her glory after World War I, "the last of the last," as the French optimistically referred to it then. One day in the twenties, André Maginot, he of the Line of the same name, asked her to come to his war ministry and cater an important dinner. She snorted and complained, but eventually agreed, and tramped across town with her own casseroles and knives, refusing to touch the least bit of the equipment of the ministry's own cooks. Without so much as a by-your-leave, she moved into the kitchen and took over as if she were occupying conquered territory, and brooking no sass from the natives, either. By the end of the morning she had made life so impossible for the ministry's staff that the chief cook marched up to the very office of *Monsieur le ministre,* knocked on the door and announced that if Madame Gênot stayed an hour longer he was handing in his resignation.

Maginot went down to the kitchen himself to try to calm the storm, but the terrible old lady threw him out.

"She's really impossible," he sighed to his guests as the dinner began. "I shouldn't have brought her in." But when it came time for the main course the waiters carried in Madame Gênot's famous *épaule de mouton aux salsifis*, and suddenly all the assembled big-shots were like infants with pacifiers stuck in their mouths. At the end of the dinner, Maginot summoned her into the dining room and kissed her on both cheeks. But he never did invite her back.

Through the Second World War and into the period of post-war reconstruction and boom, various *mères lyonnaises* continued to lavish their goodness upon the lucky inhabitants of that blessed corner of the earth, but they were getting old and no one was coming around to take their places. Inspired by the economic explosion all around them, seduced by the idea of a "real" career like the men, rejecting the old ways as backward and degrading, not to mention tiring, the young women stayed away from the *bouchons* in droves. Unexpectedly, terrifyingly, the eaters of Lyon found themselves with hardly any more female presence at the stoves of their beloved *bouchons*. The last of the old-line was Léa of La Voute, a hole in the wall between the opera and the River Saône. Lea's stewed tripe specialty known as *tablier de sapeur* (a nicely double-edged vulgar name, but the joke is too complicated to explain) was a Lyonnais monument of infinitely better taste than the monstrous, turreted basilica of Notre-Dame-de-Fourvière that squats, Byzantine and medieval at the same time, on the hill above the river, and her poached sausage and cold *lyonnaise* salad of marinated lambs' feet with mayonnaise were cult objects which Bocuse would send his more esteemed customers to taste after they had eaten their fill of three-star fare up in Collonges. If they went to the banks of the Saône on market day, and if they were lucky, they could catch the extraordinary sight of Léa doing her shopping, pushing her way through the crowd behind a three-wheeled cart which was adorned with a hand-lettered sign: *faible femme, forte en gueule*, which means, roughly, "little woman, big mouth." When the shoppers along her route tarried too long over the artichokes or horse kidneys, blocking her way, she would clear passage by squeezing the rubber bulb of the old car horn she had mounted by her right hand: *pouet-pouet.* Léa, too, has taken her retirement now, and a man is presently defiling her kitchen. As hard as he tries, the results just aren't the same.

But there is always a balance in life: the women are starting to return. Some of the more perceptive young ones, in the manner of Dr. Richard, the lawyer who decided she would rather sell cheese in *les halles* than argue divorces or chase after ambulances, have begun a back-to-the-kitchen movement by setting themselves up in new little *bouchons* scattered around Lyon. A few of them have already made their way into the guides, and their example seems to be contagious. Just the other day I supped on a green salad with chicken livers, a *gratin de macaroni* and a *sauté d'agneau* at Le Temps Perdu, a one-room wonder on a hillside street above the Rhône, and watched through eyes misted with tears as Nicole Daru, the slender blonde *patronne*, put it all together for me and perhaps twenty-five other guests with only a single assistant at the open kitchen a couple of yards away from us. With any luck, Lyon will once again be teeming with *mères* of this sort. Yea teem!

To Lyon's everlasting shame, however, it was in Paris that the postwar rebirth of feminine gastronomy took place. The capital city's two last "mothers" of the old-school, traditional sort had been *la Mère Michèle*, sainted for her poached fish and the faultless *beurre blanc* with which she inevitably accompanied it, and Madame Cartet, whose regal bearing was so intimidating that she looked a very duchess and no one ever dared call her anything but Madame: never, never, was she known as *la Mère Cartet*.

Until her recent retirement, Madame Cartet was the *doyenne* and uncontested figurehead of the *cuisinières parisiennes*, and the court to which she admitted serious admirers was barely big enough for twenty fanatics of Pantagruelesque lunches, which was the only meal she deigned to prepare, locking up tight at night to indulge her passion for the opera and theater. She cooked in what appeared to be a closet, and her pastel miniature restaurant was like a hallway. The grandeur of these premises on the rue de Malte, behind the

Place de la République in the 11th *arrondissement* (a district of the city which offered no other valid reason for the setting of one's foot), barely allowed room for her single serving lady to squeeze through the space between the tables and the back wall as she shuttled back and forth. The crowding, the lunch-only *diktat*, her high prices and the difficulty of making a reservation discouraged many, but those who persisted were treated to the perfection of solid lyonnais-style food, dishes like *boeuf à la mode*, roast lamb with fresh spring vegetables, stuffed shoulder of lamb, *boeuf à la ficelle*, crab soufflé or *brandade* of cod, served in unbelievably generous portions. It was a good idea to get all your day's work done before you went to Madame Cartet's, because lunch usually went on until four o'clock or so, and you were in no shape to perform after that.

Fernande Allard, too, has taken leave of her kitchen, on the rue Saint-André-des-Arts, just behind Saint-Germain-des-Prés, where Juliet Greco's troubling contralto crooning used to vie with *le jazz hot* for the attention of audiences in overheated *cave* nightclubs, while Sarte looked down upon it with wall-eyed existential contempt, denounced it all as bourgeois frivolity, and longed for the day when the wrath of the political commissars would come down upon them. (I'll bet he never enjoyed a meal in his life, and perversely that pleases me.) With its turn-of-the-century style, its sawdust on the floor, its waiters in long black aprons, Le Restaurant Allard was like a Hollywood set for a Paris bistrot, and for several years it became virtually impossible to gain entrance without reserving weeks in advance. The food was strictly traditional and orthodox, and it was kept that way by Fernande, who had the solid build, unblinking brown gaze and intransigent character of a Burgundian peasant. You didn't find any tiny raw fish with caramel or kiwi soufflés in Fernande's kitchen, but there was plenty of tripe the way they like it in Dijon, and guinea hen with lentils, and duck with olives, and an inimitable salad of *pissenlits au lard*, tender dandelion leaves with hot chunks of salt pork, scraped right out of the frying pan directly onto the salad, with all that deliciously cholesterol-laden pig fat. Fernande's staff numbered four, and they were all men, because that was the way she wanted it: there was a lot of heavy hefting to do in there to keep forty clients fed, and she needed some strong arms. No back talk, though: Fernande dominated her assistants with the same ease that she did her husband, Albert, who was in charge of the wine cellar. Yes, dear. Anything you say.

"I break my cooks in," she once explained to me, without an ounce of humor. "When men come to work for me, I impose my cooking on them. I want that and nothing else, and they do what I want. I make them do home cooking—women's cooking. If they don't, I fire them."

I believed her.

With Madame Cartet and Fernande out of the picture, one typical traditionalist of the *mères* school of cooking remained to make the liaison with the modern school: Adrienne Biasin was her name, but she was better known as *la vieille* (the old lady), a nickname she had carried ever since she was twenty-seven years old and waiting on tables in a restaurant in the middle of the old Paris Halles district. When Adrienne finally got her own place, a ground-floor cubbyhole in the one-block-long rue de l'Arbre Sec, near the Seine on the right bank, she naturally named it La Vieille. It was even smaller than Madame Cartet's, and the kitchen was across a corridor, down which tenants of the building passed on the way to their apartments, but the cooking was the kind of nourishment that had made the Lyonnais love *la Mère Fillioux:* terrines, pâtés and *rillettes* of her own confection, stuffed tomatoes the way every Frenchman likes to think his mother made them (and most likely didn't), *pot-au-feu, boeuf aux carottes, navarin d'agneau* and the "ordinary" desserts at which most male cooks turn up their noble noses as not complex enough, and hence unworthy of their attention. Who wants to eat a vulgar *mousse au chocolat* these days, they ask rhetorically, or a mere *crème caramel* or a *tarte aux pommes?*

I do, I do.

Justement, it was largely because of the overpowering snobbery that reigns in the capital city that few Parisians developed the affection and intimacy with the older generation of women cooks which the Lyonnais had always felt for their holy *mères*. Paris was too big, too anonymous, too wealthy and too narcissistic for that kind of small-town relationship, preferring the brittle joys of fickle fashion to the steady, slow-burning warmth of the mothers. As a result, the city paid little more than passing attention when Madame Cartet walked out of her closet for the last time, or when Fernande quit Le Restaurant Allard. But the one thing that the Parisian adores above all is novelty, and it was probably because of this willingness (this *need*) to harbor change that the phenomenon of the young generation of *cuisinières* developed there rather than in the provinces. Beginning in the late sixties with a few timid first steps and growing in importance ever since, the movement of feminine—although not necessarily feminist—gastronomy is now firmly installed throughout France, and the end is not in sight. But the young women who are proliferating within the world of French cuisine are not replays of the old *mères*. Their style is more daring, their approach resolutely modern. It looks like the days of modesty are numbered: these kids don't intend to be epiphenomena in a male world. Times are changing.

The movement's two most important pioneers, the one who broke the ground in which the other *parisiennes* are now flowering, came to restaurant cooking cold, with no background in the trade, no preconceptions and, luckily, no idea of how hard it would be. Both are intelligent and attractive, born cooks who didn't realize their talents until it was too late to back out. One of them is a fawn-eyed brunette in bangs, and the other a tiny blonde who looks like something out of a fairy tale, with large blue-green eyes, a fine, full mouth, just the thing for kissing frogs, and tresses long enough for a hungry Prince Charming to shinny up for a little bite. They are named, respectively, Dominique Nahmias and Christiane Massia.

These new-style *mères* were more like *demoiselles* at the outset, since they both began exceedingly young—Dominique (bangs) at twenty, with a restaurant called Olympe and Christiane (Rapunzel) at nineteen with Le Restaurant du Marché. Neither one really needed to go to work for a living (Albert Nahmias was teaching sociology at the University of Paris, and Christiane's husband, Michel, was a successful businessman), but both, glory be to God, felt the impulsion to express themselves in a manner more satisfying than watching TV while waiting for hubby to come back from work.

"I want a restaurant," Christiane announced one day, just like that, already bored with the housewifely condition while still only a teenager, and Michel had the good judgment to go out and get it for her. With the Nahmiases, it was Albert's idea to change professions—the future of social sciences at the Sorbonne looked windy and boring—and Dominique, who is an astonishingly calm, offhand sort of dame, said, sure, why not. You'll do the cooking, suggested Albert, and I'll handle the other side. Okie doke, hon, said Dominique. What the hell.

This cavalier attitude in a city like Paris, which has the bitchiest collection of eaters and gastronomic critics in the world, ought to have spelled commercial suicide, but Dominique proved to possess such an Olympian calm and such inventiveness that the gourmet establishment began falling all over itself with compliments almost from the moment she and Albert opened shop. Today, she admits that she never really believed it was going to happen until opening day, on the morning of which she decided she'd better get cracking, ho hum. With zero experience and slightly less training, she began with the basic "vocabulary" of curried crayfish, braised suckling pig, chicken with tomatoes and rabbit in cream, and found herself hailed as "the discovery of the year" before Olympe was two weeks old. Such hyperbole is enough to turn many a pretty little head, but Dominique just shrugged and plugged on. She became a radio and television star with her cooking lessons and a culino-literary *lionne* with her cookbooks, and the new Olympe (the first one turned out to be too small for the demand), in a corner of town behind Montparnasse, has become *the* fashionable place for name-droppers, the way the Tour d'Argent is for Japanese tour groups and l'Archestrate, Alain Senderens's research laboratory behind the Invalides, was for those with an unlimited fortune at their disposal. (They may now deposit their gold lingots at Senderens's new address, the ancient and honored Lucas-Carton.) For Francis Ford Coppola, Dominique will cook Italian style, and for Roman Polanski she will turn her delicate hand to *barszcz wigilijny,* while Robert de Niro is said to prefer her fresh egg noodles and Warren Beatty *pigeon au miel.* For Catherine Deneuve, she sautés *langoustines,* but then again, so would I. I would also stand on my head if she asked me. And wiggle my ears.

Like all the best of the women cooks, Dominique avoids the interior-decorator silliness of the "new" cooking, but it is difficult to hang a label on her highly personalized style. There are a few broad characteristics which are common to all the members of this exciting new sisterhood, though, and they get me as close as I can come to defining a specific approach as "female cooking": instinctive rather than academic, and inventive rather than rule-bound. The reason for this is simple: with few exceptions, they have all learned by themselves rather than in hotel schools or as apprentices in the large male kitchens, from which young girls have been generally excluded in France. With no academic baggage behind them, they invent as naturally as birds fly, and the results are sometimes surprising and always interesting. And unlike the *mères,* the girls of today have turned their backs on classical, "home" cooking and are striking out in all manner of odd and unpredictable directions.

Lulu Rousseau, feisty, skinny, bright-eyed and outrageous in the day-glo purple *beret basque,* which she prefers to wear in place of the *toque,* draws herself up to her full five and a half feet and puts up her dukes if you so much as mention the words "home cooking" in the confines of her tiny restaurant, L'Assiette, on the rue du Château in Paris. A classic case of *mauvais caractère* who is probably a reincarnation of Madame Gênot, Lulu will gladly tell you and the other seventeen persons squeezed within her four narrow walls all about the years and years she spent as an anonymous chef in someone else's place, because no big-name male chef would have her in his *brigade,* even as a learner, even as an apprentice, she who possessed the professional qualifications of at least a *sous-chef.* Shut out from the classical route, then, Lulu learned on her own, and the result is an unexpected but absolutely first-rate mixture of tradition and freewheeling, bearing her own stamp and no one else's. Like all the good ones, Lulu cooks her own fresh foie gras, makes her own terrines and *rillettes*, and if you remain indifferent to her roast guinea hen, served with a perfect wedge of fresh, green, sweet cabbage, you are nothing but a churl, and Lulu will tell you so herself.

"All art and no science," is the way one gastronomic professional summed up for me the style which Lulu and her peers have developed within the last decade or so.

"Women cooks have been hurt by their modesty," Christiane Massia adds to the analysis, in the same whispery voice with which she directs her kitchen staff, miraculously making herself heard over the clatter of pots and the screams of dying oysters. "Women are becoming more audacious now, and a lot less shy about inventing. Little by little, the difference between male and female cooking is disappearing. And, anyway, most of the dishes and techniques that male cooks take for their inventions are just the things that the women had been doing all along. Paul Bocuse didn't invent everything."

Aha. There it comes. Nothing could better symbolize the difference in styles and the curious, fidgety state of diplomatic relations between the sexes in French cuisine today than this, the matchup of Christiane, the most delicate and feminine of cooks, with Bocuse the macho monster, the very one who had universally outraged feminists by his declaration that he would rather have women in his bed than in his kitchen, and then proceeded to aggravate the case against him by following it up with a bit of logic that was as heinous as it was irrefutable: "Wouldn't you prefer to have them smelling of Chanel No. 5 rather than cooking fat?"

Most women should be as attractive in evening gowns and Arpège as Christiane in work clothes and cooking fat! Or as successful: she cooked so well, and with such a plethora of fine products, at Le Restaurant du Marché that she was able to buy another place down the street in the backwoods of the 15th *arrondissement* and bring it to a popularity equal to the Marché, not to speak of a star in the *Guide Michelin*. It was in this second restaurant, L'Aquitaine, that Bocuse charged into Christiane's life a few years back, when she was awarded the Order of Agricultural Merit, in recognition of her exemplary promotion of French products. Apparently repentant for all the deliberate provocation which he had visited upon women's movements everywhere, the Bad Boy from Lyon offered to make a pilgrimage to the big city and pin the medal upon Christiane's snowy breast his very self. What better gesture of reconciliation and humility could one hope for? And so it came to pass that Bocuse did appear at the award ceremony, and bearing with him a generous peace offering, too: a five-gallon keg of Brouilly, chosen from George Duboeuf's best lots. Inscribed on the front of the keg was a touching dedication:

For Christiane Massia

From Paul Bocuse

in recognition of women's cooking

Bocuse entered the restaurant surrounded by a hyperbolically feminine honor guard composed of ten dancers from Le Crazy Horse Saloon, dressed only in aprons and chefs' *toques.*

"Now, *that's* the way I like women cooks to be," he cried from within a thicket of limbs and bodacious curves, as the photographers snapped away and Christiane wondered what in hell was going on.

The empty keg is still there today, decorating the entrance to the restaurant, which at least proves that Christiane can take a joke, but everything else about her operation is the opposite of the Bocuse style. In both the Marché and L'Aquitaine the kitchen staff is exclusively feminine—and that includes the cat, Valkyrie, too, a critter of high-class tastes who dines on turbot and filet of sole. Christiane's helpers in L'Aquitaine, Salma (Vietnamese), Natividad (Portugese), Lisette (Guadeloupean) and Claire, Laurence and Isabelle (French), are organized not into the specialized, military-style *brigades* of men's kitchens, but in an informal first-come, first-served approach, in which any one of them might handle an hors d'oeuvre, a salad, a main course or a dessert, depending on who is available and who feels like it. Somehow, the system works fine, and Christiane neither screams nor disciplines nor delivers *coups de pied au cul*. She doesn't believe in that. That's not ladylike. She has a better system.

"I hate it when a girl transforms me into a cop," she admits. "I can't shout and bawl them out. That's not my style. So when a girl has made me angry, I pout. It's very effective. After two or three days of that, she really wants to speak to me again."

Christiane's policy of hiring only women for her two kitchens might be taken for feminist militancy, but she sees it as nothing more than a small gesture in the direction of redressing the ancient injustices of *grande cuisine,* which has always kept her sex on the outside looking in, or relegated them to the status of marginal curiosities. "As *mères* they can accept us," she says, "but as chefs, they look down on us."

Poor Christiane. She is capable of brief sallies like that, dukes up, chin out, but fighting is quite against her constitution. Try as she might, she remains sweet and kind and good, as warm-hearted as she is attractive, and her benevolent nature always gets the better of her. Even in rush hour, the atmosphere in her kitchen resembles a kaffeeklatsch more than a salt mine: the girls chat and giggle and gossip as they clean fish, stir sauces and chop shallots, and the gear they cook with is just the ordinary frying pan and casserole, the same kind as any home cook uses. The rhythm of work steps up as more orders come in, but there is never the least sign of panic or ill-humor. The jokes and the wisecracks continue as the hands fly over the *piano,* and, effortlessly, the dishes come together and zip up the dumb waiter when they're called for. Christiane works bare-headed, a little concession to vanity and her conviction that the *toque* is ugly, and beneath her apron and white blouse she is wearing a black dress, some nifty black stockings and high heels. Wowee.

A mother in spite of herself—and she has two daughters—she chides Isabelle for cooking a steak too fast because she knows the order is for a kid. Children don't like the taste of charred meat, she explains, and then she lifts the meat off the grill and trims the edges back. They don't like the fat, either.

"There's always something to learn about cuisine," she says.

"It's never finished. I never do a dish for my clients without wondering whether it's good for their health. I've got to be very careful. My clients are my babies."

I'd like to find a male cook who could make that statement.

Might I have discovered with that the secret to and the definition of women's cooking? I will leave this for you to judge, according to your political convictions and allegiances in the War of the Sexes, as you make your way through the long list of wonderful establishments where the hand in charge of the cuisine is feminine. You should start your pilgrimage with Madame Point in Vienne, of course, because she is the grandest of the *grandes dames* and a monument in herself. True, she has never been in the kitchen, but she oversees the food of La Pyramide just as acutely as Fernand used to do. When you leave Vienne, you will go only a few miles downriver to discover the admirable Beau Rivage of Madame Castaing, who has been cooking for more than fifty years, and who has earned two stars in the Michelin. I suggest you test yourself with *St. Pierre à la Côte Rôtie, mousse de brochet aux écrevisses* and *lapin à la gousse d'ail* to see whether the taste is male or female. Something tells me that by the time you have polished off every last scrap and sopped up the gravy with your bread, you won't care.

There are so many other ladies worthy of your visit that I feel shame for not naming them all, and I apologize in advance for omitting dozens of members of the sorority who deserve to be on any discriminating list. Naturally, you can't miss Marie-Claude Gracia in Poudenas, and Édith Remoissenet in the village of Vignolles, next to Beaune, has absolutely swept the gruffest of gnarled old gastronomic grumps off their flat feet with her Petit Truc. In Chaumont-sur-Tharonne, just south of Orléans, Gisèle Crouzier continues the tradition in La Croix Blanche, where women have been doing the cooking for more than two hundred years, and up next to the Seine, forty miles west of Paris, Caroline Beyssier is the fourth generation of her family's women, all of them named Caroline, to run the kitchen of the Auberge de Senneville. In the Champagne country village of Sept-Saulx, near Reims, Laurence Robert, who was trained by Madame Castaing, has a Michelin star for her *truite au bleu* and *émince de boeuf au coriandre* and at Firminy, near Saint-Étienne, in La Table du Pavillon, you will order your wines from Danièle Carré-Cartal, who in 1978 won the coveted title of the Best Sommelier in France, the first to break the masculine strangle hold on matters oenological.

And of course there is Madame la Baronne, the great, the marvelous, the unique Jeanne Gouttebaron. Don't look for Jeanne in any guide to *relais de campagne* or château hotels, because that's not her style, in spite of her grace and her aristocratic demeanor. Jeanne lives in a hamlet named Vendranges, fifteen kilometers south of Roanne (Troisgros City), perched in La Châtaigne, her whitewashed *auberge*, a rambling, low-ceilinged building that used to be the village bakery, overlooking a vista of rolling hills, farmhouses and Charolais cattle. Twelve rooms, creaking wooden floors, rustic antiques, a few thousand books and miraculously low prices, *La Châtaigne* is everybody's image of what a French country inn ought to be, and Jeanne is the one who holds it together, giving the place more class than all the Parisian palaces combined. The dining room is rustic but elegant, the atmosphere informal, the conversation spirited, and the *carte* limited to a few *plats du jour*, prepared with equal ease and simplicity by Jeanne or Jean, her husband, Monsieur le Baron, whichever one happens to be available for the moment.

If you are lucky enough to spend a few days in La Châtaigne, the chances are good that you will become an honorary member of the family, and perhaps you will taste the long-simmering *joue de boeuf en daube*, or a mushroom omelet whose raw materials Jean has gathered in the environing fields and copses, followed by fresh goat cheeses, dimpled and dripping whey, from farms where the families still speak in a *patois* that bears only a passing resemblance to French. If the place strikes you as a little bit unkempt or archaic—there's no television, no tennis, no swimming pool, no sauna, and no staff outside of Jeanne, Jean and the cleaning lady—then La Châtaigne is not for you. But if you care for art, literature, history or the rural folklore in which Vendranges is awash, put yourselves in the hands of Madame la Baronne. She'll even let you go for a meal or two *chez* Troisgros. She's much too much of a lady to be possessive.

Oh, God. As I go along, others tumble into my mind, crying for attention. Like Madame Chestier—how could I forget her, when she saved my life one dour, louring April day in 1984? I was motoring through the Sancerre district, valiantly ignoring the siren call of the seductive names that cried out at me as I rolled past: Pouilly-sur-Loire, Sancerre, Bue, Crézancy, Sury-en-Vaux, all of them pointing to the indubitable truth that a chilly glass of Savignon, white veering lightly to yellow, flinty, sharp and revivifying, was a million times preferable to the wheel of a Volkswagen and the idiotic quiz show on the radio. Luckily, lunchtime rolled around, as it must, and I found myself in the farm village of Vailly-sur-Sauldre, population 875. I fled in terror from the first place I found, an interior decorator's dream whose menu was replete with *kiwisine* flourishes, and plodded on down the deserted street to a superannuated façade with a little sign indicating Hôtel-Restaurant du Cerf. Ah, what a good choice! Instinct wins again.

It looked closed, because no one was up in the front room, but I continued onward, pushed the door to the dining room—and there discovered the reason why the street was deserted: the town was here, having lunch. A large, square room it was, with peeling paint, a few old mirrors and a desultory poster or two announcing a local tombola or bicycle race, but the tables were packed with a kaleidoscopic collection of Berrichon society, ranging from farm hands to traveling salesmen to hungry family groups. *They* knew about the relative merits of tradition versus flighty fashion, and they had made their choices long before me. No sooner was I seated than a smiling young lady—Madame Chestier's daughter Claudine—handed me the *carte*, which showed menus at the approximate equivalent of $3.50 to $4, offering no-nonsense fare like *pâté en croûte, bavette aux échalotes, andouillettes grillées, lapin farci* and *langue de veau, sauce ravigotte*. Everything was made *à la maison*, everything was succulent and the portions were generous enough to sate a foundry laborer.

After lunch, tranquilized by *pâté maison* and good old *boeuf bourguignon* (and a little carafe of Sauvignon, too), I stammered my thanks to Madame Chestier, who said *pas du tout, pas du tout,* it's only normal. But how, I wondered, did she manage to do so well for so little money? Oh, you know, she said, I prepare everything myself, which cuts the price down, and then I save on personnel, too, because there's only me in the kitchen and Claudine *en salle.* I would have liked to have an apprentice to help out in the kitchen, she sighed, but every time I requested one from the regional authorities they turned me down. Why? Well, because the place isn't elegant enough, I guess. So Claudine and I do everything ourselves. Which only goes to prove that bureaucrats, even French bureaucrats dealing with the sacred categories of restaurants and *hôtelleries,* can be as thick as oxen. I can only suggest that you do your part to alleviate this injustice by going to Vailly-sur-Sauldre as soon as possible, ordering Madame Chestier's most expensive menu (stifle your disbelieving laughter), and informing her that she is soon to be beatified, even if the labor authorities are inimical and the guides ignorant. If there had been more women like Madame Chestier in America, our civilization might not have succumbed to the tyranny of the burger and the chili dog.

And, yes, the gloomy reality is that even in France the totalitarian jackboots of the franchised food forces, their allies the industrial packagers and their cohort of running-dog ad men can be heard marching across the country. Here, though, there are at least some obstacles, and the defenses have not been entirely breached: surrender to the enemy is not necessarily inevitable. The resistance continues, then, but if the death struggle against the industrial tidal waves is to be won, it will require a lot more than the few isolated oases at the top level of three-star gastronomy. What's needed is more Châtaignes and more Hôtels du Cerf.

We can be certain that there will always be Guérards, Bocuses and Chapels in France, the *hauts couturiers* of nourishment, the stars who cook for stars, national symbols who maintain and justify four centuries of gastronomic pride. But will the great traditions that underlie the glitter survive as well, the ancient habits of eating well and eating right, of taking joy in the preparation and presentation of food? Maybe we can find an indication and an encouragement in today's burgeoning *cuisine de femme*. Anyone who doesn't cheer loudly for this needs to have his or her head examined, because it is the women who pass on the traditions and set the family examples which develop the tastes of generations. The more Jeanne Gouttebarons and Madame Chestiers we have, the fewer burgers and the less slovenly eating we will have.

It's just a pity that there weren't more of them in America to join in the noble fight back when the franchised hyenas first moved in with their asinine little paper hats, but America has always been terrific at comebacks, so I haven't given up hope that the young generation will see the light and save us. Meanwhile, we have France in the thick of the battle. You can combine a good deed for humanity with your own personal pleasure and edification by showing the *femmes en cuisine* how much you appreciate them. The list goes on and on, every place better than the last, and I can only wish you the time and the appetite to try them all. The *mères* and the *filles* will be waiting for you. Give them my love.